Regulating New Media in Africa

BCMCR
New Directions in Media and Cultural Research

Series editors: Oliver Carter, Kirsten Forkert, Nicholas Gebhardt, Annette Naudin and Nick Webber
Print ISSN: 2752-4515 | **Online ISSN:** 2752-4523

The Birmingham Centre for Media and Cultural Research's 'New Directions' book series aims to advance research and teaching in the broad range of media and cultural studies and to serve as the focal point for a community of scholars who are committed to critical inquiry and collaborative practice. Books in the series engage with developments in the field, showing how new theoretical approaches have impacted on research within both media and cultural studies and other related disciplines. Each volume will focus on a specific theme or issue, as well as exploring broader processes of social and cultural transformation. The series is committed to producing distinctive titles that challenge traditional disciplinary boundaries and question existing paradigms, including innovative scholarship in areas such as the creative industries; media history, heritage and archives; games studies; gender and sexuality; screen cultures; jazz and popular music studies; media and conflict; song-writing studies; and critical theory. The editors are also keen to encourage authors to experiment with non-standard approaches to academic writing.

In this series:

Regulating New Media in Africa: Politics, Law and Governance, edited by Vincent Obia, Sulayman Bah, Yemisi Akinbobola and Oliver Carter (2026)

Nuclear Gaia: Media Archives of Planetary Harm, by Agnieszka Jelewska and Michał Krawczak (2025)

Media Materialities: Form, Format, and Ephemeral Meaning, edited by Iain A. Taylor and Oliver Carter (2025)

Popular Music Ethnographies: Practices, Places and Identities, edited by Sarah Raine, Shane Blackman, Robert McPherson and Iain A. Taylor (2025)

Encountering the Plague: Humanities Takes on the Pandemic, edited by Wojciech Sowa and Tony Whyton (2024)

Under the Counter: Britain's Trade in Hardcore Pornographic 8mm Films, by Oliver Carter (2023)

Regulating New Media in Africa

Politics, Law and Governance

EDITED BY

Vincent Obia, Sulayman Bah,
Yemisi Akinbobola and Oliver Carter

intellect
Bristol, UK / Chicago, USA

First published in the UK in 2026 by
Intellect, The Mill, Parnall Road, Fishponds, Bristol, BS16 3JG, UK

First published in the USA in 2026 by
Intellect, The University of Chicago Press, 1427 E. 60th Street,
Chicago, IL 60637, USA

EU GPSR Authorised Representative
LOGOS EUROPE, 9 rue Nicolas Poussin, 17000, LA ROCHELLE, France
E-mail: Contact@logoseurope.eu

A catalogue record for this book is available from the British Library.

Copy editor: MPS Limited
Cover designer: Natalie Thomas
Production manager: Debora Nicosia
Typesetter: MPS Limited
Indexer: Janet Andrew

Hardback ISBN 978-1-83595-244-3
ePDF ISBN 978-1-83595-246-7
ePUB ISBN 978-1-83595-245-0

Part of the BCMCR New Directions in Media and Cultural Research series
Print ISSN: 2752-4515 | Online ISSN: 2752-4523

This is a peer-reviewed publication.

Contents

Tables

Acknowledgements

The journey that led to this edited collection started at the Birmingham Centre for Media and Cultural Research (BCMCR), where two Ph.D. students (now Drs Vincent Obia and Sulayman Bah) collaborated with their supervisors, Dr Yemisi Akinbobola and Prof Oliver Carter, to organize a conference. Like most conference organizers, we envisioned a special issue journal or co-edited book coming out of the Regulating African Media conference proceedings, which we held on 3–4 May 2022. Publishing the co-edited book just four years later is a testament to everyone's commitment.

We extend our deepest gratitude to the esteemed authors whose groundbreaking research has enriched this book with insights on various African countries: Dr Hayes Mabweazara, whose Keynote address at the conference took us on a continent-wide journey. Also giving a continent-wide contribution was Dr Vincent Obia. Dr Muthoni Esther King'ori and Dr Maureen Syallow, both of Strathmore University, then offered a focus on Kenya. From Kenya we were taken to Zambia by Dr Ndawana Youngson (University of Zambia), Dr Joanne Knowles (Liverpool John Moores University), and Dr Elastus Mambwe (University of Zambia). Then to Ghana by Dr Kobina Ano Bedu-Addo (Ghana Institute of Journalism and the University of Westminster). Three of the co-editors also had chapters that gave us insights in The Gambia (Dr Sulayman Bah), Nigeria and South Africa – thanks to Dr Trust Matsilele (Birmingham City University), who co-authored a chapter with Dr Yemisi Akinbobola and Dr Vincent Obia, and who also provided additional support and encouragement. We are also grateful to our interviewees whose insights gave wider context to the scholarly discussions. Many thanks to Guilherme Canela de Sousa, Chief of the Section on Freedom of Expression and Safety of Journalists at UNESCO's headquarters in Paris, Churchill Otieno, a veteran digital media practitioner in Kenya, president of the Africa Editors Forum and former managing editor of the Nation Media Group. We also thank H.E. Latifa Akharbach, president of Morocco's High Authority for Audiovisual Communication (HACA), and David Diaz-Jogeix, senior director of programmes at Article 19. And finally, thanks to Dr Winston Mano (University of Westminster) for his concluding remarks.

Beyond the book's valuable insights, we hope that the collaborative approach, leadership and vision demonstrated by the co-editors of this book serves as inspiration for other Ph.D. students and supervisors on the importance of such engagements in academia.

Thank you for reading.

Foreword

Oliver Carter

Each year, the Birmingham Centre for Media and Cultural Research (BCMCR) at Birmingham City University, United Kingdom, dedicates its research program to a particular theme. For the 2021–22 academic year, we selected the theme 'disruption'. Curated by Dr Craig Hamilton, a postdoctoral researcher in the Centre, the purpose of this theme was to develop ideas that consider how and why we do the work that we do; where and under which conditions that work takes place; what forms our work takes; why it matters; and who it matters to. Looking back, it seems obvious why we chose disruption as our annual theme, given the disruptive nature of global events such as COVID-19 and climate change, as well as more local issues, like Brexit. Typically, for media and cultural studies scholars, disruption is often viewed through a binary lens, either as a force for progress or as a destabilizing threat. It has been associated with new technologies, particularly in terms of technological innovation and the transformations it brings to media industries, production practices and audience experiences.

Our edited collection records how two of BCMCR's research clusters – Creative Industries and Media and Place – contributed to this theme. With two of our outstanding doctoral researchers, Sulayman Bah and Vincent Obia, sharing a common interest in African media regulation, Dr Yemisi Akinbobola and myself collectively decided to hold a two-day conference in 2022. This provided a space for the now Drs Bah and Obia to develop their leadership in this area, bringing together scholars from all over the world to discuss the disruptive relationship between new technologies and media regulation in the Global South. Nowhere is this disruption more complex and layered than in Africa, a continent whose diverse histories, cultures and political landscapes have long been shaped by the ebb and flow of technological change, colonial legacies and the dynamics of globalization. In practice, the reality is far more intricate. Disruption has the potential to democratize access to information, amplify marginalized voices and foster new cultural expressions. At the same time, it raises critical questions about governance, the protection of local cultures and the risks of deepening existing inequalities. These tensions are at the heart of this book's inquiry, providing an exploration of how new media technologies are regulated across Africa's varied socio-political contexts.

Through a range of contributors, we bring into focus the unique challenges and opportunities that media disruption poses to Africa, examining how the regulation of new media technologies intersects with broader social, political, legal and cultural transformations. We see it contributing to ongoing debates around 'regulatory disruption', a concept that explores 'the gray space between regulation and its absence, exposing incongruity between the law as written and the present state of a changing world' (Grimm 2022: 354). As the world becomes increasingly interconnected, the regulation of new media in Africa carries global significance. Africa's experience underscores how media disruption cannot be understood in isolation from issues of power, sovereignty and cultural integrity. The role of both state and corporate actors in regulating digital spaces is critical in determining whether these technologies will empower or exploit, liberate or control. The chapters in this book ask difficult yet essential questions: How do we balance the need for regulation with the promise of innovation? How can African societies protect cultural diversity while embracing technological advancements? What are the responsibilities of local governments, international corporations and global institutions in ensuring fair and equitable digital futures?

At a time when discussions about media disruption are dominated by the experiences of the Global North, this book offers a much-needed counter-narrative. The voices and perspectives contained within remind us that disruption, especially in Africa, is not just about technology; it is about people, histories and futures. In examining Africa's encounter with new media technologies, this book provides critical insights into how these technologies can be harnessed to build more just, inclusive and vibrant societies. We also hear valuable non-academic voices, those who are either directly or indirectly involved in regulation.

As you engage with the ideas presented in these pages, we the editors invite you to consider the broader implications of media disruption. This work challenges us to rethink how we understand power, participation and representation in an increasingly interconnected world. In doing so, it opens up new possibilities for reimagining the future of new media regulation and its impact on global cultures.

Dr Oliver Carter
Professor of Creative Economies
Birmingham Centre for Media and Cultural Research

REFERENCE

Grimm, Daniel (2002), 'Against regulatory disruption', *Jurimetrics*, 62, pp. 347–96, https://ssrn.com/abstract=4240191. Accessed 19 August 2024.

Introduction: Regulating Digital Media in Africa – Politics, Law and Governance

Vincent Obia and Sulayman Bah

In May 2022, we, the editors of this collection, hosted a virtual conference named Regulating African Digital Media at the Birmingham Centre for Media and Cultural Research, Birmingham City University. We aimed to incorporate African perspectives into worldwide discussions regarding the governance of emerging media technologies. We saw the need to create a space for African scholars to network and share their research at a time when governments around the world are attempting to regulate digital media technologies, from social media to artificial intelligence. In the conference call for papers, we recognized the reality of the 'regulatory turn' (Flew et al. 2021) – the increasing move by governments to institute digital regulation and not rely on the service terms of the major platforms, most notably Facebook (now Meta), Google, Apple, Amazon and Twitter (now X). This is also the case in many African countries, from Egypt to Zambia, where governments have introduced laws, guidelines and policies seeking to regulate the media ecosystem. In the conference call for papers, we argued that the shift towards greater regulation warrants investigation in scholarly circles as it exemplifies the struggle over the appropriation and exercise of power over collective voices, with consequences for democracy, plurality, independence, dissent and freedom.

This book collects some of the contributions from the conference. It is particularly noteworthy that the majority of the contributions included here are from scholars based in African institutions, pointing to the need to establish the book collection in the shared perspectives of researchers who are 'on the ground' and to promote localized sources of knowledge – as a way of bringing African voices to the centre. Also included in the collection are four interview transcripts that highlight the views of stakeholders in the digital media regulatory landscape in Africa. Our goal was to bring together conventional scholarly works and the perspectives of stakeholders directly involved in journalistic and regulatory practice. As a whole, the contributions reflect Milan and Treré's call to de-westernize the fields of new media, data studies and social science in general and to explore 'the richness and the diversity of meanings, worldviews, and practices in the [Global] Souths, as well as their specific challenges and inherent problems' (Milan and Treré 2019: 323). We also note Sampaio-Dias et al.'s (2019: 3) argument on the relevance of 'decolonial shifts' in African scholarship, research and education. Although western empirical and theoretical perspectives offer important insights for researching digital media regulation in the Global South, we believe that attentiveness to contemporary regulatory trends and themes in Africa is fundamental. Again, such a focus is needed because of the tendency for academic work related to the internet and datafication – and their regulation – to be centred on liberal democracies of the West, while the Global South is neglected (Milan and Treré 2019).

We see this neglect in Flew and Martin's (2022) edited collection on 'global perspectives on internet governance' – perspectives that, although described as 'global', do not include examining regulatory practices and views from Africa. Instead, research on digital media regulation typically considers American debates relating to issues like the First Amendment (Fagan 2018) or Section 230 of the Communications Decency Act (Overton 2020), the emerging European approach of digital constitutionalism (Manganelli and Nicita 2022) or overt Chinese censorship (King et al. 2013). To some extent, this is portrayed in Bradford's (2023) work, which conceptualizes the American, European and Chinese regulatory systems as digital empires. Each of these empires has its regulatory model that it seeks to export to other parts of the world, either in material or abstract forms (Bradford 2023). For America, the goal is to export a free market idea of regulation; for China, it seeks to spread the notion of state-based regulation driven by its digital infrastructural export; and for Europe, the emphasis is on a right-based regulatory model that it aims to extend to the globe. Scholarly investigations such as these (Flew and Martin 2022) that take a broad sweep of global regulatory practices then overlook Africa, indicating that the continent largely exists as a recipient of regulatory ideologies that come from elsewhere.

By compiling this edited collection, however, we make the case for de-westernizing and decolonizing the field, given that Africa possesses its unique regulatory context based on its history of media policy and state-citizen distrust (Ogbondah and Onyedike 1991; Obijiofor et al. 2016). What we know is that regulation on the continent tends to focus on censorship and the targeting of free speech, as the contributions to this collection demonstrate. Beyond this, we note that regulation also underscores the need to define acceptable behaviour in online spaces and manage the influence that platforms wield – an exercise fraught with challenges, not least the allowance it could provide for states to introduce draconian policies that limit online freedoms. This points to the importance of designing regulatory solutions that strike the right balance between combatting digital media misuse and protecting civil liberties. Related here is the global balance of power realities that Africa faces in attempting to regulate the use of technologies headquartered outside the continent. These are the issues that the book collection focuses on, seeking to spark discussions on the approaches to regulation in Africa, how they contribute to global debates on regulation and the possible alternatives that African countries can consider in their attempt to regulate digital media technologies. And although we refer to digital media regulation in Africa generally, it is important to note that we do not see the continent as a monolithic bloc, where one rule of thumb applies across the board. This is why virtually all the contributions focus on individual cases and countries in Africa.

In seeking to catalyse these discussions, we acknowledge the contributions that previous compilations have made to understanding approaches to digital media regulation in Africa and their limitations. Examples include Chan-Meetoo's (2013) edited collection on media ethics and regulation in Africa. Having little to do with digital media regulation, the collection focuses on how journalists negotiate media regulation and imbibe the required ethics. Sampaio-Dias et al.'s (2019) special issue also follows the same theme, aiming to Africanize knowledge of media regulation. However, we note its overwhelming focus on regulation as it relates to journalism practice, not digital media regulation per se. There is also Dwyer and Molony's (2019) edited collection, which gives attention to how Africans use social media for political engagement and social movements, even though it also considers surveillance tactics and legislations like cybercrime laws used as means of repression. Kperogi's (2022) edited collection also follows the same line, exploring how people in Africa use social media to express themselves and resist state overreach and how governments respond using censorship tactics, including internet shutdowns.

Our collection builds on these previous compilations, but more importantly, it charts a bold line of inquiry into digital media regulation in Africa, identifying it as a primary concern. It is the close of a journey that we began three years ago when we released the call for the conference. Demonstrating the need to go beyond Global North perspectives, the collection extends our work (see Obia 2023a; Bah 2023) and draws broadly from political economy ideas to shed light on regulatory practices in African countries, their effect on people and the conceptualization by which all these can be understood as part of contributing to a fuller comprehension of global debates on digital media regulation.

Examining Political Economy and Power in Relation to Regulation

Seven months before our conference in May 2022, Facebook found itself amid what Rochefort (2020: 228) calls a 'legal and social reckoning'. One of its former employees, Frances Haugen, had copied and leaked internal research files that show Facebook's complicity in the spread of harmful content on its platform. On 5 October 2021, Haugen testified before the US Senate, noting that the underlying problem of online harms on Facebook was the profit-driven algorithmic design interface that the platform uses, describing it as Facebook 'buying its profits with our safety'.[1] The conclusion of her statement was a call for stronger regulation of platforms like Facebook by the US government. This call has gained increasing acceptance in research and policy circles. We see this, for instance, in Flew and Gillett's (2021) assertion that the hands-off approach to regulation has increasingly lost its appeal, given what they describe as the perceived failing of the self-regulatory paradigm. The Haugen story is then symptomatic of other crises moments that social media platforms have faced – the proliferation of 'deepfakes', for instance – reinforcing what Baccarella et al. (2019) see as the dark side of technology. Based on this, Flew (2022) submits that nation-state regulation of platforms will increasingly become the case in both liberal and authoritarian countries, as the demand for greater accountability and transparency grows.

As if in tow, states and supranational entities have responded as predicted. Consequently, digital media regulation has emerged out of concerns regarding monopoly over the internet, fake news, online hate speech, abuse and harassment, and the need to stem the tide of terrorist and extremist content (Kaye 2019). From Australia with its News Media Bargaining Code to the European Union with its Digital Services Act, digital platforms have come under regulatory oversight from different quarters, even if the power ordering means that platforms still wield immense influence. This power ordering points to political economy considerations and the role that platformatization plays in concretizing platform power in the digital ecosystem (Mansell 2004; Balkin 2004). It underlines rapid developments in digital media technologies, resulting in what Glasius and Michaelsen described as a 'renegotiation of the boundaries of state power' (Glasius and Michaelsen 2018: 2). Political economy is, therefore, central to much of the discussion in the chapters of this collection, as it underscores the examination of 'how media and communications are organised and in doing so pay particular regard to regulations and governance' (Hardy 2014: 177).

For African countries, we note that political economy points to power imbalances that they face, first in relation to platforms and then in relation to Global North countries (Obia 2023a). When it comes to platforms, Fuchs and Sandoval (2015) observe that social media networks have essentially become oligopolies, dominating social media use and making it difficult for alternatives (e.g. non-corporate social media) – that question the capitalist model on which they are founded – to be developed. Platforms also set the rules of engagement in their terms of service, which Suzor (2018) describes as constitutional documents that affect how our social spaces are governed, placing considerable power in the hands of platforms and serving their business interests. The reality, therefore, is what Klonick (2018) refers to in calling platforms the New Governors of online speech. These Governors service the needs of users across the globe, and they draw on this reach as a way to deter state regulation:

> The New Governors are part of a new model of free expression: a triadic model. In this new model, online speech platforms sit between the state and speakers and publishers. They have the role of empowering both individual speakers and publishers (as well as arguably minimizing the necessity of publishers to speaking and amplification), and their transnational private infrastructure tempers the power of the state to censor.
>
> (Klonick 2018: 1664)

We note the relevance of the transnational influence that Klonick (2018) refers to, since this is perhaps the greatest limitation that African countries face in their attempt to design a regulatory architecture for the internet. Hence, we see that the regulatory relationship that African governments share with internet service providers (ISPs) is different from their relationship with digital platforms. For ISPs, they primarily operate within the national context and are subject to a political-economic ordering that specifies that they can be put out of business should they refuse to submit to government control – a reality that the contributions to the collection underscore in the way that internet shutdowns are implemented in Africa. The case is different for platforms that enjoy enormous power, backed up, in part, by the difficulties that issues of jurisdiction present. Schlesinger and Kretschmer (2020), for instance, point out that the United Kingdom, with the Online Safety Act, will have to grapple with jurisdictional challenges since the tech companies that it intends to regulate are based primarily in the United States or China or other European countries. For African countries, the disadvantage that issues of jurisdiction present is even more pronounced since the platform power imbalance is even more stark.

What this underscores, therefore, is the link between platform power and the power of the countries where they are based. Kwet alludes to this by noting that the ownership and control of pillars of the digital ecosystem – software, hardware and network connectivity – 'vest the United States with immense political, economic, and social power' (Kwet 2019: 4). An example is the way that American legal principles such as the First Amendment and Section 230 of the Communications Decency Act have shaped how digital media technologies are used and governed (Klonick 2018) and how this affects Africans, who have no say in American constitutional affairs. We explore this theme in the collection by considering references the chapters made to the imbalance that African countries face – a pointer to the continuation of Galtung's (1971) structural imperialism. This is a situation where decisions related to digital media technologies are largely made by platforms and governments in Global North countries, while those in Global South regions such as Africa supply obedience. It is perhaps for this reason – the inability of African governments to wield control over multinational digital platforms given the global balance of power realities – that they turn instead to target their citizens with regulatory measures that border on censorship and repression.

The Approach to Digital Media Regulation in Africa

The discussion above outlines how regulation finds expression in the context of platform power and the influence wielded by Global North countries, and this is a theme that the contributions to the collection explore. However, we are mindful of the overwhelming emphasis that contributors gave in examining state power in relation to the control that African governments seek to maintain over the information space. Again, this underscores the importance of political economy since it considers how digital media content and systems are related to broader structures in African societies. This includes investigating how, why and in whose interest governments act or fail to act. It is a theme that the collection pursues, particularly in demonstrating the existence of an ulterior motive in the regulations that African governments prescribe. Related here is the political economy of media capture, where, as Cardenas et al. (2017) observe, the media in regions such as Africa cannot afford to report on information that is displeasing to state authorities. Legislations can then be introduced to facilitate media capture by promoting a system built on self-censorship as journalists become wary of violating vague provisions, usually based on national security. What the contributions to the collections show, therefore, is that a similar level of repression has been extended to online media outlets. Sulayman Bah, in Chapter 11, for instance, points to a policy of incorporation (a kind of revolving door strategy) in The Gambia, where prominent journalists are employed by the media regulator to become defenders of repressive digital media laws. Our interview in Chapter 9 with Churchill Otieno, a veteran online journalist, also highlights draconian laws that limit journalism practice in places like Kenya and Uganda.

What our collection points to, therefore, is an approach to regulation that is based on state overreach. Cunliffe-Jones et al. (2021) refer to this in their report on misinformation laws in Africa. They found that one-third of the laws penalize publications regardless of whether harm may be caused. Also, the laws and regulations do not address the key types, drivers or originators of harmful false information and they have minimal effect in curbing harm. This is related to what we present here, emphasizing the fact that although regulations are justified on the need to combat harmful online content, they, in effect, serve as censorship tools. Cunliffe-Jones et al. (2021) further refer to the application of broad and vague terms, which make misinformation laws on the continent open to partisan abuse. Beyond laws, there is also the use of overt censorship tools such as internet shutdowns. Kaun and Treré describe these as 'digital connection as repression' (Kaun and Treré 2020: 704), highlighting its top-down nature and its collective consequences for people. We also note the political undertone that shutdowns come with since they serve as 'communicative ruptures' typically implemented around politically sensitive periods such as elections (Wagner 2018: 3919) – a point that Hayes Mabweazara reiterates in Chapter 1. Related also is the increasing attention that African governments are giving to surveillance laws and practices (Roberts et al. 2021) by sometimes enacting duplicitous laws. The discussion of these regulatory practices is what we consider in this collection.

Overall, our argument, based on the aggregation of contributions, is that while there is a need to combat the use of digital media technologies to spread harmful content, African governments tend to see this need as an opportunity to introduce legal and technical measures that stifle free expression and reinforce their control over the information landscape. As a result, governments cannot strike the nuanced balance needed to introduce the kind of regulation that citizens want – regulation that combats online harms and protect civil liberty concerns such as freedom of expression and privacy. This scenario exacerbates state-citizen distrust as far as regulation is concerned, further widening the gap between the government and the governed.

The Way Forward

Beyond considering the approach to digital media regulation in Africa, our collection further seeks to map the way forward for policy and research in the field. In doing this, we recognize McMillan's (2019) submission that state regulation of any kind is bound to limit free expression. The point is that regulation happens in living systems and cannot be separated from political interests (Lodge and Wegrich 2012). Regardless, the singular bold call that our collection makes is for research that highlights the role that the ruling elites in Africa have to subject their political and economic interests to the service of the broader social good as far as digital media regulation is concerned. Kobina Bedu-Addo, in Chapter 6, highlights the central nature of this in observing the need for the Ghanaian government to update digital broadcasting laws – something which can only happen if the elites place national interest above their political and economic considerations. As long as this does not materialize, an ulterior motive in regulation will prevail; the effect is that people second-guess government regulatory intent and are poised to resist state action. We see this in the Kenyan example, where Esther King'ori and Maureen Syallow, in Chapter 8, note that civil society groups have organized opposition to cyber legislation both online and in the courts.

Cyber legislations have become increasingly widespread in Africa, and perhaps for good reason – safeguarding cybersecurity and critical national information infrastructure should be a priority. But as Youngson Ndwana, Joanne Knowles and Elastus Mambwe show in Chapter 4, the cybercrime law in Zambia has been used to introduce punitive measures that violate civil liberties. Going forward, therefore, one key concern that policymakers on the continent will have is ensuring that cybercrime and other digital media legislations are robust enough to address the challenges that online harms pose while being sensitive enough to protect constitutional rights, especially freedom of expression. It points to the need to maintain the precarious balance between state policy and human rights – preserving the thin line between necessary regulation and punitive censorship. And for that to happen, our collection shows that political interests and regime security must be subdued.

Minimizing political considerations also means broadening the pool of stakeholders who shape digital media regulatory policies on the continent, an argument that King'ori and Syallow emphasize in Chapter 8. This points to multi-stakeholderism. To make it work, Guilherme Canela, in Chapter 2, emphasizes the need for meaningful participation by all stakeholders, including civil society actors. It also means including other stakeholders, such as academia, policy experts, and the general citizenry, in national policymaking to build regulatory trust and acceptance. The goal here is for policymakers on the continent to go beyond tokenistic inclusive measures to ensure that policy actions are co-created from the start with all groups. Again, it emphasizes the salience of placing the broader national interest above narrow political considerations. Multi-stakeholderism is also required globally, with Obia (2023b) suggesting that African governments need to advocate a protocol that is inclusive, systemic and flexible. Without this inclusivity, we note that African governments will likely not have much of a say in shaping regulatory outcomes at multistakeholder bodies like the Internet Governance Forum, a point that Calandro et al. (2016) buttress.

For research, it remains important for scholars working on digital media regulation in Africa to continue to investigate the issues highlighted above, especially in relation to decolonialization and de-westernization as scholars have canvassed for (Mano and Milton 2021; Govenden 2023). Winston Mano particularly emphasized this focus on decolonization, including the importance of elevating African voices, in the concluding chapter of this collection. We also note the need for researchers to extend the scholarship in aspects such as the contest of competing interests, ulterior motives, censorship and broad-based participation. Relevant here is an examination of how to create a balance between regulating online harms and protecting civil liberties. But, as Vincent Obia notes in Chapter 3, researchers will need to go beyond these areas to investigate the global balance of power dynamics as far as regulation is concerned. It will equally be important to expand the focus of regulation from state policymaking to the various ways that regulation occurs in interpersonal and group settings and how these interplay with formal regulation. Finally, the collection urges for scholars to expand their focus to consider emerging areas of technology and digital media regulation in Africa in relation to areas such as data privacy, artificial intelligence and the Internet of Things. By doing this and more, scholars will be contributing to giving Africa the place it deserves in global conversations on the regulation of digital media technologies.

Structure of This Collection

This collection is divided into three parts comprising 11 contributions to capture scholarship on digital media regulation and practices in Africa and map the way forward for researching the field. All three parts contain seven manuscripts and four interviews with Guilherme Canela, Latifa Akharbach, Churchill Otieno and David Diaz-Jogeix. We have gone with this approach to place academic work on regulation side by side with the perspectives of stakeholders and experts who are directly involved in these activities. Our goal is to provide an avenue for the researchers and stakeholders to be in conversation and we hope that readers will appreciate the structure we have provided for this. Readers should note that we transcribed the interviews verbatim, although we edited the transcripts for added clarity and comprehension. It is also important to recognize that the transcripts vary in tone, style and depth of expression. This was down to the manner and language form in which each interviewee responded to our questions. The first part, 'Regulatory Trends and the Research Landscape', contains one of the verbatim interviews. The part explores the regulatory landscape in Africa and maps the state of research into internet governance on the continent. It begins with Hayes Mabweazara's conceptual interrogation, which was the keynote speech at our 2022 conference. Mabweazara traces the history of internet governance, from the techno-optimist era of the late 1990s and the early 2000s to the present moment, where platform power and online harms now underscore the need for regulation of social media and broader internet usage. But African states have missed it by introducing repressive regulatory measures that limit freedom of expression, pointing to what we see as the need to explore appropriate regulations that are attuned to Africa's realities and not merely a rehash of western approaches, even as they remain consistent with prevailing international principles.

Following this, in Chapter 2, Guilherme Canela of UNESCO extols the importance of human rights in the enactment of digital media laws, arguing that the concern of regulators should be how to balance regulation with freedom of expression considerations. This balance, Canela observes, requires a complex arrangement where different approaches exist side by side, approaches such as platform self-regulation, co-regulation, user empowerment and multistakeholder governance. The key thing, therefore, is to ensure that all stakeholders are able to participate meaningfully in multistakeholder dialogues and that information is seen as a public good. The first part ends with Vincent Obia's systematic analysis, which maps the research field, finding that research into digital media regulation in Africa can be classified into five broad areas: laws or policies targeting free expression, internet shutdowns, online harms, internet governance/multi-stakeholderism and data privacy in that order. The result, Obia argues, underscores the focus that African scholars have given to matters related to censorship and internet bans. Obia further discusses the findings in light of issues around research methodology, place, publication types and time, outlining what these portend for the future of research into digital media regulation in Africa.

In Part 2 of the collection, we turn our focus to 'State Policy Approaches and Regulatory Challenges', as we consider policy and legal instruments that restrict digital freedoms and the perspectives of regulators on the prospects and challenges of digital policymaking. These legal instruments prohibit specific online content including incitement to violence, indecency, hate speech, seditious publications, libellous speech, blasphemy, terrorism promotion, threat to national security and political dissent. The part begins, in Chapter 4, with Youngson Ndawana, Joanne Knowles and Elastus Mambwe, who focus on cybersecurity laws and media freedoms in Zambia. Their chapter investigates the 2021 Cyber Security and Cyber Crimes Act, which they argue, points to media repression, vague legislations and digital authoritarianism (including internet shutdown), representing the government's desire to maintain control over the public sphere. Ndawana and colleagues further observe that the Act has consequences for freedom of expression, privacy and the balance between regulation and securitization, especially as it relates to the securitization of morality. Following this is Chapter 5, an interview with Latifa Akharbach, president of the High Authority for Audiovisual Communication (HACA), the media regulator in Morocco. Akharbach provides insights into

Morocco's approach to regulating digital media, noting that the country seeks to balance innovation and economic growth with the protection of users' rights and the public interest. She adds that while a specific legal framework for social media platforms is still under debate and discussions around an AI strategy are ongoing, existing laws covering areas like personal data and hate speech are in operation. There is also a focus on Pan-African cooperation and global digital governance, especially regarding the accountability of major tech platforms.

Next is Kobina Bedu-Addo's chapter on digital broadcasting in Ghana and the need for convergence in the regulatory framework. Bedu-Addo shows that Ghana's broadcasting regulation has not caught up with the changes that digitalization and convergence have brought, and this is because the political and economic elites want it so. Even though Ghana implemented the digital switchover in 2020, the government has continued with the regulatory status quo (with laws that were established in the 1990s), implying that analogue-era regulation is still being used in the digital era. This effectively means that there has been convergence in the way the media operates, but not in the regulation. Bedu-Addo argues that this state of affairs serves the interest of the political and economic class who want to maintain control over broadcast media practices, even in the era of digital transition. To end Part 2, Yemisi Akinbobola, Vincent Obia and Trust Matsilele consider the regulation of traditional and online broadcasting in Nigeria and South Africa in the years after the transition to democratic governance, following the legacies of military rule and apartheid, respectively. The chapter finds that the regulations in both countries revolve around themes such as vague interpretation, contradictions and (in)dependence of the regulators. It also analyses stakeholder remarks regarding how broad the regulations are, the inconsistencies in enforcement and ulterior motive concerns, with consequences for state-media relations. The chapter synthesizes all these to argue that what matters in evaluating the nature of traditional and online broadcasting regulation in post-transition countries like Nigeria and South Africa is the character of the political system, not necessarily whether the system is democratic or autocratic.

Following this is Part 3, titled 'Digital Media Censorship: Frictions, Tensions, Reaction'. Here, we highlight the perspectives of those who are the targets of regulation (e.g. journalists) and others who campaign for 'good' regulation (e.g. civil society actors) to demonstrate the tensions that digital media regulation precipitates and how people respond. The part begins, in Chapter 8, with Esther King'ori and Maureen Syallow's chapter on the analysis of Kenya's Computer Misuse and Cybercrimes Act of 2018. They examine the intentions behind the law, the process that led to it, the stakeholders who took part in the process and the complaints that arose after the law was enacted. Describing the law as repressive and overly broad, they note that the drafting of the Act lacked broad-based participation as it excluded the voices of citizens, civil society, social media influencers, bloggers and international organizations. In their argument, they suggest that although the law is needed for cybersecurity, drafters took advantage of this window to introduce politically motivated provisions to limit freedom of expression. After this, we present an interview with Churchill Otieno, a veteran online media journalist, who offers his perspective on digital regulation as it affects citizens and journalists in countries like Kenya. Otieno's interview reminds us that there are laws in the statute books that can be adapted to the digital space, noting that the new laws being introduced for social media internet communication largely serve the interest of the ruling elite. The solution, for Otieno, includes self-regulation and ethical standards for the media. But more than this, what is needed is not just user empowerment but also user agency – the people themselves must assert their rights when necessary to guard against state encroachment and protect civil liberties in online spaces.

Next is an interview with David Diaz-Jogeix of Article 19 on digital media regulation and freedom of expression in Senegal. Diaz-Jogeix sheds light on the regulatory landscape, highlighting both positive aspects like media diversity and negative aspects such as state interference and restrictive press codes. The interview also explores the challenges faced by online media, the role of government in censorship and the impact on citizen journalists. It further considers the importance of aligning Senegalese legal frameworks with international standards, the need for self-regulation, the potential for regional cooperation through bodies like ECOWAS and the African Union and a realistic appraisal of digital media regulation in Senegal in the future. Sulayman Bah ends the part, with a focus on what he terms 'evasive journalism', where online journalists circumvent regulation in The Gambia in order to report the news. The central law that the chapter interrogates is the 2013 Information and Communication Act, which The Gambian government has used to censor journalists in the country and beyond. Bah also notes that successive Gambian governments have maintained colonial-era laws such as sedition and criminal defamation, with which they repress the media, pointing to postcolonial influences and the need to decolonize digital media regulation in Africa. The reaction of Gambian journalists has been to evade censorship by establishing online news websites that operate from the diaspora – Bah conceptualizes this as 'evasive journalism'. But the government also responds by introducing strict laws and instituting a policy of incorporation, where prominent journalists are brought into government as a form of media capture – pointing to the underlying state–citizen distrust that makes 'good' digital media regulation difficult to achieve in Africa.

To conclude this book collection, Winston Mano brings together all the above discussions, emphasizing the importance of a decolonial approach based on Afrokology. This includes a call for African policymakers to institute human rights and public interest principles in digital regulation on the continent. It is also a rallying cry against digital colonialism, not only through regulatory capture in Africa but also in the influence that the Global North bears on African decisions. Altogther, the focus on Afrokology underscores the need to consider other tech knowledges and lived experiences outside of the West, bearing in mind that pluliversality contributes to a decentring of the West in order that ideas from elsewhere, Africa inclusive, can find collegiate expression. This need to shift African conversations from the margins to the mainstream is what our book collection signifies as part of facilitating a greater understanding of research, policy and the practice of digital media regulation on the continent.

NOTE

1. Frances Haugen opening statement before the US Senate on the effects of social media use on children on 5 October 2021, https://www.rev.com/blog/transcripts/facebook-whistleblower-frances-haugen-opening-statement-transcript-senate-hearing-on-children-social-media. Accessed 26 October 2023.

REFERENCES

Baccarella, Christian, Wagner, Timm, Kietzmann, Jan and McCarthy, Ian (2019), 'Averting the rise of the dark side of social media: The role of sensitization and regulation', *European Management Journal*, 38:1, pp. 3–6.

Bah, Sulayman (2023), 'Media law and journalism in post-colonial Africa', Ph.D. thesis, Birmingham: Birmingham City University.

Balkin, Jack (2004), 'Digital speech and democratic culture: A theory of freedom of expression for the information society', *NYU Law Review*, 79:1, pp. 1–55.

Bradford, Anu (2023), *Digital Empires: The Global Battle to Regulate Technology*, Oxford: Oxford University Press.

Calandro, Enrico, Gillwald, Alison and Zingales, Nicolo (2016), 'Mapping multistakeholderism in internet governance: Implications for Africa', *Research ICT Africa*, https://media.africaportal.org/documents/Discussion_paper_-_Mapping_Multistakeholderism_in_Internet_Governance_-_Implic_Zr3Zlht.pdf. Accessed 12 March 2022.

Cardenas, Pamela, Declercq, Antony, Lai, Mandy and Rasquinet, Nathan (2017), *The Political Economy of Media Capture*, LSE Capstone, https://assets.publishing.service.gov.uk/media/58d131dde5274a16e8000076/1.LSE_Capstone_Final_Report_for_DFID_WB_09Mar2017.pdf. Accessed 6 June 2021.

Chan-Meetoo, Christina (2013), *Media Ethics and Regulation: Insights from Africa*, Bamenda: African Books Collective.

Cunliffe-Jones, Peter, Diagne, Assane, Finlay, Alan and Schiffrin, Anya (2021), 'Bad law: Legal and regulatory responses to misinformation in Sub-Saharan Africa 2016–2020', in P. Cunliffe-Jones, A. Diagne, A. Finlay and S. Gaye (eds), *Misinformation Policy in Sub-Saharan Africa: From Laws and Regulations to Media Literacy*, London: University of Westminster Press, pp. 99–218.

Dwyer, Maggie and Molony, Thomas (eds) (2019), *Social Media and Politics in Africa: Democracy, Censorship and Security*, London: Bloomsbury.

Fagan, Frank (2018), 'Systemic social media regulation', *Duke Law & Technology Review*, 16:1, pp. 393–439.

Flew, Terry (2022), 'Beyond the paradox of trust and digital platforms: Populism and the reshaping of internet regulations', in T. Flew and F. R. Martin (eds), *Digital Platform Regulation: Global Perspectives on Internet Governance*, Cham: Palgrave Macmillan, pp. 281–309.

Flew, Terry and Gillett, Rosalie (2021), 'Platform policy: Evaluating different responses to the challenges of platform power', *Journal of Digital Media & Policy*, 12:2, pp. 231–46.

Flew, Terry, Gillett, Rosalie and Cole, Rachel (2021), 'Editorial – Platform governance: Power, diversity and accountability', *Journal of Digital Media & Policy*, 12:2, pp. 207–14.

Flew, Terry and Martin, Fiona (eds) (2022), *Digital Platform Regulation: Global Perspectives on Internet Governance*, Cham: Palgrave Macmillan.

Fuchs, Christian and Sandoval, Marisol (2015), 'The political economy of capitalist and alternative social media', in C. Atton (ed.), *The Routledge Companion to Alternative and Community Media*, London: Routledge, pp. 165–75.

Galtung, Johan (1971), 'A structural theory of imperialism', *Journal of Peace Research*, 8:2, pp. 81–117.

Glasius, Marlies and Michaelsen, Marcus (2018), 'Illiberal and authoritarian practices in the digital sphere', *International Journal of Communication*, 12, pp. 3795–3813.

Govenden, Prinola (2023), 'The media decolonial theory: Re-theorising and rupturing Euro-American canons for South African media', *Communicatio*, 49:2, pp. 1–30, https://doi.org/10.1080/02500167.2023.2219872.

Hardy, Jonathan (2014), *Critical Political Economy of the Media: An Introduction*, London: Routledge.

Kaun, Anne and Treré, Emiliano (2020), 'Repression, resistance and lifestyle: Charting (dis)connection and activism in times of accelerated capitalism', *Social Movement Studies*, 19:5–6, pp. 697–715.

Kaye, David (2019), *Speech Police: The Global Struggle to Govern the Internet*, New York: Columbia Global Reports.

King, Gary, Pan, Jennifer and Roberts, Margaret (2013), 'How censorship in China allows government criticism but silences collective expression', *American Political Science Review*, 107:2, pp. 326–43.

Klonick, Kate (2018), 'The new governors: The people, rules, and processes governing online speech', *Harvard Law Review*, 131, pp. 1598–1670.

Kperogi, Farooq (ed.) (2022), *Digital Dissidence and Social Media Censorship in Africa*, Oxon: Routledge.

Kwet, Michael (2019), 'Digital colonialism: US empire and the new imperialism in the Global South', *Race & Class*, 60:4, pp. 2–26.

Lodge, Martin and Wegrich, Kai (2012), *Managing Regulation: Regulatory Analysis, Politics and Policy*, London: Red Globe Press.

Manganelli, Antonio and Nicita, Antonio (2022), *Regulating Digital Markets: The European Approach*, London: Palgrave Macmillan.

Mano, Winston and Milton, Viola (2021), 'Decoloniality and the push for African media and communication studies', *Routledge Handbook of African Media and Communication Studies*, London: Routledge, pp. 1–18.

Mansell, Robin (2004), 'Political economy, power and new media', *New Media & Society*, 6:1, pp. 96–105.

McMillan, Imara (2019), 'Enforcement through the network: The Network Enforcement Act and Article 10 of the European Convention on Human Rights', *Chicago Journal of International Law*, 2:1, pp. 252–90.

Milan, Stefania and Treré, Emiliano (2019), 'Big data from the South(s): Beyond data universalism', *Television and New Media*, 20:4, pp. 319–35.

Obia, Vincent (2023a), 'Regulatory annexation and the matrix of dependence: The regulation of social media in Nigeria', Ph.D. thesis, Birmingham: Birmingham City University.

Obia, Vincent (2023b), 'Regulatory annexation: Extending broadcast media regulation to social media and internet content', *Communication Law and Policy*, 28:2, pp. 99–123.

Obijiofor, Levi, Murray, Richard and Singh, Shailendra (2016), 'Changes in journalism in two post-authoritarian non-Western countries', *The International Communication Gazette*, 4:79, pp. 1–21.

Ogbondah, Chris and Onyedike, Emmanuel (1991), 'Origins and interpretations of Nigerian press laws', *African Media Review*, 5:2, pp. 59–70.

Overton, Spencer (2020), 'State power to regulate social media companies to prevent voter suppression', *UC Davis Law Review*, 53:4, pp. 1793–1830.

Roberts, Tony, Mohamed-Ali, Abrar, Farahat, Mohamed, Oloyede, Ridwan and Mutung'u, Grace (2021), 'Surveillance law in Africa: A review of six countries', *Institute of Development Studies*, https://www.ids.ac.uk/publications/surveillance-law-in-africa-a-review-of-six-countries/. Accessed 23 July 2022.

Rochefort, Alex (2020), 'Regulating social media platforms: A comparative policy analysis', *Communication Law and Policy*, 25:2, pp. 225–60.

Sampaio-Dias, Susana, Mabweazara, Hayes, Townsend, Judith and Osman, Idil (2019), 'Practices, policies and regulation in African journalism: Mapping a research agenda', *African Journalism Studies*, 40:3, pp. 1–9.

Schlesinger, Philip and Kretschmer, Martin (2020), 'The changing shape of platform regulation', *LSE Media*, 18 February, https://blogs.lse.ac.uk/medialse/2020/02/18/the-changing-shape-of-platform-regulation/. Accessed 13 February 2022.

Suzor, Nicolas (2018), 'Digital constitutionalism: Using the rule of law to evaluate the legitimacy of governance by platforms', *Social Media + Society*, 4, pp. 1–11.

Wagner, Ben (2018), 'Understanding internet shutdowns: A case study from Pakistan', *International Journal of Communication*, 12, pp. 3917–38.

PART 1

REGULATORY TRENDS AND THE RESEARCH LANDSCAPE

1

Regulating Digital Technologies in Africa: Navigating a Shifting Tech Landscape

Hayes Mawindi Mabweazara

Introduction: Setting the Scene

The conversations in this volume on regulating new media technologies in Africa are both timely and essential. Like much of the Global South, Africa has often been sidelined in major debates on digital media regulation nor have the minority voices driving these discourses on the continent made significant inroads in shaping mainstream discourses on the regulation of digital technologies. In equal measure, research in this area within the region remains 'limited, fragmented, and typically undertaken as isolated and disconnected projects' (Gillwald 2003: 34). This lack of relevant critical discourse from the region and a broader research coherence, compounded by the absence of comprehensive regulatory precedents in the region, perpetuates a fragmented understanding of digital media's impact and the regulatory terrain, thereby hindering the development of cohesive and robust frameworks that address the unique challenges (and potential) of Africa's digital landscape. Gillwald's observation from several years ago that, '[u]nlike other parts of the world committed to participatory policy formulation processes, there are few independent local agencies contributing to public policy processes in the broader public interest' (Gillwald 2003: 34) remains strikingly relevant today, highlighting a persistent gap in the region's digital policy landscape. Without cohesive, context-specific studies and a unified dialogue, digital policy formation risks relying predominantly on imported models that may not align with the diverse realities across Africa, leaving crucial regulatory issues insufficiently addressed and the continent's digital future potentially compromised. This scenario is exacerbated by rapid technological advances driven by opaque and powerful multinational Tech Giants, which leave the region in a continual state of catch-up.

In addition to the above circumstances, the digital regulatory terrain across regions has exposed deep fissures of 'digital divides' while also illuminating extant geopolitical power imbalances and tensions among nation-states. This is further compounded by the fact that, in some contexts, laws and regulations have not kept pace with technological advancements, exacerbating disparities in governance approaches. Consequently, powerful digital regimes, such as China, the United States and the European Union, have assumed a dominant role in shaping the global regulatory agenda for digital technologies. This is particularly evident in efforts to confront the deepening disruptive power of Big Tech platforms. As Bradford (2023) outlines, these digital superpowers – or 'empires', to use her own term – have established regulatory trajectories that have become global models. They include China's state-driven model, the United States' market-oriented approach and Europe's rights-driven model. One can also add Australia's pragmatic and adaptive regulatory approach, responding to emerging risks while maintaining a pro-business environment (Flannery 2023). These regulatory models not only reflect differing perspectives on the relationship between markets, the state, and individual and collective rights (Bradford 2023) but also highlight the unique socio-political and economic conditions that shape how 'digital superpowers' regulate digital technologies – conditions that do not always align with realities across Africa.

The frameworks, particularly those emerging from western countries, including the United States and the EU, not only serve as key benchmarks for assessing the 'battle' to regulate digital technologies in Africa, but also influence regulatory approaches across the continent. Many African countries adopt and adapt a diverse range of digital regulatory frameworks, using them as reference points to shape their own policies. For instance, Ferracane et al. observe that the adoption of data protection laws in the region 'is often modelled after the EU's General Data Protection Regulation' (Ferracane et al. 2025: 1). Thus, writing about Africa's digital policy issues in the early 2000s, Munyua highlights that '[m]ost telecommunications policies developed in Africa have been the result of adoption of "best practice" recommendations from international organisations and developed countries' (Munyua 2003: 14). Making similar observations, Gillwald avers that most of the understanding of the information age, including discourses on regulating digital platforms, 'comes from the [...] experiences gained in the developed world. Africa produces little in the way of independent, primary research feeding into [digital] policy and regulatory processes' (Gillwald 2003: 34). Consequently, the region has often had to wait for developments elsewhere before adding its voice to these discussions. However, as noted above, while western empirical and theoretical perspectives offer valuable insights into the regulation of digital media, critical nuances require attention to contextually rooted dynamics, trends and issues that speak directly to African experiences. This 'one-way travel of legal and regulatory influence', as Sampaio-Dias et al. (2019: 2) contend, should be interrogated.

Therefore, my objective in this chapter[1] is to examine the key issues that have arisen as governments across the African continent navigate the social, economic, political and cultural implications of digital platforms. I explore questions around the dominant concerns regarding the influence and impact of digital media (the internet and its associated technologies) and the evolving approaches to governing and regulating them. In doing so, I consider how these concerns have been framed and debated over time. After over two decades of discourses largely shaped by perspectives from western liberal democracies (Flew et al. 2019; Murray 2019), shifting attention to one of the least developed regions of the Global South is particularly important as it helps us to better understand the complex dynamics of the challenges and opportunities that digital governance presents in varied contexts. Against this backdrop, I ask: why have questions of internet governance and regulation gained prominence since the late 2000s and remained relevant today? What are the implications of the rise in 'platform power' and the closely associated developments in artificial intelligence (AI), and the role of algorithms within social media platforms?

Rather than seek to offer definitive answers to these questions, I take them as entry points to a much broader discussion on the evolving regulatory landscape of digital technologies in Africa, a subject that remains highly contested, developing unevenly across the continent and raising more questions than settled conclusions, as this volume broadly demonstrates. The overarching aim, therefore, is to provide a historical contextualization of the current tech regulatory landscape in Africa by tracing its evolution from the techno-optimist era of the late 1990s and early 2000s to the present context, where the rise in 'platform power' and its social impact underscores the pressing need for firm regulatory mechanisms. I must stress, however, that I do not aim to provide a comprehensive socio-historical genealogy of Africa's digital regulatory landscape, as such an endeavour would require a far more extensive treatment than the scope that this chapter allows. Instead, I offer a broad 'analytic generalisation' (Yin 2003: 40) that captures an overview of the continent's current digital regulatory trajectory.

The chapter broadly draws on exploratory observations informed by data and insights from published peer-reviewed studies (journal articles and book chapters) and unpublished sources (research and policy documents), all collectively evaluated as making important advances to the understanding of the intricacies of digital media regulation in Africa. To beef-up, insights from these secondary sources, I also draw on my longstanding research, which broadly centres on the adoption of digital technologies within the context of African journalism but resonates across wider spheres of Africa's digital media landscape (see Mabweazara 2011, 2015, 2021).

It is also important to note that, while I use the terms *regulation* and *governance* interchangeably in this chapter, the two concepts have distinct nuances. *Regulation* typically refers to formal policies enacted by governments or government agencies – such as laws, bills, codes and statutes. In contrast, *governance* involves collaboration between various organizations beyond the government, including the private sector, civil society and international bodies. It is guided more by shared principles, rules and decision-making processes that shape the development and use of the internet and related technologies (Tunis Agenda for the Information Society 2005). One must also stress that in the broader scheme of things, the meaning of these terms varies according to the background and objectives of those who invoke them, often with 'many ambiguities and misunderstandings in defining the field and the issues at stake' (Brousseau and Marzouki 2012: 368).

A key point to emphasize is that, while this chapter occasionally refers to Africa as a single entity, it is crucial to recognize the continent's vast socio-economic and political diversity, alongside its intricate historical and infrastructural complexities – factors that significantly influence the adoption of digital technologies and the regulatory landscape. There are marked differences and gradations between countries, including distinct national digital trajectories, each of which has important implications for regulation. So, we cannot talk of Africa as one homogeneous entity with uniform developments on the digital front. Despite these differences, there is a consensus among communication scholars that Africa, like the rest of the world, is experiencing the disruptive impact of digital platforms (Mabweazara 2013; Moyo et al. 2020). The region has not been immune to the complexities and challenges that come with the rapid development and adoption of digital technologies across various social spheres – a process that gained momentum across much of the continent in the late 1990s, significantly later than in the developed economies of the Global North.[2] Understanding these contextual issues is crucial for examining the evolution of digital technology regulation in Africa. The following section, therefore, examines the defining features of early regulatory approaches, their underlying rationale and their development in response to the rapid advancements in digital technologies.

Shifting Ideas on New Tech Regulation: From Euphoria to Polycentricism

As previously intimated, any discussion on contemporary digital regulatory developments in Africa must consider a pivotal historical period – the late 1990s to mid-2000s – the era of an open or libertarian internet (Flew 2021). This era was defined by an optimistic, largely *technicist* or *deterministic* view of the internet and its associated technologies – the belief that simply introducing technology into society would trigger dramatic transformations, enabling it to 'leapfrog' traditional development stages by bypassing established infrastructure, practices and the conventional path of gradual progress (Berger 2005). It was a period of wonderment and excitement over the liberatory potential of the internet – a 'eureka moment' of sorts. This digital euphoric moment or 'honeymoon' period set the backdrop for contemporary developments in the digital sphere.

Discourses on governance and regulation were more inclined towards 'leapfrogging' Africa into the digital era than to controlling or policing usage. The era was conveniently described using countless catchy metaphors. Some of the earliest included the internet as a *frontierland* 'full of opportunities for navigators, explorers and other adventurers' (Information Society 2003: n.pag.) and fancy terms like the *information superhighway*, which reflected the ambitious vision for an interconnected, accessible digital landscape likened to highways – suggesting a fast, efficient pathway for communication and connectivity globally. These metaphors were bandied about in public discourse and were frequently used in popular media, policy debates and legal opinions in reference to digital communication systems and the internet (Perritt 2001). The excitement was partly driven by the Modernization paradigm's idea that development depended on 'external aid' and that everyone needed to be part of the *superhighway* in order to provide the information-impoverished with access to the wealth of (western) information, thus enabling them to transform their lives (Berger 2005).

During these early developments, in 1997, Rhodes University in South Africa established a very vibrant annual international conference under the name 'Highway Africa', a partnership between the Rhodes School of Journalism and Media Studies and the South African Broadcasting Corporation, with support from a variety of partners, including government, development agencies and corporate sponsors. It became the largest hub for debates on the impact of digital technologies on journalism and the media, and by extension, society. The conference grew into the largest gathering of African journalists and communications experts worldwide, bringing together around 500 delegates for discussions and training on new media and the Information Society. It arguably became a flagship event for championing what we could possibly do with digital technologies to transform lives and indeed the practice of journalism and communication in the broader sense within the continent.[3]

Discussions and debates at the conference prominently featured issues of internet governance and the funding of digital infrastructure, particularly in response to Africa's increasing engagement with new technologies (see Everett 2009). The conference also served as a key platform for representing African interests at global conventions such as the World Summit on the Information Society (WSIS) –

a two-phased summit initiated by the United Nations to establish a multistakeholder forum addressing digital inclusivity, with a particular focus on the internet. As Everett (2009) observes, a notable example of this engagement was the effort made by conference organizers and participants to influence the second phase of WSIS, held in Tunisia in November 2005, which culminated in the submission of a statement aimed at preventing the marginalization of Africa's digital concerns while advocating for the continent's active involvement in the deliberations of this influential United Nations-led initiative. This context is particularly important for two closely connected reasons: first, as Everett rightly observes, the Highway Africa Conference played a significant role 'in advancing ICT development and infrastructures across the African continent over a period of years' (Everett 2009: 194). Second, this significance is further highlighted when considered against the backdrop of Rhodes University's instrumental role in introducing and developing internet connectivity in Africa, having been granted the first South African IP address in 1988 (see Lawrie 1997; Nyirenda-Jere and Biru 2015).

As noted earlier, the dominant discourses during this period were largely underpinned by techno-solutionism – the idea that most, if not all problems, could be solved by technology. Questions of access to digital technologies, bridging digital divides and leapfrogging the continent into the so-called information superhighway were at the forefront. Similarly, during this period, internet governance was largely decentralized at the international level (Information Society 2003). However, western liberal democracies played a dominant role in shaping the agenda and discourse on how the internet should be governed. In fact, many developing nations at the time complained that 'the world's most visible internet governance body – the US-based Internet Corporation for Assigned Names and Numbers (ICANN) – [did] not adequately represent their interests and should be scrapped' (McGuire 2003: n.pag.). So, as well as the deregulatory economics and the 'countercultural idealism' that characterized that period (Flew 2021: 18), this was a period of 'polycentric regulation' of the internet at an international level without being fixed in any geographical sphere (Scholte 2017: 168). The regulatory approach was underpinned by 'the idea that governments can and should be largely kept at bay in matters of regulating the internet' (Flew 2021: 18).

The prevailing view was that the best decisions were those made by a rough consensus in a multistakeholder forum, where governments were relatively uninvolved in the process of governing the internet. This perspective stemmed from the excitement surrounding the internet and its associated technologies as a liberatory space, where individuals could freely express themselves, guided by the belief that minimal government involvement was ideal. This spirit of limited governmental interference was famously captured in John Perry Barlow's (1996) bold 'Declaration of the independence of cyberspace' and was evident in key summits such as the WSIS referred to above. One of the key resolutions of its first gathering in Geneva, Switzerland, in 2003 – where the summit solicited ideas and recommendations for a global effort to bridge the 'digital divide' – was highlighted in paragraph 50 of The Geneva Declaration of Principles and Geneva Plan of Action (2003). This emphasized a coordinated approach to the international governance of the internet, proposing the establishment of a multisectoral and multiregional working group on internet governance:

> [I]n an open and inclusive process that ensures a mechanism for the full and active participation of *governments, the private sector, and civil society from both developing and developed countries, involving relevant intergovernmental and international organisations and forums*, to investigate and make proposals for action, as appropriate, on the governance of the Internet
>
> (The Geneva Declaration of Principles and Geneva Plan of Action 2003: 11, emphasis added)

This approach aimed to foster regional and international cooperation, ensuring broad participation in the development of the digital space (Information Society 2003; Nyirenda-Jere and Biru 2015; Scholte 2017), with the overarching goal of achieving a common vision and commitment to building a people-centric, inclusive and development-oriented Information Society, in which everyone could create, access, utilize and share information. This polycentric model of internet governance, characterized by the involvement of multiple institutions and communities, supported a diverse and adaptive regulatory landscape. However, as the internet's influence expanded and concerns over security, data privacy and market dominance intensified, governments began to assert greater control. This shift towards a more centralized and stringent regulatory framework marks the new realities of what has been termed the *regulatory turn.*

New Realities and the Regulatory Turn

While the techno-optimism of the 1990s and early 2000s has undoubtedly been realized in most parts of Africa – albeit in deeply disproportionate ways – through the redefinition of 'the very fabric of human [communication] experience', vastly expanded communication channels and hitherto unseen access to content and data with 'immeasurable benefits for individuals and societies' (Bradford 2023: 2), a point needs to be made here that, as elsewhere, the region is witnessing the gradual erosion of the aforementioned long honeymoon period – the period of polycentric governance of the internet, as national regulatory frameworks begin to take firmer shape, albeit in an uneven and evolving manner.

One might thus ask, as this volume broadly does, where Africa – in all its complexities – is headed in the regulation of digital technologies. And by extension, what regulatory direction is the region taking? Answers to these questions are multifaceted and too broad to fully address in the space available here, but one might argue, as seen elsewhere across the globe, that the African continent is at a point where we are witnessing a *critical regulatory turn* in relation to the internet and its associated technologies. The regulatory turn marks the shift from viewing the internet as a self-regulating space to recognizing the need for external regulation, partly driven by concerns over the social impact of digital platforms, thus prompting national authorities to introduce new oversight frameworks (Flew 2021). It could further be asserted that over the past decade or so, this shift has intensified, particularly with the emergence and entrenchment of 'platform power', a point also noted within the western context (see, for example, Schlesinger 2020; Tambini 2018; Flew 2021); I return to this topic in the following section.

This 'regulatory turn' coincides with a surge in the publication of a key set of polemic texts – far too many to mention here, such as Morozov's (2011) powerful critique of 'cyber-utopianism', boldly showing that the internet is not always what it appears to be. Rather than purely promoting democracy, it can also reinforce authoritarian regimes and make democratic efforts more challenging. Similarly, McChesney (2013) also offers a foresighted examination of the relationship between the internet and the economy – arguing that capitalism's colonization of the internet has spurred the collapse of credible journalism and made it an unparalleled apparatus for government and corporate surveillance. The book brings to the fore the close and complex relationship between digital and social inequalities, and the very lived consequences of digitization. By the same breadth, Curran also challenges readers to realize that 'society exerts, in general, a greater influence on the internet than the other way around' (Curran 2012: 59) and calls for greater reflection as to what role we should assign this powerful digital medium.

The list of the foregoing critical polemic texts is growing, and stretching beyond the academy to include digital policy practitioners, all pointing to the increasingly complex connections between technologies and society, and the dilemmas if not inadequacies around polycentric regulatory approaches and structures that are not fixed in any geographical sphere with 'unclear and contestable lines of command between regulatory institutions' as well as lacking 'an ultimate decision point' (Scholte 2017: 172). This shift towards polemic discourses about the internet shows that the 'bubble' of excitement has finally burst. The unrestrained excitement of the 1990s and early 2000s has gradually faded over the past decade as civil society actors, academics, digital policy practitioners and other stakeholders have increasingly reconsidered the internet, its associated technologies – particularly Big Tech platforms – and their impact on society.

So, *the regulatory turn*, along with an increasing understanding of developments within the sector, within the digital sphere, demonstrates that the online environment, long perceived as beyond the reach of government policy and oversight (Scholte 2017; Flew 2021), can, in principle, be regulated, and that the internet and its related technologies are not necessarily as inherently liberatory as once imagined. While the move towards tighter regulation of online spaces clearly stems from a confluence of factors rather than a single moment, in the Global North, the 2016 US presidential election served as a key catalyst, intensifying debates about the role of digital platforms in democratic processes. The period between the Obama and Trump administrations saw a notable evolution in digital governance discourse. However, concerns over data privacy, misinformation, digital incivility and platform accountability, among other issues, had already been growing, as highlighted by the widely publicized 2013 Edward Snowden revelations about the extent of US National Security Agency surveillance (Flew and Martinand 2022: 1) and the European Union's adoption of the General Data Protection Regulation (GDPR).

In contrast, in Africa and much of the Global South, identifying the origins and trajectory of this regulatory shift is more complex, due to limited and often fragmented research. Nevertheless, concerns over political stability, threats to ruling power, national security, data protection and the broader societal impact of the internet have been central to regulatory efforts. While awareness of the internet and its associated technologies influence – particularly the role of Big Tech – has shaped policy debates on misinformation, hate speech and digital sovereignty, regulatory frameworks have largely been driven by domestic political and security considerations. Thus, while some factors behind the regulatory turn in Africa mirror those in other regions, regulation is also shaped by deeper tensions between state authority and fundamental rights, particularly freedom of expression and access to information. Governments frequently justify stricter digital controls as necessary for security and stability (Munoriyarwa and Mare 2022).

As elsewhere, there is a growing realization among governments in the region that there is a need to protect citizens' personal data and regulate how public and private entities use personal data. This is linked to a need to establish, as we see in some countries, data protection authorities that are tasked with helping to control how data are appropriated and used. In countries like Kenya, Rwanda and South Africa, we have seen the development of comprehensive data protection laws, which, in a typical fashion, share some elements found in the European Union's 2016 GDPR. However, in several countries, these laws also serve as instruments for consolidating and 'securitizing data protection-related matters' (Munoriyarwa and Mare 2022: 101), hence aligning with the state's broader strategy of power preservation and consolidation.

Consequently, as noted above, the growing control and regulation of digital platforms is accompanied by increasing tensions between freedom of expression and the restrictions imposed on digital platforms. In other words, old ways of regulating and controlling the communication environment are, in some countries, being directly transferred into the governing and regulation of digital spaces. Consequently, some policy and regulatory responses, such as Uganda's Social Media Tax 2018 and Tanzania's Online Content Regulations 2018 (amended 2020), have been perceived as tools for suppressing political activism and restricting online freedom of expression, while also reinforcing existing mechanisms for controlling and suppressing free speech (see Namasinga Selnes and Orgeret 2020; Ubena 2020). This trend increasingly highlights the abuse of the legislative process and the criminal justice system in several countries, as arrests of ordinary citizens for cybercrimes, including alleged social media abuse, have become commonplace. The shift towards *digital authoritarianism* or *repression* is also associated with a range of digital restrictions, including internet shutdowns and signal jamming. Such measures have been observed in countries like Eswatini, Kenya, Zambia and Zimbabwe, but are widespread across the continent, particularly during civil protests and elections. In the same manner, questions of surveillance and censorship have also become critical ways of controlling the internet across the continent (see Munoriyarwa and Mare 2022).

From the above overview, it is evident that the regulatory approach to the internet in Africa has undergone a significant transformation since the late 1990s when the first documented gathering on internet governance in the region was convened by the African Internet Group shortly after the establishment of ICANN (Nyirenda-Jere and Biru 2015). Throughout the late 1990s and early 2000s, internet governance followed a decentralized, global and multisectoral approach primarily focused on building institutions to *support internet expansion and accessibility rather than regulating usage and content.* In contrast, the unfolding regulatory landscape places increasing emphasis on tighter controls and governance frameworks that address content regulation, digital rights and platform accountability. This shift underscores the growing role of African nation-states as key 'sovereign actors' in shaping discourses on the regulation of digital technologies.

The Era of Platformization

A crucial dimension of contemporary internet governance in Africa is the impact of *platformization* – a growing shift and concentration of online interactions and engagements within a relatively small number of dominant corporate social media platforms such as Facebook, a phenomenon some scholars also describe as the rise of 'platform power' (Gillespie 2018). This marks a sharp departure from the internet's earlier vast and decentralized nature towards a landscape shaped by fewer but more powerful and widely used digital actors. When one looks across Africa, there is widespread evidence that platforms such as WhatsApp and Facebook have gained ground on the continent relative to what we see in the Global North. Take Facebook for instance. The number of Facebook users in Africa was estimated at 124.6 million at the end of 2015 (Willems 2016) and by 2022, there were 271 million users, a number forecast to reach over 377 million by 2025 (see Bhanye et al. 2023; Galal 2024).

A key driver of the growing power of social media platforms on the continent is mobile internet, which has gained traction thanks to the widespread availability of 'basic "feature phones", which do not have the full range of apps [...] but have some Internet access and popular apps such as WhatsApp and Facebook' (Mabweazara 2021: 358) as well as attractively priced prepaid social media 'data bundle packages' (Willems 2016: n.pag.). In countries such as Zambia, Zimbabwe and many others in the region, mobile phone operators are often trying to outcompete each other in providing affordable services to their customers. As a result of this, as Willems (2016) observes, in most countries in the region, the nature of internet experience is not only largely determined by social media but also predominantly takes place within the walls of platforms such as Facebook. Regulatory frameworks have evolved to respond to this growing dominance of digital platforms, which as noted earlier, has come with multiple challenges, for example, concerns over disinformation, data privacy, digital incivility, market dominance and a pronounced role in shaping political processes, including elections thus leading to governments in countries such as Burundi, Chad, Congo, Uganda and Zimbabwe ordering mobile phone operators to 'block access to social media during periods of elections or protests, frequently citing concerns over national security' (Willems 2016: n.pag.).

It is also worth highlighting that these platforms are strongly imbued with the Silicon Valley ethos of platformatizing free speech and user engagement for economic ends. This is the DNA of their business model, their underlying philosophy. This explains their longstanding reluctance to manage online interactions in ways that address both civic concerns and what we might call the 'customer interest'. This tension is evident in repeated clashes between platforms and various governments, particularly in the Global North, where platform executives have occasionally been summoned before parliamentarians after incidents exposing their failure to protect users. Some, however, dismiss these hearings as mere 'symbolic action' rather than meaningful efforts to reform platforms (see Napoli 2021).

These considerations highlight why the immense power wielded by these platforms must be accompanied by significant social responsibility. Given their ability to control and gatekeep communication in the networked age, this responsibility cannot be overlooked. Moreover, as the platforms increasingly shape political discourse on the continent (Bosch et al. 2020), the urgency of addressing their role in governance and accountability, among other issues, becomes even more apparent. This raises pressing questions: where do the main points of contention lie? What are the core concerns when it comes to platform power? The chapters in this collection engage deeply with these issues, illustrating the vast and complex landscape of challenges involved in integrating social responsibility into the governance of digital platforms in Africa.

Thus, while the era of 'platform power' can be seen as broadly signalling an expansion of communication capabilities in Africa as well as highlighting the sheer endless possibilities emerging with the era of interactive digital technologies (Mabweazara and Mare 2021), it has also ushered in new challenges and entrenched 'age old' normative dilemmas in communication ecosystems. In short, the era of 'platform power' has become both a catalyst for unprecedented connectivity as well as a 'prime site of the normative crisis' (Duff 2008: n.pag.) facing African communication in the digital era. As new threats emerge and longstanding ethical concerns take on renewed significance, the imperatives and complexities of digital regulation to protect citizens in individual countries become increasingly pressing and multifaceted. From the range of issues discussed in this book, it is clear that the list of key concerns is extensive – far too long to cover in the space available here. However, for illustrative purposes, I will isolate a few notable ones.

Privacy, Security, Disinformation and Cyberpropaganda

As highlighted above, the immense power of platforms brings with it unsettling disruptions and challenges that demand significant social responsibility. Central to this responsibility, among other issues, are concerns about *privacy* and *security* as well as the spread of *disinformation* which have become topical issues, most frequently raised when talking about the normative dilemmas posed by platforms in Africa and elsewhere (Mare et al. 2019).

Concerns about the potential loss of the right to personal privacy are not only prevalent but perhaps also one of the reasons why most governments in Africa have sought to curb and control the internet and its associated technologies. Privacy issues have plagued almost all platforms, most notably Facebook in the scandal surrounding Cambridge Analytica, a now-defunct British political consulting firm that gained notoriety for its misuse of personal data harvested from Facebook to influence political processes, including in some African countries like Nigeria and Kenya (see Ekdale and Tully 2019). The 2016 US presidential race and the UK Brexit referendum were also implicated (Brown 2020). These scandals exposed unethical data mining and microtargeting practices, which led to the company's closure in 2018 amid widespread public and regulatory backlash.

This breach of privacy by platforms and their growing influence and interferences with electoral processes has unsurprisingly intensified calls for their governance and regulation. Also, in relation to questions of surveillance practices, scholars like van Dijck (2014) have spoken about 'dataveillance' – the monitoring of citizens based on their data traces online, representing the continuous tracking of citizens. This is more prominent in some countries than others. In countries like Zimbabwe, this question of dataveillance has been enhanced due to technologies that have been imported from China (Munoriyarwa and Mare 2022). This connects to the observation that every online interaction produces a data trail which can, in turn, inform further economic transactions. And debates have emerged around what has been referred to as data colonialism or digital capitalism (Couldry and Mejias 2019; Kwet 2019), or, as Zuboff (2019) calls it, surveillance capitalism.

As noted earlier in this chapter, security concerns have often been used as justifications for controlling or regulating digital platforms in Africa. Several African governments have cited national security, cyber threats or the protection of citizens from harmful online content as reasons to impose stricter controls on the internet and social media platforms. While these regulatory overtures and actions often stem from genuine concerns about national security and protecting citizens from cyber threats, it has also been observed that they are sometimes used as tools to stifle free expression, limit access to information or suppress political opposition (see Munoriyarwa and Mare 2022). Therefore, the balance between national security and individual freedoms remains a contentious issue in many African countries.

Another issue that underscores the need to regulate these platforms relates to questions of disinformation and cyber propaganda – what was popularized as 'fake news' in the first Trump Administration. In the African context, there have been growing concerns about the use of digital technologies to spread disinformation (Mare et al. 2019; Tully et al. 2022), particularly during elections and in moments of civil unrest. We see this often in South Africa when it comes to xenophobic attacks fuelled by disinformation that circulates on digital platforms, including WhatsApp (Chenzi 2021). This has been facilitated, in part, by the generic affordances of interactive digital technologies, particularly their spreadability, to use Jenkins et al.'s (2013) concept.

Online Hate Speech, Harassment and Accountability

There are also concerns around online incivility associated with hate speech and harassment – particularly their amplification through social media platforms.

These issues have been identified as significant and growing concerns within the African context (Mabweazara and Mare 2021). Indeed, one of the most insidious forms of what has been referred to as 'dark forms' of digital participation in Africa is the systemic harassment of female journalists, particularly in patriarchal, toxic and polarized political media environments (Msimanga et al. 2023). In light of these concerns, when one talks about the need to regulate digital platforms, one of the key points that warrants consideration is the role of AI and algorithms. Given these developments – specifically, the growing risks associated with online incivility, the weaponization of digital platforms for harassment and the increasing influence of AI-driven decision-making – I would argue that the next big challenge for African countries is to shift attention to the regulation of AI and its implications in structuring the conduct of digital platforms and their impact on human behaviour.

Questions of accountability and agency will have to be considered within this mix. Key among these is the extent to which AI can be regarded as accountable, and, more broadly, what agency should we give to technology? There are also questions of bias, fairness and transparency that must be incorporated into the debate about AI, alongside legal and ethical issues. This raises a critical question: Can AI – or even algorithms – make decisions that can be challenged legally? Complicating matters further, due to the underlying nature of AI and algorithms – the very fact that they sit underneath complex global supply chains and interactions – it may be difficult to grasp exactly how they operate (Mabweazara and Mare 2021). Moreover, when we consider questions of digital media literacy in the African context, where, arguably, literacy levels are lower than those observed elsewhere (Open Knowledge Network 2024), the implications become even more concerning. In such environments, it becomes even more worrying to see how AI can be used to reinforce existing inequalities, for instance, through biased content moderation, automated censorship or discriminatory algorithmic profiling. People use digital platforms potentially without understanding that behind the scenes – deep within the architecture of platforms – their actions, how they engage, what they see and what they share are largely shaped, influenced and even manipulated by 'hidden' non-human actors (Mabweazara and Mare 2021). Therefore, in addressing the regulation of digital platforms in Africa, I would argue that the next level of intervention should shift attention towards AI and algorithms in a more comprehensive manner.

Concluding Thoughts and Charting a Way Forward

Based on the discussion above, we can see why there are growing calls for greater regulation of online activities, all justified by the need to reduce social harms (Flew 2021). These calls are difficult to argue against. And hardly will you find scholars who advocate for a return to the late 1990s–early 2000s euphoric moment when the internet was basically left unchallenged. There is a clear consensus across regions on the need to regulate digital platforms to curb their power. From the above discussion, a series of regulatory questions emerge, including the need to ask what regulatory approaches work best for African countries. Other related questions logically follow: Do twentieth-century communication and media policies still have any relevance in the current environment? Are nation-states' regulatory frameworks still viable given the global networked nature of digital platforms? We can also ask who should be involved in the regulation of content on these platforms? Should governments be involved at all? Can it be an approach that involves co-regulation? Or should it be about self-regulation – allowing platforms to regulate themselves?

These are questions that we have not definitively answered, partly because the digital space comes with a high level of innovation, including regulatory innovation. We see examples in what platforms themselves are attempting, although that has led to further contentions and debates. For instance, Facebook's Oversight Board presents a case of how approaches have been devised to regulate what happens on these platforms (Klonick 2020). In Africa, the emphasis among non-governmental groups still largely rests on the need for an open internet, coinciding with a freedom-of-speech mandate that platforms uphold. As a result, what we often see across the continent is that any attempt to regulate digital platforms is sometimes challenged, particularly by civil society organizations, quite vigorously. This is evident in countries like Zimbabwe, where organizations like the Media Institute of Southern Africa have been vocal in terms of what needs to be regulated and who should be involved in the regulation of platforms.

But what I would argue here is that above all, the golden rule is that any limitation of rights should be lawful and be within existing statutes. It should be proportionate and necessary in that democracy – in other words, it should be contextually rooted and not just a blind adoption of policies developed elsewhere, particularly in the Global North. It should also be based on questions of transparency and openness, especially given the opacity that generally pervades the terrain around platforms and how they conduct their business. Social justice elements should also be considered, i.e. questions of human dignity, equality and freedom. In trying to apply these principles, we should be mindful that getting the balance right will not be easy, especially given the fact that the difficulty that surrounds digital media regulation in Africa partly revolves around re-establishing public confidence in state regulation and foregrounding the public interest value of these regulatory practices.

In conclusion, the regulatory landscape of digital technologies in Africa is vast and evolving, and this discussion has only scratched the surface. While key aspects have been highlighted, many complexities and nuances remain beyond the scope of this essay. Notably, growing concerns over platform market dominance and the impact of AI demand deeper analysis in terms of the state of play. Future research must grapple with these pressing issues to provide a fuller picture of the unfolding regulatory challenges.

NOTES

1. An earlier version of this chapter was presented as a keynote at the Regulating African Digital Media conference, Birmingham Centre for Media and Cultural Research, Birmingham City University, May 2022. My sincere thanks to the editors for transcribing the presentation and helping to transform it into a coherent chapter.
2. To put this into perspective, while the internet originated in the 1960s with the US-based Advanced Research Projects Agency Network, a pioneering long-haul network funded by the US Department of Defence, sub-Saharan Africa's first network did not emerge until nearly three decades later (Nyirenda-Jere and Biru 2015).
3. I had the privilege of attending and actively participating in a number of these conferences – initially as a student at Rhodes University and later as a conference delegate presenting papers – contributing to research that shaped aspects of the conference deliberations, including early discussions on how Southern African journalists were adopting digital technologies (see Mabweazara 2005).

REFERENCES

Barlow, John P. (1996), 'A declaration of the independence of cyberspace', Electronic Frontier Foundation, 8 February, https://www.eff.org/cyberspace-independence. Accessed 10 December 2024.

Berger, Guy (2005), 'Powering African newsrooms: Theorising how Southern African journalists make use of ICTs for newsgathering', in G. Berger (ed.), *Doing Digital Journalism: How South African News Gatherers Are Using ICTs*, Grahamstown: High Way Africa, pp. 1–13, https://guyberger.ru.ac.za/fulltext/Doing_Digital_Web.pdf. Accessed 11 February 2025.

Bhanye, Johannes, Shayamunda, Ruvimbo and Tavirai, Rungamai C. (2023), 'Social media in the African context: A review study on benefits and pitfalls', in R. Baikady, S. M. Sajid, J. Przeperski, V. Nadesan, M. R. Islam and J. Gao (eds), *The Palgrave Handbook of Global Social Problems*, London: Palgrave Macmillan, pp. 1–32, https://doi.org/10.1007/978-3-030-68127-2_366-1.

Bosch, Tanja, Admire, Mare and Ncube, Meli (2020), 'Facebook and politics in Africa: Zimbabwe and Kenya', *Media, Culture & Society*, 42:3, pp. 349–64, https://doi.org/10.1177/0163443719895194.

Bradford, Anu (2023), *Digital Empires: The Global Battle to Regulate Technology*, Oxford: Oxford University Press.

Brousseau, Eric and Marzouki, Meryem (2012), 'Old issues, new framings, uncertain implications', in E. Brousseau, M. Marzouki and C. Méadel (eds), *Governance, Regulation and Powers on the Internet*, Cambridge: Cambridge University Press, pp. 368–97.

Brown, Allison J. (2020), '"Should I stay or should I leave?": Exploring (dis)continued Facebook use after the Cambridge Analytica Scandal', *Social Media + Society*, 6:1, 2056305120913884, https://doi.org/10.1177/2056305120913884.

Chenzi, Vincent (2021), 'Fake news, social media and xenophobia in South Africa', *African Identities*, 19:4, pp. 502–21, https://doi.org/10.1080/14725843.2020.1804321.

Couldry, Nick and Mejias, Ulises A. (2019), *The Cost of Connection: How Data Is Colonizing Human Life and Appropriating It for Capitalism*, Stanford: Stanford University Press.

Curran, James (2012) 'Rethinking the internet', in J. Curran, N. Fenton and D. Freedman (eds), *Misunderstanding the Internet*, London: Routledge, pp. 34–65.

Duff, Alistair (2008), 'The normative crisis of the information society', *Cyberpsychology: Journal of Psychosocial Research on Cyberspace*, 2:1, n.pag., https://cyberpsychology.eu/article/view/4207/3248. Accessed 10 December 2024.

Ekdale, Brian and Tully, Melissa (2019), 'African elections as a testing ground: Comparing coverage of Cambridge Analytica in Nigerian and Kenyan newspapers', *African Journalism Studies*, 40:4, pp. 27–43, https://doi.org/10.1080/23743670.2019.1679208.

Everett, Anna (2009), *Digital Diaspora: A Race for Cyberspace*, Albany: State University of New York Press.

Ferracane, Martina F., Ugarte, González S. and van der Marel, Erik (2025), 'The Brussels effect in Africa: Is it beneficial for intra-regional trade in digital services?' *Journal of International Economic Law*, 28:1, pp. 1–22, https://doi.org/10.1093/jiel/jgae059.

Flannery, Angela (2023), 'Regulation of digital platform services in Australia: Tracking the European Union', *International Bar Association*, 24 July, https://www.ibanet.org/regulation-of-digital-platform-services-in-Australia. Accessed 10 December 2024.

Flew, Terry (2021), *Regulating Platforms*, London: Polity.

Flew, Terry and Martin, Fiona (2022), 'Introduction', in T. Flew and F. Martin (eds), *Digital Platform Regulation: Global Perspectives on Internet Governance*, Cham: Palgrave Macmillan, pp. 1–21.

Flew, Terry, Martin, Fiona and Suzor, Nicolas (2019), 'Internet regulation as media policy: Rethinking the question of digital communication platform governance', *Journal of Digital Media and Policy*, 10:1, pp. 33–50.

Galal, Saifaddin (2024), 'Social media in Africa: Statistics and facts', *Statista*, 10 January, https://www.statista.com/topics/9922/social-media-in-africa/#dossier-chapter1. Accessed 17 January 2025.

Gillespie, Tarleton (2018), *Custodians of the Internet: Platforms, Content Moderation, and the Hidden Decisions That Shape Social Media*, New Haven: Yale University Press.

Gillwald, Alison (2003), 'Development by default', *Rhodes Journalism Review*, 23, pp. 34–35.

Information Society (2003), 'Internet governance: Cyber-empires and digital divides', preview of the booklet published in February 2004, The World Summit on the Information Society.

Jenkins, Henry, Ford, Sam and Green, Joshua (2013), *Spreadable Media: Creating Value and Meaning in a Networked Culture*, New York: New York University Press.

Klonick, Kate (2020), 'The Facebook Oversight Board: Creating an independent institution to adjudicate online free expression', *The Yale Law Journal*, 129:8, pp. 2418–99.

Kwet, Michael (2019), 'Digital colonialism: US empire and the new imperialism in the Global South', *Race & Class*, 60:4, pp. 3–26.

Lawrie, Mike (1997), 'The history of the internet in South Africa: How it began', hmvhDOT-net website, http://archive.hmvh.net/txtfiles/interbbs/SAInternetHistory.pdf. Accessed 17 February 2025.

Mabweazara, Hayes M. (2011), 'The internet in the print newsroom: Trends, practices and emerging cultures in Zimbabwe', in D. Domingo and C. Paterson (eds), *Making Online News: Newsroom Ethnographies in the Second Decade of Internet Journalism*, New York: Peter Lang, pp. 57–69.

Mabweazara, Hayes M. (2013), 'Normative dilemmas and issues for Zimbabwean print journalism in the "Information Society" era', *Digital Journalism*, 1:1, pp. 135–51.

Mabweazara, Hayes M. (2015), 'African journalism in the "digital era": Charting a research agenda', *African Journalism Studies*, 36:1, pp. 11–17.

Mabweazara, Hayes M. (2021), 'Towards reimagining the "digital divide": Impediments and circumnavigation practices in the appropriation of the mobile phone by African journalists', *Information, Communication and Society*, 24:3, pp. 344–64.

Mabweazara, Hayes M. and Mare, Admire (2021), *Participatory Journalism in Africa: Digital News Engagement and User Agency in the South*, London: Routledge.

Mare, Admire, Mabweazara, Hayes M. and Moyo, Dumisani (2019), '"Fake news" and cyber-propaganda in Sub-Saharan Africa: Recentering the research agenda', *African Journalism Studies*, 40:4, pp. 1–12.

McChesney, Robert W. (2013), *Digital Disconnect: How Capitalism Is Turning the Internet Against Democracy*, New York: New Press.

McGuire, David (2003), 'UN summit to focus on internet', *Washington Post*, 4 December, https://www.washingtonpost.com/archive/business/2003/12/05/un-summit-to-focus-on-internet/e87ea7aa-2a8e-4185-a666-52bf6112e06d/. Accessed 20 June 2023.

Morozov, Evgeny (2011), *The Net Delusion: The Dark Side of Internet Freedom*, New York: Public Affairs.

Moyo, Dumisani, Admire, Mare and Mabweazara, Hayes M. (2020), 'Editorial: Social media, the press, and the crisis of disinformation in Africa', *Communicatio*, 46:4, pp. 1–6.

Msimanga, Mbongeni J., Tshuma, Lungile A., Matsilele, Trust and Jamil, Sadia (2023), 'Contending with sexual harassment: A study of Southern African female journalists' experiences', *Journal of Communication Inquiry*, 0:0, pp. 1–25, https://doi.org/10.1177/01968599231210790.

Munoriyarwa, Allen and Mare, Admire (2022), *Digital Surveillance in Southern Africa: Politics, Politics and Practices*, Cham: Palgrave.

Munyua, Alice (2003), 'On the table: Africa's issues', *Rhodes Journalism Review*, 23, pp. 14–15.

Murray, Andrew (2019), *Information Technology Law: The Law and Society*, Oxford: Oxford University Press.

Namasinga Selnes, F. and Orgeret, Kristin S. (2020), 'Social media in Uganda: Revitalising news journalism?' *Media, Culture & Society*, 42:3, pp. 380–97.

Napoli, Philip (2021), 'The symbolic uses of platforms: The politics of platform governance in the United States', *Journal of Digital Media & Policy*, 12:2, pp. 215–30.

Nyirenda-Jere, Towela and Biru, Tesfaye (2015), 'Internet development and internet governance in Africa', *Internet Society*, https://www.internetsociety.org/wp-content/uploads/2017/08/InternetInAfrica-2015070820Final.pdf. Accessed 6 February 2025.

Open Knowledge Network (2024), 'Digital literacy, not just access, is Africa's biggest problem', 18 June, https://blog.okfn.org/2024/06/18/digital-literacy-not-just-access-is-africas-biggest-problem/. Accessed 24 February 2025.

Perritt, Henry (2001), *Law and the Information Superhighway*, New York: Apsen Law and Business.

Sampaio-Dias, Susana, Mabweazara, Hayes M., Townend, Judith and Osman, Idil (2019), 'Practices, policies and regulation in African journalism: Mapping a research agenda', *African Journalism Studies*, 40:3, pp. 1–9.

Schlesinger, Philip (2020), 'After the post-public sphere', *Media, Culture & Society*, 42:7–8, pp. 1545–63, https://doi.org/10.1177/0163443720948003.

Scholte, Jan A. (2017) 'Polycentrism and democracy in internet governance', in U. Kohl (ed.), *The Net and the Nation State: Multidisciplinary Perspectives on Internet Governance*, Cambridge: Cambridge University Press, pp. 165–84.

Tambini, Damian (2018), 'Social media power and election legitimacy', in D. Tambini and M. Moore (eds), *Digital Dominance: The Power of Google, Amazon, Facebook, and Apple*, New York: Oxford University Press, pp. 265–93.

The Geneva Declaration of Principles and Geneva Plan of Action (2003), World Summit on the Information Society, Geneva, 10–12 December, https://www.itu.int/net/wsis/docs/promotional/brochure-dop-poa.pdf. Accessed 22 February 2025.

Tully, Melissa, Madrid-Morales, Dani, Wasserman, Herman, Gondwe, Gregory and Ireri, Kioko (2022), 'Who is responsible for stopping the spread of misinformation?: Examining audience perceptions of responsibilities and responses in six Sub-Saharan African countries', *Digital Journalism*, 10:5, pp. 679–97, https://doi.org/10.1080/21670811.2021.1965491.

Tunis Agenda for the Information Society (2005), World Summit on the Information Society, Geneva 2003–Tunis 2005, https://www.itu.int/net/wsis/docs2/tunis/off/6rev1.html#:~:text=34.,and%20use%20of%20the%20Internet. Accessed 17 February 2025.

Ubena, John (2020), 'The bolts and nuts of online content regulation in Tanzania', *Information & Communications Technology Law*, 29:1, pp. 45–65.

van Dijck, Jose (2014), 'Datafication, dataism and dataveillance: Big data between scientific paradigm and ideology', *Surveillance and Society*, 12:2, pp. 197–208.

Willems, Wendy (2016), 'Beyond free basics: Facebook data bundles and Zambia's social media internet', Africa at LSE blog, 1 September, https://blogs.lse.ac.uk/africaatlse/2016/09/01/beyond-free-basics-facebook-data-bundles-and-zambias-social-media-internet/. Accessed 20 November 2024.

Yin, Robert K. (2003), *Case Study Research: Design and Methods*, London: Sage.

Zuboff, Shoshana (2019), *The Age of Surveillance Capitalism: The Fight for a Human Future at the New Frontier of Power*, London: Profile Books.

2

Human Rights, Freedom of Expression and Multi-Stakeholderism in the Governance of New Media Technologies in Africa – Interview with Guilherme Canela

Vincent Obia

Guilherme Canela is the director of the Division for Digital Inclusion and Policies and Digital Transformation at UNESCO headquarters in Paris. He has expertise in media, communication and regulation in the Global South, particularly in Latin America. He played a pivotal role in developing the UNESCO Guidelines for the Governance of Digital Platforms, which also covers Africa; the Guidelines were launched in November 2023. In this interview, which took place on 8 August 2023, he outlines his perspectives on the need to balance regulation with freedom and the importance of multistakeholder governance as the regulatory approach that African countries should adopt.

VINCENT OBIA: What is your view about social media regulation globally, particularly given the role played by big tech companies and platforms, and the attempts by government entities and the need to consider how to address issues around digital harms?

GUILHERME CANELA: This is of course the one-billion-dollar question of the moment, and it requires a very complex answer. There are a few elements that are important to structure this debate in a more reasonable way. The first thing that is important to underline is that this space is already regulated. It is not that the regulation is a new thing. For instance, if you look at the United States where there is a big debate about Section 230, the one that guarantees the non-intermediary liability for these companies, which is an important aspect to protect among other things, freedom of expression. It is a government issue, since it is a legal and statutory instrument, establishing rules of the game for this digital ecosystem. So, the first thing we need to do to demystify this debate about regulation is its current status. Sometimes, I hear that we have a non-regulated market and that there is a need to go to a regulated market. For others, there is a need to keep self-regulation. This is certainly not true. This market is already regulated in many ways. Maybe the question is whether the existing regulation is enough or is too much or is it the right regulation. This is the first important element.

The second important element is that when we look into a more comprehensive set of rules that could be called the governance of this digital ecosystem, you have different things that are in place. You have certain areas where there is more self-regulation, which is different from statutory regulation that is enforced by law enforcement agencies or regulators or independent regulators. There are some scenarios where you have core regulatory arrangements where some of the issues are implemented by the regulated market and others are implemented under the oversight of the regulatory authorities. So, the other important element is that there is already a complex ecosystem of governance and again the question is, is this system working? Should we provide new guidance for that? Should different things be put in place? So on and so forth.

The third point is that it is true that maybe the most comprehensive new institutional structure to deal with these problems or the challenges offered by the digital ecosystem is the current European regulation – that is the DSA (Digital Services Act), the DMA (Digital Markets Act) and so on. So, the European effort is currently the most comprehensive attempt to reorganize the existing elements with new rules of the game trying to deal with or to tackle the problems that this space was offering for different reasons. And the European effort which is a regional effort with a regional body with different characteristics has somehow triggered discussions about regulation in other jurisdictions. Although during COVID-19, there was an acceleration of different kinds of regulation of the digital space, particularly in trying to deal with some content problems like disinformation or misinformation. We saw an explosion of the so-called anti-fake news laws or things like that in the digital ecosystem. The problem with this is unfortunately the problem with several of the draft legislation that is here and there being proposed. Several of them unfortunately are not aligned with international human rights standards, particularly freedom of expression standards.

In a nutshell, our challenge is to recognize that the digital ecosystem has offered the most incredible opportunities for the expansion of freedom of expression since Gutenberg invented the printing press. Our challenge is how to keep supporting, fostering and enhancing these opportunities while dealing with the negative externalities that this ecosystem has also generated – things like the expansion of disinformation. It is not that the digital system has invented disinformation, but it has expanded it for different reasons that we can discuss. So, we need to foster the opportunities, we need to mitigate the risks and eventually it may be necessary to prosecute the harms if they go over a certain threshold.

This is the challenge in a very broad manner. This challenge won't be solved only with one solution. There is no simple solution for complex problems. The likelihood of addressing this is a complex system where we will need to have different approaches, operating in the same boat with their different added values. Some practices will be self-regulatory, meaning the companies will need to do a lot of better things themselves. Some of these will be co-regulatory arrangements – negotiations that the companies will have with regulators in a public manner. And some of these things will require statutory regulation. The balance of those different components will depend on the jurisdiction, the context, and whether there is a regional human rights system in place with further protections for human rights in general and for freedom of expression in particular.

Regardless of what is possible and what is desirable in terms of these different contexts etc, there are some elements, and this is the UNESCO view, that should be in place no matter what. There are some key principles in dealing with this and if we do not have them, the regulation or the governance including regulation, co-regulation, self-regulation, whatever it is will fail. First and most important is that they should be human-rights-driven. The first step of the process is to make sure that whatever is being done is based on international human rights law. The second element is that we need to have in place a very strong and meaningful process of transparency with clear rules on what we mean; what does it mean to have more transparency, more transparent companies and more transparent regulators. The third element is that we need to require human rights due diligence when new things are being put in place or when you have specific situations when the companies are developing a new product or if they are dealing with a new context like, for instance, elections in a country. What is the human rights due diligence they are implementing to cope with whatever is the situation and of course based on human rights standards? Finally, we also need to have a strong component of user empowerment. What are the rules of the game in terms of empowering the users so they can take informed decisions on what is going on?

And when it comes to statutory regulation, by which I mean laws approved by parliament to give powers to governmental authorities, two things are very important. First, we need to start with the obligations of the states not the obligations of the companies and those obligations are very important – these are the things that the state should not do, not the things they should do. For instance, states should not go for internet shutdowns to deal with this problem. States should not criminalize freedom of expression to deal with these problems and so on and so forth. But also, there is an institutional element that is very important; that is, if any regulatory measures are being established and are to be implemented by a particular bureaucracy or agency, these regulators should be independent from political power and independent from the regulated sector to avoid what is known in the literature of regulation as the risk of capture. In a nutshell, these are the drivers we need to consider when we are looking into this kind of debate.

VO: When we consider those drivers, those contexts, and the global framework perspective, how would you describe the trajectory of digital and online media regulation in Africa?

GC: Well, I am not an expert in the African continent, so I guess I am not the most reliable person to respond to that question, but I can tell you a bit of the trajectory globally speaking. Since the beginning of the United Nations system and universal system of human rights when we are dealing with technologies that can have an impact, positive or negative, on freedom of expression. The starting point is Article 19 of the Universal Declaration of Human Rights and the regulatory mechanism of that article in terms of international law is Articles 19 and 20 of the ICCPR, the International Covenant on Civil and Political Rights. If you look into the history of regulating different technologies during the twentieth century and the twenty-first century from the perspective of the universal system of human rights, these regulations have a dialogue with both Article 20 of the Universal Declaration and Articles 19 and 20 of the ICCPR plus all the international jurisprudence related to the actual implementation of those instruments. So, we are talking about the decisions of international human rights courts, we are talking about the decisions of the committee of civil and political rights, and so on and so forth. The trajectory of this discussion is always a balancing act on how much should be regulated to protect freedom of expression while dealing with the eventual externalities that freedom of expression can generate, and these things are already there underlined in Articles 19 and 20 of the ICCPR.

Of course, the language is still very much vague in the sense that it is important to also look into jurisprudence. The courts have been interpreting the implementation of these different kinds of regulations or even judicial decisions and so on at the national level, establishing tools like the three-part test or the Rabat Plan of Action. So, it is important how you establish thresholds in the sense of understanding the ways that the regulatory elements that restrict freedom of expression (and here a very important parenthesis – restriction does not mean elimination neither does it mean censorship). When you say that, for instance, a particular content on television can only be broadcast after a certain hour to protect children, this is not censorship. You are not saying that the content can't be broadcast, you are just saying that there is a need to broadcast that content just after – I do not know whatever time – so you can guarantee families the possibility of being at home to say to the children, 'Look this is too violent for you or this is too pornographic', or whatever it is the reason that the family will decide that children can't have access to that content.

So, when we say that restrictions can be in place to protect freedom of expression and other rights, it is not necessarily that the restriction should be an elimination of the content. It is more about the rules of the game. The trajectory was always about looking into this balancing act: freedom of expression *vis-à-vis* other rights. And also, the best way to do that to protect freedom of expression.

Of course, when you had the broadcasting system since the electromagnetic spectrum is a limited public resource, in a way, it was easier to do these kinds of regulations because you could deal with a lot of that within national boundaries or national frontiers. The internet disrupted this possibility of dealing only with these in a national context. You need to look broader than that and that's also the beauty of the internet. Now the trajectory also needs to look into what happened at the regional level. So although I do not know the details of the African context, if you look into the regional system of human rights – so for instance the inter-American system of human rights with the Inter-American Commission and the Inter-American Court of Human Rights or the European system with the European Court of Human Rights (but the African system is similar with the African Court of Human Rights but also the regional courts like ECOWAS for Western Africa or the Eastern Court of Justice for East Africa), you will see that several cases throughout the last years and decades were analyzing the actual implementation of these kinds of regulations by different member states. And the international courts reacted to that saying whether this is okay or not *vis-à-vis* the international instruments that these countries have already ratified.

To take the African case, the ECOWAS court took important decisions saying to governments that they can't do internet shutdowns. So, the trajectory is a trajectory of trying to keep the principles and then you have this important decision of the Human Rights Council saying that the rights we have offline should be applied online. And the last many years were actually a strong attempt to apply this kind of things. The problem is that in the last few years, this accelerated so much – I mean the characteristics of the digital ecosystem, which again are some of the very positive things. They come with serious impacts on important processes for our democracies, for instance. These things impact on elections or the way you manage a pandemic or whatever it is.

And then of course there are the content issues in what we call the four V's known as volume, velocity, virility and verisimilitude – because the problem is not that this information is a new thing. What is new is how big this can be, how fast this can be, how viral this can be, and also how it looks like truth or deepfake. And now with generative AI, it is even a bigger problem. So, it is not that it is that simple to identify; it is not only about fact checking; it is not only about teaching people media and information literacy. It is about everything. It is all these things plus regulatory measures plus transparency and so on. This, I think, the global trajectory that in a nutshell looks into three components. How we qualify the demand for quality information; how we empower the users to interact with the digital ecosystem, so they are capable to then do that in a critical way – to know that, 'Let's not forward this thing because it's fake or whatever it is.' So, this is one part of the problem – the empowerment of the users and citizens of all ages. But, of course, it is very unfair to put all the weight on the shoulders of the citizens when we are dealing with trillion-dollar companies with all their lawyers. So, this is one part but it is not the only part.

The second element of this puzzle is how to foster and enhance the supply side – how we stimulate good content. Good content here is basically content that was checked and produced in a professional and accurate way. For these, we need to support the suppliers of information. We need to have policies to protect journalists, to protect the news media, to protect the scientists, to protect the artists, to protect the teachers – all the people that are producing content that will offer to the digital ecosystem things that are relevant to counter bad content, by which I mean disinformation, hate speech, or whatever it is. But unfortunately, only protecting the demand and the supply is no longer enough, we need to discuss the transmission chain. The transmission chain is the companies, the social media companies, the internet companies and so on and what they should bring to the table to again foster the opportunities for freedom of expression but mitigate the risks for freedom of expression and other human rights. So, we are now in the moment that it is more or less clear that the problem we have is what are the different pieces of the puzzle that we need to look into and how exactly to do that. There is no consensus and there are legitimate concerns regarding any course of action regarding the different pieces of the puzzle.

VO: In terms of the African context and globally, what role do you see the users playing in Africa when it comes to shaping the regulation or being part of the regulatory process? And how is this affected by what we would call the politics of locationality – the fact that most of these big platforms are located in countries like the US or maybe China, and then countries in Africa having to navigate challenges around power imbalance?

GC: In our approach – I mean the UN approach including UNESCO – in terms of the governance of these systems in order to protect human rights, while we are dealing with these problems and including freedom of expression, one of the safeguards that are necessary to be in place is the multistakeholder characteristic of these governments. Which means that the different stakeholders, including the users, should participate actively in this process, not only being consulted but there should be ways that the different voices that are relevant for this – they should have concrete institutionalized ways of putting their concerns, suggestions, and comments on the table. When these things are being decided and are being implemented and looking into this complex story of the digital ecosystem.

Virtually every stakeholder has a say. So, if you look into the problems, it is understandable that freedom of expression is what digital rights groups are more concerned or maybe they are more conservative when talking about expanding regulatory provisions, for instance. But when you look into the children's rights movements or the women's rights movements etc., maybe they are interested in how they can deal with the actual real problems that children or women or others are facing with all the complex and bad content you have against women or against children in this space. So, it is not that one group is more important than the other. The issue is how to find a balance and the balance should be fine with dialogue, and actual participation in a meaningful way. In terms of taking these decisions, if the countries want these discussions to be aligned with international human rights standards, they need to know that from the outset. These processes should be multistakeholder processes with some meaningful participation of all the relevant stakeholders. Then you have of course the structured civil society organizations and the companies themselves. You have the academics like you guys, technicians, engineers, but also the users organized in different ways.

And so, on your other question, the issue is that the more countries go into very lonely solutions for this, the less likelihood to succeed. And second, even if they succeed, they can have a very bad result and fragmented internet – something that's not interoperable. It is completely redesigning something that actually has very good impacts in a positive way for humanity in many fields, not only on the freedom of expression front. So, if these countries are serious about getting the best outcome, and the best outcome for us is further protection of human rights – for us, the way is agreeing on common principles on how to do that. Because if the principles are similar, then the companies have an interest in applying them because this will reduce their transactional costs. Of course, it is a nightmare to deal with 194 regulations if you take only the number of member states of UNESCO. But if these regulations are very similar and are based on key principles that are the same, then it is much easier to implement. In the end, it becomes more difficult for the companies to say, 'Oh, we can't deal with that.'

So again, I think – in this case you asked me about Africa – if there is a Pan-African discussion to really support these principles of transparency, human rights, due diligence, and dealing with these things in a certain characteristic, then of course there will be specific things. Like, for instance, in our Guidelines, we are talking about the specificity of languages when we are dealing with content moderation – that the company should invest to offer content moderation tools in different languages. This is the specificity when looking into a particular country, but the principle is the same. It is the principle of diverse investment in terms of multilingualism, etc. Our approach even *vis-à-vis* the countries that are the headquarters of these big companies is that if there is an international effort to look into common principles that are human-rights-based, this will be a win-win game for everyone. If the players started going alone, the chances that we will have a very bad result in many ways is high.

VO: Could there be a holistic approach that can serve as a balancing act of international criminal law and international human rights law when it comes to digital regulation?

GC: The first thing is that governments can always misuse international standards when they are applying them in concrete cases which does not mean that the standards are bad. I mean the issue is that if you apply the standards like this, you are going to have these results in terms of protection of human rights. But if you misuse them, you can't expect to have the same results. That's why when I was responding to the question on the trajectory, I mentioned that we need to look into the principles that international law has – Article 19 of the UDHR and Articles 19 and 20 of the ICCPR, plus international jurisprudence in terms of how you implement those different provisions. In Article 19, you will see that public order and national security are one of the elements that the Article considers as a criterion for eventual restrictions to freedom of expression. However, the international courts have underlined that in doing that, you need to have certain rules of the game. Some of them are that the restrictions should be narrowly defined in a particular law, approved by parliament so that national security can't be broadly evoked.

You need to say in the law what exactly you mean for national security. And then when you are applying that to restrict freedom of expression, you need to follow the three-part test: you need to follow the idea of legitimacy, legality, and necessity and proportionality. This is where countries normally fail the test, because you see that a particular measure is neither necessary nor proportional to the harm that is being dealt with. Article 19 is not about prohibitions of speech; it is about restriction – regulating speech, which is not saying you can't publish something. It is after you publish, how we deal with that, so it is an ex post facto decision by the regulator or by the judges. The only Article that deals with prohibitions is Article 20, which has only two elements: propaganda for war and incitement to hatred.

And in terms of the incitement to hatred, we need to know what is hate speech and what is not. If you look into the Rabat Plan of Action – that is another element of the international jurisprudence – the Rabat threshold has not only three parts as the three-part test that I already explained; it has six parts to take a decision when there is a hate speech element being analysed either by the judge or by the regulator. So, this is a long preamble to say that I do not think it is possible to deal with the provisions of international standards while not keeping the protection of freedom of expression. If you follow the standards in a comprehensive manner and not picking and choosing specific elements of the international standards that can serve the issue that you have at hand. This unfortunately is what happened in several cases. If you look into the jurisprudence of the internet of the inter-American Court of Human Rights or the European Court of Human Rights, you will see that those two courts have again and again been telling national jurisdictions that the way they are interpreting, for instance, national security provisions are not aligned with international human rights standards.

So, it is not enough to just say, 'Oh I did that because it's national security.' You need to pass the public interest test, the threshold test, and so on. That's why in our view for the digital ecosystem if there are a detailed set of principles that could be applied in a common ground, this could help those countries that want to do things well to do things well but for those that do not want to do things well, these principles can assist the civil society to hold these governments accountable. Because they can say, 'Well, what you are saying here, that it is national security, it's not. Or that this regulator you have established is not an independent regulator because it's missing the characteristic a, b or c. Or what you are asking the company it's not allowed by international standards' and so on and so forth. And also to help to hold companies accountable when they say, 'Oh we are transparent.' Okay everyone wants to be transparent but when you look into the detail, you can say, 'Okay but what you are saying you do for transparency is not what this international guidance is actually highlighting as true meaningful transparency.'

Of course, I am not naïve. It is easy to say it is difficult to implement, but I think we need to be very clear that the misuse of international standards does not invalidate the international standards. What we need to do is to expose the misuse. It is very important to have a clause on public health in terms of one of the elements that can eventually generate restrictions to freedom of expression. I mean you can't, based on freedom of expression, allow a party in front of a hospital because you will disturb the public health of that hospital. But in that case, you have all the components of the three-part test applied in this balancing act. And then the judge needs to assess it because if the noise that is generated in front of that hospital is a protest because the doctors are being accused of corruption, then this should be allowed and then the public health clause is not valid in this case because the necessity and proportionality test will be checked for this. So, it is not that the system developed by the international human rights standards is a bad system; what is bad is sometimes the actual implementation in real cases.

VO: UNESCO is developing a system known as the Regulatory System, a kind of multi-stakeholder system. Based on this, what kind of regulatory system do you think Africa should then go for in terms of multi-stakeholderism and embracing a multi-stakeholder approach to regulation?

GC: First just a small clarification: UNESCO is not developing a multi-stakeholder regulatory system; we are developing guidance so that for those who want to develop a system, they will have the elements based on international human rights law on how to do it. We are not a regulator; we are a standard-setting organization. So, we can offer the standards but then it is up to the different stakeholders to take them on board or not. That clarification made, I think it is not a question that can have an answer on a regional basis, not even national. I think it will depend on the strategy regarding the different stakeholders involved. So, for instance in the process that we did for developing these guidelines it was a multi-stakeholder process, we had global consultations, and I was very much impressed by the amount of comments and suggestions and criticisms we received from stakeholders based in Africa – all different kinds of stakeholders. We had even consultations organized by children in Africa, and some were children from 13 to 17 years old who read the UNESCO text and sent back to us their comments.

Now to this process and this can be useful for Africa but also for other regions. What we need to do when we are conducting multistakeholder processes (we at UNESCO but also the governments, or whoever is trying to put a multi-stakeholder system in place) is to make sure that you offer the conditions for the different stakeholders to participate in a meaningful way. Of course, the big companies have their battalions of lawyers or whatever engineers, and they can quickly react. Governments, in different sizes, have their diplomats, their experts who can join. But if you want civil society to participate in a meaningful way, you need to offer the conditions for that, otherwise it will be an unfair game. So, for instance, what we did in this process, we launched the call for small grants so those organizations that wanted to participate but needed some funds – sometimes it was to just organize a coffee break. Sometimes it was to translate the document of UNESCO in a local language, participants to travel from one city to another, and sometimes it was to buy a Zoom license. So, we provide grants so that they could participate, and these kinds of barriers were not an impediment for them to actually join. This is a very small example to say that any serious multistakeholder process or institution should consider what are the needs of the different stakeholders to participate in these processes in a meaningful way.

Now you mentioned the African challenges. Although I am the global head of freedom of expression, and I am not a particular expert in the African situation, but I think it is very important based on what I have observed in these many years that I have been doing these things is how to build regional networks. Because these regional networks empower the stakeholder voices. One thing is if you go alone as the stakeholder of the country a, b or c; the other thing is if you go together with the stakeholders of several countries facing similar challenges, they are not always the same, but they are similar. So, I would say that from the stakeholder perspective, they should always try to join forces to create synergies because this is the way they will have more wins to have their voices considered in these different processes that are ongoing either in the international arena or in the national arena.

VO: We are in a world where we have new tech, artificial intelligence, machine learning and other emerging technologies. How do we learn from the past? What are the things from your perspective and your years of expertise in this area that governments, tech and other stakeholders need to be very conscious of as we go forward in regulating these new technologies?

GC: I think we discussed a lot of those drivers during this session, but to add something – 30 years ago when we were facing a new wave of democratizations after the fall of the Berlin Wall, one of the big questions was, what are the characteristics of the media ecosystem that actually should be reinforced to really consider a media ecosystem, one that is democratic and plural. There was a meeting in Windhoek, a very pivotal seminal meeting in 1991 where this discussion took place and the stakeholders who were gathered in Windhoek in 1991, they came up with what is known as the Windhoek Declaration. The 1991 Windhoek Declaration established three key concepts for answering this question: What is the media ecosystem that can deal with this new world of a more democratic nature, with new democracies coming? And the three concepts were the need to have an independent, free and pluralistic media.

So, in the last 30 years, there was a lot of investment from all the stakeholders, the UN system including UNESCO, the government and civil society with the academics, to say, 'Okay have we really protected these three things: independence, freedom and pluralism?' So, 30 years later in 2021, we decided to come back to Windhoek and say, 'Okay, the Windhoek Declaration had a lot of impact in shaping the discussion during these three decades and these three things are still important: independence, freedom and pluralism. But what else do we need with the changes of the digital ecosystem among other changes?'

So, we, all the stakeholders, produced a new document called the Windhoek Plus 30 Declaration, and this new document underlines a very important thing that I think is central to the dialogue with your question – that is, recalling that information is a public good, therefore, journalism is a public good.

And when you have public goods like clean air, like the oceans, or things like that, you need to develop a series of policies to protect these public goods that are things collectively used by the shared humanity. In the Windhoek Plus 30 Declaration, there was an emphasis on three concepts to build this idea of information as a public good. One is the thing you mentioned – the producers of information as a public good – they need to be viable; they need to exist. I mean you need to fund journalism; you need to fund science; you need to fund things that are producing this. The viability of the producers of information is a key element for this new era because the usual business model that was funding these kinds of things is no longer working. The second element is the transparency of the players, particularly the tech companies. If we want to produce evidence-based policy in this area, we need evidence, and to have evidence, we need these companies to be more transparent than they are. The third element is user empowerment, the media and information literacy, the capacity of every one of us to deal with these news stories, the old ones and the new ones and generative AI, whatever it is.

In a nutshell, our bet here is that we need to reinforce this idea that information is a common good and a public good. And how we protect that, how we advance this will be the challenge. It is the current challenges and will be the challenge of the next years. It is very much related to the other big challenge we have on this planet; which is saving the planet itself. So, we currently have two existential problems on this planet: we need to save the planet, climate change, the environment and so on, and we need to save freedom, we need to save democracies. And for both things, information as a public good is essential because part of the problem in convincing governments and people and so on that the climate story is an issue. It is the level of information that we have about climate change and all these problems. It is like the democratic story. So, if we do not engage in a meaningful and collective way to protect information as a public good, these two big existential threats we are facing – the planet and democracies – won't survive. They will have problems, so we need to move ahead with this discussion.

NOTE

1. A link to the 'Guidelines' is available here: https://unesdoc.unesco.org/ark:/48223/pf0000387339. Accessed 10 December 2023.

3

Mapping a Research Agenda for Digital Media Regulation in Africa: A Systematic Analysis

Vincent Obia

Introduction

Academic research into digital media regulation in Africa has become more pronounced since the Arab Spring uprising that swept across North Africa and the Arab world. The uprising signalled an activist reawakening and prompted governments in the region to impose policies such as internet shutdowns (Gerbaudo 2013), resulting in increased research interest into how shutdowns function as a tool of censorship. The interest has only grown ever since, and scholars who work in the African context have widened their focus to include multistakeholder governance frameworks (Calandro et al. 2016; Nonnecke 2016) and the policies of national governments justified on the need to combat harmful online content (Olaniyan and Akpojivi 2021). Researchers have also considered the role that private platforms play in shaping how we use technologies by investigating issues around content moderation (Ayalew 2021) and data privacy on the continent (Bryant 2021). This breadth shows how far the scholarship has come, underscoring how vital it is to aggregate and synthesize studies on digital media regulation in Africa to provide a definitive statement on what the general body of knowledge indicates, where the gaps are and what the way forward is. These are the issues that I consider in this chapter, which is based on a systematic review of studies on digital media regulation in Africa.

I argue that such a focus is essential, given that Africa is at a crossroads as far as digital media regulation is concerned. Countries on the continent have found themselves having to regulate the usage of social media networks that are mainly owned by western or Chinese companies. In this sense, regulation has involved introducing punitive laws that, research has demonstrated, largely miss the mark (Cunliffe-Jones et al. 2021; Obia 2023). Still, technology is progressing into new forms, such as artificial intelligence and the Internet of Things (IoT), posing challenges for countries in the Global North, especially Africa. A starting point for the continent would be to learn lessons from existing research on digital media regulation to inform future regulatory policies. Doing this requires bringing together the somewhat disparate research in the field, and this is what I have done in this chapter, which asks the question: what is the state of research into digital media regulation in Africa?

Answering this question entails asking other sub-questions: What is the spread in terms of duration (year) and type (e.g. article) of the research in the area? What countries/regions do they focus on? What methodologies do they use? What subject areas (e.g. data privacy) do they highlight? What are their findings/recommendations? What are the gaps in knowledge? What is the way forward? In addressing these questions, I employ systematic analysis, and the next section outlines my steps. This is followed by the chapter's findings, including an overview of research in the field and the understanding gleaned from their collective outcomes. Seen in the broader context of this book, the chapter underscores the research significance and landscape of digital media regulation in Africa, setting the stage for the research that currently exists in the field. By so doing, it brings together what we know about regulatory action and intent, in areas such as state-citizen distrust, political self-interest, broad application of laws, digital authoritarianism, power asymmetry between the Global North and South and the need for measures that balance regulation with civil liberties and are based on broad-based multistakeholder participation and the application of international human rights principles in policymaking across the continent.

Methodology

To synthesize research on digital media regulation in Africa, I used systematic review as the study's methodology, which I adapted based on the procedure outlined in previous research (Petticrew and Roberts 2006; Xiao and Watson 2019). It involved searching relevant databases, such as Scopus, for research on digital media regulation in Africa. The instrument that guided my search was the review protocol, which two external researchers validated; it served as a methodological guardrail that determined what studies I included or excluded. Below, I indicate the principal features of the content of the protocol, evident in the process that I followed.

Inclusion criteria: I included studies (both empirical and conceptual) that consider digital media regulation in one or more African countries. I did not include studies that were based on comparisons between countries in Africa and countries in other continents to ensure that I got a picture as accurate as possible on regulation in Africa. Regulation, as used here, comprised social media policy, data privacy, internet governance and controls on internet communication as it broadly relates to content. Since I was interested in scoping the entire field, I included all types of academic publications, including journal articles, books or book chapters, conference papers, reports, theses, dissertations, policy briefs and discussion papers. All the research were published in English.

Literature identification: This refers to the search terms that I used, the databases searched and the start and end dates. There was no start date precisely because I wanted to include the earliest studies in the field. The end date was May 2023, which was when I carried out the search of the literature and began analysing the data. The databases included Scopus, Web of Science, Google Scholar and Google Search in that order. I also searched the following journals: *Journal of African Media Studies*, *Communication Law and Policy* and *Journal of Digital Media & Policy*. I found some studies in these journals, except for *Communication Law and Policy*. This is an indication that research into digital media regulation in Africa has not found a home in *Communication Law and Policy*, one of the flagship journals in the field. I searched the UK's Electronic Thesis Online Service (EThOS) for Ph.D. theses but found no relevant entries.

I note that the lack of entries in *Communication Law and Policy* represents a blight on the *Journal*'s global reach, as it points to the exclusion of African voices and scholarship, although most likely indeliberate. There are at least three possible reasons for this lack of entries. First, the *Journal* has not been receptive of studies that focus on Africa; second, African scholars are not aware that the *Journal* exists; third, African scholars are aware that it exists but are not open to publishing their works in it. The third reason is most plausible, given that *Communication Law and Policy* subsequently published my study on regulatory annexation in Africa (Obia 2023), a sign also that African scholars are aware of the Journal. Perhaps what the *Journal* needs is to reach out more to African scholars. This is important because of the need to secure a greater diversity of voices in the wider scholarship, ensuring that no part of the world is missing in debates relating to digital media regulation. It also points to the importance of regular mapping exercises such as the present study, where gaps like this can be identified.

As for the lack of entry in EThOS, this is not surprising, given that I found only one thesis in my general search. It shows that digital media regulation in Africa may not have been of particular interest to doctoral candidates, within or outside the continent.

Search terms: I used the following keywords to search each database:

- 'New media regulation in Africa';
- 'Social media regulation in Africa';
- 'New media governance in Africa';
- 'Social media governance in Africa';
- 'Internet regulation in Africa';
- 'Internet governance in Africa';
- 'Internet censorship in Africa';
- 'Regulating fake news in Africa';
- 'Regulating hate speech in Africa.'

I am conscious of the limitation of using these search terms – the fact that they are not exhaustive. In particular, I restricted the terms to specific mentions of 'Africa', meaning studies that focused on specific African countries without using the words 'Africa' or 'African' may have been inadvertently excluded. Regardless, I note that some of the studies that were included in the review focused on specific African countries as opposed to Africa as a whole, showing that my usage of 'Africa' in the search terms was useful in identifying as many studies as possible, using an approach that was manageable and not overly cumbersome.

For the search itself, I began with Scopus, where searches using the keywords yielded 96 studies, which became 43 studies after duplicates were removed. I proceeded to Web of Science, where I found 50 studies, which became 30 studies after duplicates were removed. In Google Scholar, I searched the first ten pages for each search term and found 127 studies, which became 102 studies after duplicates were removed. In Google Search, I also searched the first ten pages and found 50 studies, which became 36 studies after duplicates were removed. This brought the total number of studies I found in the databases to 211. After removing duplicates across the databases, this number became 156 studies.

In my search of the journals, I found one additional study in *Journal of Digital Media & Policy*; this brought the number of studies found to 157. It should be noted that I found other studies in *Journal of African Media Studies,* studies that I had previously located in my search of the databases.

Screening for inclusion and eligibility: This involved reading the abstracts and keywords of the 157 studies I extracted to establish their suitability and skimming through the studies themselves to evaluate their quality and eligibility.

After doing this, I removed 84 studies based on the following reasons:

- 27 studies did not consider digital media regulation.
- 19 studies did not examine regulation as it relates to internet content.
- 24 studies explored cases beyond Africa.
- 7 studies explored cases in the Middle East even when done in comparison with North Africa.
- 1 study focused on traditional media regulation.
- 1 book contained some individual chapters that had already been included.
- 4 items were either a blog post, newsletter or newspaper article.
- 1 item was an unpublished report.

The removal meant I was left with 73 studies. During this process, I found two more studies in *Information, Communication & Society*. I found one study from the book *Digital Dissidence and Social Media Censorship in Africa,* edited by Farooq Kperogi, bringing the number of eligible studies to 76.

Iterations: This included additional searches, i.e. backward and forward searches. Backward search is the screening of publications that a particular article cites, and forward search is the screening of publications that cite the article of concern (see Xiao and Watson 2019). For backward search, I scoured the bibliographies of the 76 studies, focusing primarily on bibliographic entries related to social media regulation, digital media regulation or internet content. This meant that entries relating to data privacy and cybercrimes were not included, so I could manage the final count. In the end, I found 11 studies through backward search. I also carried out forward search, which involved searching studies that cite the 76 studies – no new study was found. Hence, the final count of the studies that I reviewed was 87.

Data extraction and analysis: For each of the 87 studies, I extracted information on the study type, the region the study examined, the methodology used, the subject area (e.g. studies that consider internet shutdowns) and the findings/recommendation. The data extraction, coding and analysis were done using NVivo.

Findings

As the previous section shows, I located 87 studies considering digital media regulation in Africa (Table 3.1 lists these studies). The studies are further sub-divided into five subject areas as follows: Research that considers laws or policies targeting free expression (*n*=26), internet shutdown (*n*=21), online harms (*n*=20), internet

TABLE 3.1: Studies in the dataset showing type, region and method (sorted by year).

Studies	Type	Region	Method*
Mthimkhulu (2011)	Master's dissertation	South Africa	Yes – Document analysis and interview
Van Vuuren et al. (2012)	Conference paper	South Africa	No – Policy analysis
Souter and Kerretts-Makau (2012)	Report	Kenya	Yes – Policy analysis and interview
Martin (2013)	Ph.D. thesis	Eastern Africa	Yes – Case study – document analysis and interview
Gerbaudo (2013)	Article – *Westminster Papers*	Egypt	No – Interview
Bitso (2014)	Article – *South African Journal of Libraries and Information Science*	South Africa	Yes – Content analysis of news items
Borena et al. (2015)	Conference paper	Africa	No – Critical literature review
Orji (2015)	Conference paper	Africa	No – Policy analysis
Calandro (2015)	Discussion paper	Africa	No – Policy/document analysis
Nyirenda-Jere and Biru (2015)	Report	Africa	No – Review
Kanjo and Jere (2015)	Conference paper	Africa	Yes – Participatory observation and document review
Kiai (2015)	Master's dissertation	Kenya	Yes – Survey
Gumede (2016)	Article – *Journal of African Media Studies*	Africa	No – Commentary
Hwang et al. (2016)	Report	Sub-Saharan Africa	No – Policy analysis
Calandro et al. (2016)	Discussion paper	Africa	No – Policy/document review

(Continued)

TABLE 3.1: Studies in the dataset showing type, region and method (sorted by year).

Studies	**Type**	**Region**	**Method***
Nonnecke (2016)	Article – *Telecommunications Policy*	Eastern Africa	Yes – Policy analysis, observation and interview
Holden and Van Klyton (2016)	Article – *Government Information Quarterly*	Africa	Yes – Policy and content analysis and interview
Abraha (2017)	Article – *Information and Communications Tech Law*	Ethiopia	No – Policy analysis
Vareba et al. (2017)	Article – *International Journal of Media, Journalism and Mass Communication*	Nigeria	No – Review
Turianskyi (2018)	Report	Africa	No – Policy analysis
Darch et al. (2018)	Book chapter	South Africa	No – Policy analysis
Rukundo (2018)	Article – *International Journal of Law and Information Technology*	Uganda	No – Policy analysis and case study
Freyburg and Garbe (2018)	Article – *International Journal of Communication*	Sub-Saharan Africa	No – Qualitative comparative analysis
Nkrumah (2018)	Article – *Alternation*	South Africa	No – Technological, legal and political frameworks
Stork and Esselaar (2019)	Report	Africa	No – Case study
Cross (2019)	Book chapter	Tanzania	No – Interview and content analysis
Powell and Schonwetter (2019)	Book chapter	Africa	No – Policy analysis
Sugow (2019)	Article – *Strathmore Law Review*	Kenya	No – Policy analysis
Sive and Price (2019)	Article – *South African Law Journal*	South Africa	No – Policy analysis

(Continued)

TABLE 3.1: Studies in the dataset showing type, region and method (sorted by year).

Studies	Type	Region	Method*
Kakungulu-Mayambala and Rukundo (2019)	Article – *African Human Rights Law Journal*	Uganda	No – Policy analysis
Olukolu et al. (2019)	Article – *University of Baltimore Journal of Media Law and Ethics*	Nigeria	No – Policy analysis
Ayalew (2019)	Article – *Information and Communications Technology Law*	Ethiopia	No – Review
Southern Africa Litigation Centre (2019)	Report	Southern Africa	No – Review
Marchant and Stremlau (2019)	Report	Africa	No – Workshop
Open Technology Fund (2019)	Report	Egypt	Yes – Case study
Ogunlana (2019)	Article – *Journal of Strategic Security*	Nigeria	Yes – Policy analysis and interview
Boxell and Steinert-Threlkeld (2019)	Article – *African Human Rights Law Journal*	Uganda	Yes – Social media analysis
Gravett (2020)	Article – *African Human Rights Law Journal*	Africa	No – Commentary
John (2020)	Article – *Information and Communications Technology Law*	Tanzania	No – Policy and case law analysis
Nothias (2020)	Article – *Media Culture & Society*	Africa	No – Content analysis, video reviews and use of VPN
Alunge (2020)	Conference paper	Africa	No – Policy analysis
Abdulrauf (2020)	Book chapter	South Africa	No – Policy analysis
Salau (2020)	Article – *African Human Rights Yearbook*	Africa	No – Policy analysis

(Continued)

TABLE 3.1: Studies in the dataset showing type, region and method (sorted by year).

Studies	Type	Region	Method*
Rutenberg and Sugow (2020)	Article – *SLJ*	Kenya	No – Policy analysis
Ayalew (2020)	Article – *African Human Rights Law Journal*	Ethiopia	No – Policy analysis
Parks and Thompson (2020)	Article – *International Journal of Communication*	Tanzania	No – Policy analysis and document review
Rydzak et al. (2020)	Article – *International Journal of Communication*	Africa	No – Review
Ngwenya and Ngoepe (2020)	Article – *Security Privacy*	South Africa	No – Review
Marchant and Stremlau (2020a)	Article – *International Journal of Communication*	Africa	No – Commentary on special issue
Marchant and Stremlau (2020b)	Article – *International Journal of Communication*	Africa	No – Review and interview
Bergère (2020)	Article – *International Journal of Communication*	Africa	No – Review and interview
Madenga (2020)	Article – *Information, Communication & Society*	Zimbabwe	No – Textual analysis of social media posts
Mare (2020)	Article – *International Journal of Communication*	Zimbabwe	Yes – Case study
Gambiza (2020)	Master's dissertation	Zimbabwe	Yes – Interview
Okunoye (2020)	Report	Africa	Yes – Interview
Mutua and Yanqiu (2020)	Article – *Journal of African Media Studies*	Eastern Africa	Yes – Policy analysis
Kalemera et al. (2020)	Report	Chad	Yes – Policy analysis and interview

(Continued)

TABLE 3.1: Studies in the dataset showing type, region and method (sorted by year).

Studies	Type	Region	Method*
Fano (2020)	Master's dissertation	Sub-Saharan Africa	Yes – Qualitative comparative analysis
Nyoni et al. (2020)	Article – *The African Journal of Info Systems*	South Africa	Yes – Survey and interview
Abdullateef (2021)	Article – *Nile Journal of Political Science*	Nigeria	Yes – Survey
Bryant (2021)	Article – *Stanford Technology Law Review*	Africa	No – Policy analysis
Selnes (2021)	Article – *Information, Communication & Society*	Uganda	Yes – Policy analysis and interview
Cunliffe-Jones et al. (2021)	Report	Sub-Saharan Africa	No – Content analysis of fact-checked materials
De Gregorio and Stremlau (2021)	Book chapter	Africa	No – Policy analysis and review
Ahmed et al. (2021)	Policy brief	Africa	No – Review
Ayalew (2021)	Article – *Mizan Law Review*	Africa	No – Review
Osakwe and Adeniran (2021)	Report	Africa	No – Review and interview
Santas and Inobemhe (2021)	Article – *MCC*	Nigeria	Yes – Desk review
Olaniyan and Akpojivi (2021)	Article – *Information, Communication & Society*	Nigeria	Yes – Interview
Mwanzia et al. (2021)	Report	Africa	Yes – Interview, survey and desk review
Obia (2021)	Article – *Makings*	Africa	Yes – Policy analysis
Delelegn (2021)	Master's dissertation	Ethiopia	Yes – Policy analysis (doctrinal and comparative legal method)

(Continued)

TABLE 3.1: Studies in the dataset showing type, region and method (sorted by year).

Studies	**Type**	**Region**	**Method***
International Commission of Jurists (ICJ) (2021)	Report	Africa	Yes – Policy analysis and interview
Bronstein (2022)	Article – *PER / PLEJ*	South Africa	No – Policy analysis
Asiedu (2022)	Policy brief	Africa	No – Policy analysis
Fombad (2022)	Article – *Journal of International & Comparative Law*	Africa	No – Review
de Veiga et al. (2022)	Conference paper	South Africa	No – Scoping literature review
Moses et al. (2022)	Article – *Journal of Digital Media & Policy*	Nigeria	Yes – Document analysis
Akinyetun and Ebonine (2022)	Book chapter	Africa	Yes – Policy and document analysis
Matsilele and Mutsvairo (2022)	Book chapter	South Africa	Yes – Virtual ethnography and case study
Boateng (2023)	Book chapter	Chad	No – Critical literature review
Munoriyarwa (2023)	Book chapter	Southern Africa	No – Policy analysis
Elega et al. (2023)	Article – *First Monday*	Nigeria	No – Review
Garbe et al. (2023)	Article – *Information, Communication & Society*	Africa	Yes – Content analysis of news items
Nakaayi (2023)	Book chapter	Africa	No – Policy analysis
Mpofu (2023)	Book chapter	Africa	No – Review of secondary data
Chari (2023)	Book chapter	Zimbabwe	Yes – Interview and survey

Notes
*Yes = methodology section included; no = lacking methodology section.

governance/multi-stakeholderism ($n=11$) and data privacy ($n=9$). The outcome underscores the considerable attention that African scholars have given to the twin issues around censorship policies and internet bans that restrict online access and freedom of expression. Data privacy has the least number of items, showing that it is a nascent, yet growing, area of research focus. Internet governance and multi-stakeholderism studies have also not received that much attention, particularly compared to studies that consider online harms such as fake news and hate speech. Online harms studies also highlight internet restrictions, as we see in De Gregorio and Stremlau (2021), who note that hate speech laws are being used to justify internet censorship.

Hence, the dominance of censorship and restrictive measures in the scholarship is clear. The first of the research across the dataset was Mthimkhulu's (2011) Master's dissertation, followed by a conference paper by Van Vuuren et al. (2012) and a report by Souter and Kerretts-Makau (2012). This indicates how recent the field is, implying that stakeholders in Africa had little to no concern regarding internet regulation in the 1990s and the first decade of this century. This trend continued in 2013 when there was only a Ph.D. thesis by Martin (2013) and a journal article (the first article) by Gerbaudo (2013). There was another article by Bitso (2014) the following year. It was not until 2015 that research in the area became more noticeable. There were six research items in 2015, and the frequency remained relatively stable in 2016 (five items), 2017 (two items) and 2018 (five items). The research became widespread in 2019 (13 items) and peaked in 2020 (23 items – a quarter of all entries) before falling in 2021 (13 items) and 2022 (seven items). A similar number of entries (seven items) were recorded in 2023 at the time of writing. Perhaps one reason why there was increased research interest in 2019 and 2020 was the rise in censorship actions, particularly the social media tax in Uganda and internet shutdowns in countries like Zimbabwe. It represents a recognition by African scholars of the need to document and potentially challenge the rise of government heavy-handedness in the area.

In terms of publication type, I found that slightly above half of the entries (51.7 per cent or 45 items) were journal articles. Twenty-five of these were published in top international journals, mainly in *International Journal of Communication* (seven items), *Information, Communication & Society* (four items) and *Information and Communications Technology Law* (three items). This underscores, at least based on the reputation of these journals, that the articles on digital media regulation in Africa are of substantial rigour and quality. It also shows that scholars in the area prefer general-purpose journals as much as they do specialist communication policy journals, if not more so. I have already reflected on the lack of entry in *Communication Law and Policy*, and the possible reasons for this. Most of the remaining twenty articles were also published in international but less well-known journals. Many of these were in Africa-based journals such as *African Human Rights Law Journal*. The remaining entries, according to the type of publication, were reports (fourteen items) and book chapters (twelve items), some of which were published as edited collections (see Mpofu 2023; Chari 2023; Nakaayi 2023, published in the book *Digital Dissidence and Social Media Censorship in Africa*). Others were conference papers (six items), Master's dissertation (five items), policy briefs (two items), discussion papers (two items) and Ph.D. thesis (one item).

The Ph.D. thesis by Martin (2013) focuses on Eastern Africa alongside journal articles by Nonnecke (2016) and Mutua and Yanqiu (2020). In East Africa, other entries consider digital media regulatory contexts in specific countries: Ethiopia (four items), Kenya (four items), Uganda (four items) and Tanzania (three items). Put together, items from the region and countries of Eastern Africa numbered 18 or one-fifth (20.7 per cent) of all items. Coincidentally, entries from the countries and region of Southern Africa also numbered 18. Most of these were studies that examine the South African national context (twelve items); South Africa also had the highest national figure across the dataset, indicating scholars' level of interest in the country. The other entries in the region focused on Zimbabwe (four items) and the broader Southern African region (two items). By contrast, West, Central and North Africa had fewer entries. In West Africa, all the entries interrogated the Nigerian context (eight items), meaning that the country ranked second behind South Africa in national entries. In Central and Northern Africa, two studies considered the Chadian and Egyptian contexts, respectively. The remaining entries examined the continent: 35 items on Africa and 4 items on Sub-Saharan Africa.

Therefore, the implication is that research into digital media regulation in Africa mainly considers the Eastern and Southern African contexts. There has been research focus on Eastern Africa because of the controversial social media taxes introduced in places like Uganda (Boxell and Steinert-Threlkeld 2019) and censorship measures such as internet shutdowns in places like Ethiopia (Ayalew 2019). Southern Africa also features because of shutdown measures in Zimbabwe (Mare 2020; Madenga 2020; Chari 2023), but more so as a result of studies that highlight data protection regulations in South Africa (Abdulrauf 2020; Ngwenya and Ngoepe 2020; Nyoni et al. 2020; de Veiga et al. 2022). Outside of these two regions, Nigeria commands the highest attention, given the focus that scholars have on areas such as the politics of social media regulation (Vareba et al. 2017; Moses et al. 2022) and the 2021 Twitter ban (Elega et al. 2023). However, one thing to bear in mind is that publication in English was a precondition for inclusion in the dataset – this could have influenced the dominance of English-speaking countries like South Africa and Nigeria. Also, as I explained in the methodology, I removed seven studies that consider the Middle East and North African context (e.g. Goldstein 1999; Houissa 2020) because the Middle East is outside the scope of my research design.

Regarding the method, I found that 56 (64.4 per cent – nearly two-thirds) of the 87 studies lacked a specific section or sub-section where the methodological approach was discussed. However, I note that some journals do not require methodology sections. Also, some researchers do not always include a methodology section, even if their work is empirical. This is noticeable in the studies that I reviewed, given that most of them contained empirical methodologies highlighted in places like the abstracts or introductions – which is acceptable. Across the dataset, only eight studies were non-empirical; they included those that employed commentaries (Gumede 2016; Gravett 2020; Marchant and Stremlau 2020a) and literature review (Borena et al. 2015; Santas and Inobemhe 2021; Mpofu 2023; de Veiga et al. 2022; Boateng 2023). Also, policy analysis based on legal interpretation constituted the most used method, reflecting a similar finding in Reinard and Ortiz (2005). My findings, for instance, showed that 38 studies (56.7 per cent) featured policy analysis, whether in a standalone or triangulated format. But triangulation was not common across the dataset, given that 23 (26.4 per cent) of the studies had mixed-methods approaches. In cases where triangulation was used, these tended to be policy analysis in conjunction with interviews, content analysis, case study, participant observation or survey.

There were rare cases where content analysis was utilized alongside analysis of video recordings and the use of a Virtual Private Network (VPN)-based method to assess the availability of Facebook's Free Basics programme in Africa (Nothias 2020) or with interview (Cross 2019), or where survey was used with interview (Nyoni et al. 2020) and virtual ethnography with case study (Matsilele and Mutsvairo 2022). Some of the studies featured the use of review. These were primarily based on the analysis of events and contexts as they pertain to regulation, not necessarily the analysis of legal documents. Others used document analysis. These were typically related to analysing news reports and other non-legal documentary evidence. One study was based on a workshop (Marchant and Stremlau 2019), and another on social media analysis (Boxell and Steinart-Threlkeld 2019). Overall, the findings show that using policy analysis based on the critique and interpretation of laws and other legal documents is dominant across the dataset, even though scholars are not always keen on making this clear in designated methodology sections. Having provided an overview of the studies in the dataset, I now discuss the five subject areas that I divide them into and what they portend for the state of research in the field of digital media regulation in Africa. As earlier mentioned, these five subject areas include laws or policies targeting free expression, internet shutdown, online harms, internet governance/multi-stakeholderism and data privacy (see Table 3.2 for a detailed description of each item based on the study areas). In reviewing the

TABLE 3.2: Description and main findings of the studies in the dataset (sorted by year).

I. Studies focusing on laws or politics targeting free expression	
Studies	**Description/findings**
Mthimkhulu (2011)	Mthimkhulu's Master's dissertation examines the relationship between internet regulation and freedom of expression in South Africa. The research underscores the concern that people have for government regulation of the internet in relation to protecting civil liberties. It concludes that the government should not use the internet as an excuse to introduce punitive regulatory measures.
Bitso (2014)	This journal article investigates internet censorship in South Africa based on the country's involvement in an intergovernmental policy proposal for the internet. The article finds that legislations such as the 2010 Protection of State Information Bill limits freedom of expression, but that action is needed to combat hacking of government websites and spams. It concludes that monitoring of governments and ISPs is crucial.
Gumede (2016)	Written as a commentary, the article appraises the rise in censorship of social media and the internet in Africa. The commentary outlines the measures that African governments take to clamp down on internet freedoms and to target activists and civil society groups. It calls on the AU and the UN to introduce stronger checks on these governments.
Hwang et al. (2016)	The report explores the suppression of social media in Sub-Saharan Africa after the Arab Spring. The report finds that international laws give African governments the discretion to limit freedom of expression for national security reasons. To strengthen freedoms in Africa, there is need for an independent media and a reform of the AU (and other regional bodies) so it can restrict prior censorship as is done in the American and European contexts.
Abraha (2017)	This journal article considers the regulation of the internet landscape in the last decade in Ethiopia. The article finds that statutory regulation, informal regulation, gatekeeping, self-censorship and regulation through 'social media army' exist in Ethiopia. It notes the challenges that the government faces in relation to exercising control over western-based platforms. Hence, regulation is done mainly through formal means such as blocking or filtering, although informal and gateway models are also being used.
Vareba et al. (2017)	Vareba et al.'s journal article highlights internet censorship in Nigeria and how it has affected digital rights and internet freedoms. The article notes that although internet censorship might be needed to combat online harms, it has been misapplied in Nigeria to muzzle anti-establishment voices and is a threat to free expression.

(Continued)

TABLE 3.2: Description and main findings of the studies in the dataset (sorted by year).

I. Studies focusing on laws or politics targeting free expression	
Studies	**Description/findings**
Rukundo (2018)	Rukundo interrogates the case of Dr Stella Nyanzi who was charged on the basis of Sections 24 and 25 of the Computer Misuse Act for calling the president 'a pair of buttocks' on Facebook. The article shows the above sections of the CMA restrict freedom of expression, and that the law represents the government's attempt to extend its offline control to the online environment.
Boxell and Steinert-Threlkeld (2019)	Boxell and Steinert-Threlkeld's article analyses the 2018 social media tax in Uganda as a tool of digital repression. Their study finds that the tax reduced the number of geo-referenced Twitter users by 13 per cent. However, there was an increase in collective action both online and offline, pointing to a backlash effect. The study adds that taxes are ineffective in repressing dissent since people can circumvent it.
Kakungulu-Mayambala and Rukundo (2019)	The article interrogates laws such as the Computer Misuse Act that directly or indirectly restrict digital activism in Uganda. The article observes that laws that are contrary to constitutional freedom and international instruments need to be abolished or amended. Still, it notes that a balanced approach is required to develop solutions that address actual harms and also protect civil liberties.
Olukolu et al. (2019)	The article highlights regulations that threaten the use of social media in Nigeria. The article shows that provisions such as the 2015 Frivolous Petitions Bill and the Nigerian Press Council Act violate media freedom and freedom of expression. It adds that the government should focus on more pressing issues in the country instead of social media regulation.
Powell and Schonwetter (2019)	In this book chapter, Powell and Schonwetter consider the positive and negative duties that African countries have with regard to protecting human rights in Africa. The chapter examines the control that African countries should not be exercising as it concerns internet censorship, the accountability that is needed to combat actual online harms and the access to the internet that countries should guarantee for their citizens.
Sive and Price (2019)	The article examines the top-down regulation of social media by South Africa's government and the role that social media platforms play in publishing or suppressing speech. Based on a model of 'regulated self-regulation', the article proposes that content removal decisions made by platforms should be subject to judicial review hinged on South Africa's common law and constitutional principles.

(Continued)

TABLE 3.2: Description and main findings of the studies in the dataset (sorted by year).

I. Studies focusing on laws or politics targeting free expression	
Studies	**Description/findings**
Stork and Esselaar (2019)	Stork and Esselaar's report examines cases of social media taxes to understand their impact. The report finds that these taxes are introduced using opaque processes without regard to cost/benefit analysis. It adds that social media taxes affect not only internet access and affordability but also economic growth, investment and productivity in the ICT sector. It concludes that taxes should be based on economic assessment.
Ayalew (2020)	Ayalew's article considers the measures that the Ethiopian government has introduced to restrict freedom of expression on the internet, using the African Charter on Human and Peoples' Rights as a benchmark. These measures include shutdowns, hate speech and disinformation regulations, and repressive laws, with the article finding that they fall short of the quadruple tests of limitation in the African Charter and the Ethiopian constitution.
Bergère (2020)	Bergère, in this article, analyses social media taxing across Africa, specifically focusing on Guinea and Benin. The article highlights how African governments repurpose digital affordances to introduce restrictive measures such as taxes. Digital technologies are easier to tax and can target specific individuals; this tax reinforces the colonial and historical relevance of taxes in the relation of subjectivity between governments and citizens.
Gravett (2020)	In this article, Gravett considers the expansion and influence of Chinese technology companies in Africa and warns that the Chinese model of internet governance could become Africa's default. The article presents this as an example of digital neo-colonialism, given the development of plans such as China Telecoms' 150,000-kilometre-long fibre optic network in 48 African countries.
John (2020)	In this article, John examines Tanzania's Electronic and Postal Communications (Online Content) Regulations to determine whether it conforms to law-making standards of legality, legitimacy, legal certainty and international fundamental rights. The article finds that the law does not conform to these standards, except in cases where it has certain legitimate purposes.
Kalemera et al. (2020)	Kalemera et al.'s report examines the trend of ICT regulation in Chad and their effect on internet freedom between 1999 and 2019. The reports find that despite the protections in the constitution, Chadian laws such as the 2015 Cybercrime Act still restrict freedom of expression on the internet. Other measures include network shutdowns, surveillance and laws that restrict data privacy protections.

(Continued)

TABLE 3.2: Description and main findings of the studies in the dataset (sorted by year).

I. Studies focusing on laws or politics targeting free expression	
Studies	**Description/findings**
Nothias (2020)	Nothias interrogates Facebook's controversial Free Basics programme aimed at increasing connectivity in the Global South. The article shows that the programme quietly expanded because of the approach that Facebook took to engage with civil society groups and because these groups were occupied with concerns around government internet censorship and shutdowns.
Ahmed et al. (2021)	This policy brief discusses the implementation of social media taxes, especially during the COVID-19 pandemic. The review demonstrates how taxes increase the cost of access to internet services, further widening the digital divide. These taxes, often introduced for short-term benefits such as debt repayments, do not meet the requirement for long-term sustained economic growth and development.
International Commission of Jurists (ICJ) (2021)	The International Commission of Jurists, in this report, notes that some governments are using measures designed to combat crime, terrorism and disorder on the internet to restrict access, freedom of expression and privacy on the internet. The report sought to develop a resource that civil society groups and lawyers could use to resist restrictive laws that are contrary to international law standards.
Santas and Inobemhe (2021)	Santas and Inobemhe's article considers the implication and challenges of regulating social media in Nigeria. The study analyses the 2019 Internet Falsehood Bill and 2019 Hate Speech Bill, finding that social media regulation is difficult since regulation of any kind will likely implicate media freedom and freedom of expression.
Selnes (2021)	The article appraises internet restrictions and their effect on journalism in Uganda. The article reveals that there are several cyber laws that the government uses to intimidate, arrest and prosecute journalists. It adds that the laws serve as control techniques to restrict internet usage among the population and that they have a negative effect on media freedom.
Asiedu (2022)	Asiedu's policy brief examines digital censorship and the relationship between the internet and democracy in Africa. The brief emphasizes that the African government lacks the capacity to control or surveil the internet as a whole, except when a shutdown order is given. It calls on stakeholders such as citizens and civil society groups to resist shutdown orders.
Moses et al. (2022)	The article investigates the practice and implication of regulating social media in Nigeria based on national security. The article finds that using the national security justification is counterproductive as it limits freedom of expression among citizens. It views platforms as scapegoats of regulation and social media regulation as a misplaced priority, given the insecurity challenges that the country faces.

(Continued)

TABLE 3.2: Description and main findings of the studies in the dataset (sorted by year).

I. Studies focusing on laws or politics targeting free expression	
Studies	**Description/findings**
Nakaayi (2023)	In this book chapter, Nakaayi considers African countries that have introduced laws to restrict social media use. The chapter shows that the laws are worded in vague and broad terms, and that there are duplications in the laws. Some of these laws violate people's privacy protections and muzzle citizens' participation in the democratic process. A balance is needed between laws that promote order on social media and those that restrict freedom.
II. Studies focusing on internet shutdowns	
Studies	**Description/findings**
Gerbaudo (2013)	In this article, Gerbaudo discusses the effect of the internet shutdown order by Hosni Mubarak at the start of the 2011 Arab Spring. The article shows that the 'kill switch' was counterproductive, fuelling rather than disrupting the protests. The shutdown made people more sympathetic to the cause and led to a 'suicide switch' for the government.
Freyburg and Garbe (2018)	The article considers the political economy of shutdowns, that is, relationship between internet shutdowns and ownership of ISPs in Africa. The article shows that ISPs, even those that are foreign-based but in emerging markets, are more likely to comply with shutdown orders for market necessity reasons.
Ayalew (2019)	Ayalew, in this article, examines internet shutdowns in Ethiopia from 2016 to 2018, arguing that it has been used to silence dissent and civil liberties in the country. The article notes that the internet has been shut more than six times during the period, and that the government tends to use narratives instead of laws. These narratives include 'war on terror' and 'economic development' but they do not meet requirements of legality, necessity and proportionality.
Marchant and Stremlau (2019)	Marchant and Stremlau's report documents stakeholder views on internet shutdowns in countries like Burundi, Cameroon, Ethiopia, Kenya, Morocco, South Sudan, Uganda and Zimbabwe. The report suggests that shutdown should be viewed on a spectrum that considers duration, breadth, depth, speed and frequency. It notes the need for more attention on the less visible impact of shutdowns and the role of non-governmental actors. It also calls for a wider debate on the usefulness of shutdowns in protecting human rights and security.
Open Technology Fund (2019)	The report outlines digital expression violations in Egypt from 2011 to mid-2019. The report finds an increase in violations from 2016 onwards. Most cases are based on publishing false news, joining a banned group, and misuse of social media. It concludes that the legal framework in Egypt enables and legitimizes the censorship and surveillance tactics of the security services.

(Continued)

TABLE 3.2: Description and main findings of the studies in the dataset (sorted by year).

II. Studies focusing on internet shutdowns	
Studies	**Description/findings**
Southern Africa Litigation Centre (2019)	This report explores the legal considerations necessary for challenging internet shutdowns in Southern African courts. The reports note that the regulations do not give governments power to order internet shutdowns. It calls on lawyers to develop strategies that allow for fast responses to internet shutdowns.
Fano (2020)	Fano (2020), in this Master's dissertation, examines digital authoritarianism in 25 African countries and finds that 16 of them have restrictive policies. The study also examines the conditions that are present when digital authoritarian strategies are implemented: these are China's soft power, social mobilizations and internet penetration. It finds a correlation between China's influence and digital authoritarianism in Africa.
Madenga (2020)	Madenga's article considers the internet shutdown in Zimbabwe in January 2019 by analysing the Facebook posts of Baba Jukwa before the shutdown and an alternative Twitter thread of what he would have posted during the ban. The article conceptualizes this as a form of storytelling that involves everyone, a way for journalists to redefine free speech on social media and challenge internet shutdowns.
Marchant and Stremlau (2020a)	Marchant and Stremlau's contribution serves as an introduction to a special issue on internet shutdowns in Africa in the International Journal of Communication. The article considers the submissions in the issues and how they seek to reframe our understanding of internet shutdowns, why they are on the rise in Africa and how they relate to other censorship tactics and infrastructure challenges.
Marchant and Stremlau (2020b)	In this article, Marchant and Stremlau explore how internet shutdowns are currently conceptualized and argue for the need to recognize how diverse they are and why they are being used. The article outlines the frequency, duration, depth, breadth and speed of shutdowns to establish their variable nature in Africa. It also shows that governments will likely move away from blunt shutdowns to more advanced tactics.
Mare (2020)	In this article, Mare discusses why and how private telecommunication providers comply internet shutdown orders, arguing that it should be conceptualized as digital authoritarianism. The study shows that private telecoms providers comply with these orders for fear of losing their license, political harassment, victimization and imprisonment. In most cases, these private players are enablers rather than resistors of internet shutdowns.

(Continued)

TABLE 3.2: Description and main findings of the studies in the dataset (sorted by year).

II. Studies focusing on internet shutdowns	
Studies	**Description/findings**
Okunoye (2020)	The report studies the use of internet censorship circumvention tools in Africa, using Cameroon, Nigeria, Uganda and Zimbabwe as case studies. The report finds that civil society groups were crucial in motivating people to use circumvention tools and that people used innovative means such as USBs and Bluetooth to share VPNs. People also used Telegram and Signal, which were unaffected by shutdowns.
Parks and Thompson (2020)	This article analyses slow internet shutdowns in Tanzania based on a series of regulations from 2010 to 2018. This, the article notes, has reinforced state control over internet information flow and progressively reduced internet interactions by Tanzanians. This is what the article describes as slow shutdown.
Rydzak et al. (2020)	The article considers the relationship between deliberate network shutdowns and protest mobilization, to show how the latter responds to the former. The article focuses on events between 2017 and mid-2019 and finds that network shutdown leads to greater protest mobilizations. It concludes that shutdowns are counter-productive since activists use other means to continue their mobilization.
Ayalew (2021)	Ayalew's article critiques the power that states and platforms have in the digital society, observing that it has a detrimental effect on freedom of expression. The study finds that states employ digital authoritarianism in their use of internet shutdowns, national security laws and digital surveillance. It shows that platforms, on the other hand, utilize Levithan powers in their arbitrary takedown decisions and policies.
Mwanzia et al. (2021)	The report reviews internet shutdowns in ten African countries, including Cameroon, the DRC, Egypt, Ethiopia, Nigeria, Uganda, Sudan, Senegal, Zambia and Eswatini. The report considers factors such as the duration of a president's term or an election season which make shutdowns more likely. It also highlights the methods that ISPs use to implement shutdowns in their compliance with legal and licensing obligations.
Akinyetun and Ebonine (2022)	This book chapter highlights the presence of digital tools in Africa to promote mass surveillance, internet shutdown, electoral manipulation, corporate espionage and censorship. The chapter frames this as digital authoritarianism, noting that it has been done using the excuse of combatting online harms like hate speech and disinformation. It adds that this was particularly so during the COVID-19 pandemic.

(Continued)

TABLE 3.2: Description and main findings of the studies in the dataset (sorted by year).

II. Studies focusing on internet shutdowns	
Studies	**Description/findings**
Boateng (2023)	The book chapter considers the literature on digital rights restrictions and social media usage in Chad, showing how the government controls access to social media. The chapter shows that the combination of internet shutdowns and cyberlaws in Chad has the potential to restrict freedom of expression on the internet.
Chari (2023)	The book chapter explores the way that Zimbabweans experience internet shutdowns. The study considers the meaning that citizens attach to shutdowns and their interpretation of the timing and motive. It finds that citizens view internet shutdowns as a power game that highlights the government's ulterior motive, given that shutdowns target civil liberties. Internet shutdowns also disrupt economic, social and political activities.
Elega et al. (2023)	Elega et al., in this article, interrogates the 2021 Twitter ban in Nigeria, noting that it could be the beginning of digital authoritarianism in the country. The article links the ban to the Chinese model of repressive internet content regulation and the consequences of this for data politics, algorithmic governance and mass surveillance in Nigeria.
Mpofu (2023)	In this book chapter, Mpofu employs the Big Man syndrome as a lens with which to examine internet shutdowns in Africa. The chapter appraises the role played by strongmen in African politics, rulers who once led liberation movements but have become increasingly authoritarian. The citizens are effectively subject to the Big Man; so also are internet information flows.
III. Studies focusing on online harms	
Studies	**Description/findings**
Van Vuuren et al. (2012)	This conference paper considers the approach to cybersecurity legislation that is best suited to South Africa based on cases in other countries. They propose an organizational structure for effective governance of cybersecurity and the use of the CyberSAT.
Kiai (2015)	Kiai's Master's dissertation examines the perception of Kenyan bloggers on hate speech control on social media for peace building. The study shows that most bloggers disagree with monitoring and control tools (e.g. content removals by ISPs), and their perception of the use of legal means was mixed; most prefer sensitization approaches to combatting hate speech on the internet.

(Continued)

TABLE 3.2: Description and main findings of the studies in the dataset (sorted by year).

III. Studies focusing on online harms	
Studies	**Description/findings**
Nkrumah (2018)	In this article, Nkrumah assesses South Africa's unilateral, bilateral and multilateral instruments on internet hate speech regulation. The study shows that people have fears about internet content regulation, especially that require government intervention. It concludes that the government should not use the internet as an excuse to curtail civil liberties.
Turianskyi (2018)	This report highlights the state of cybersecurity and policies in Africa, focusing on Kenya and South Africa. The study argues for the need to achieve the right balance between cyber regulation and freedom of expression. It also notes the imbalance in the relationship between weak Global South countries and powerful private actors as far as the internet is concerned.
Cross (2019)	In this book chapter, Cross examines the relationship between policing and politics in the policing of social media in Tanzania. The chapter highlights how police officers implement restrictive laws and policies on social media. It finds that policing is politicized and that concerns extend beyond high-profile users to ordinary citizens, underscoring the way by policing is compromised for censorship ends.
Ogunlana (2019)	The article considers the effectiveness of technological approaches to mitigating cyber-terrorism. The study argues that terrorists are becoming adept at using new communication technologies and that multilateral cooperation is required to address terrorism in cyberspace.
Sugow (2019)	Sugow's article explores the possibility of regulating fake news without infringing on freedom of expression. The study finds that regulation can preserve freedom of expression if regulation is only brought in to address obvious harms like disinformation, while other approaches such as collaborative measures, awareness initiatives, and factchecking are introduced to checkmate fake news more broadly.
Gambiza (2020)	The Master's dissertation considers the link between fake news and social media regulation in Zimbabwe using the 2019 internet shutdown as case study. The study observes that fake news is concerning but should not be targeted except in extraordinary cases. If not, regulation (e.g. shutdowns) can lead to a chilling effect on freedom of expression.
Mutua and Yanqiu (2020)	This article was aimed at identifying challenges to online content regulation in Kenya, Uganda and Tanzania (Eastern Africa). It sees the need to incorporate digital literacy into legal frameworks and proposes the concept of content regulation and digital literacy as a viable solution.

(Continued)

TABLE 3.2: Description and main findings of the studies in the dataset (sorted by year).

III. Studies focusing on online harms	
Studies	**Description/findings**
Rutenberg and Sugow (2020)	Rutenberg and Sugow's article highlights the importance of balancing social media regulation and free speech in the context of elections. It shows that to uphold freedom of expression and democratic values, social media regulation should target platform design not content.
Salau (2020)	This article considers why the African Commission on Human and People's Rights should expand its jurisprudence into adjudicating on cybercrime laws that criminalize fake news in Africa. It shows that around twenty-three African countries have laws like this, arguing that cybercrime laws should be drafted in line with international free speech norms.
Abdullateef (2021)	In this article, Abdullateef highlights social media users' perception of Nigeria's Internet Falsehood Bill. The study finds a lack of trust between users and the government, as users fear that the government might use the proposed regulation, which contains vague criminal offences, to muzzle critical views.
Cunliffe-Jones et al. (2021)	This report considers the types and effects of change made to regulatory frameworks in relation to online misinformation. They find that out of 31 laws on misinformation in Africa, most do not address misinformation, about half of them contradiction international law and for 10 of them, alleged falsity (without evidence) is enough to warrant sanctions.
De Gregorio and Stremlau (2021)	In this book chapter, De Gregorio and Stremlau consider legal and censorship responses to online hate in the Global South, including Africa. The study notes that offline harms associated with hate speech have been used as justifications for internet censorship, including shutdowns. It calls on independent bodies such as the UN to mediate in cases where online speech might have led to significance offline harms.
Delelegn (2021)	The Master's dissertation interrogates how hate speech is regulated in Ethiopia, drawing from examples in Germany, South Africa and Kenya. The study shows that the regulation fails to strike the right balance between freedom of expression and hate speech. It recommends using a multilayered approach, which includes building trust, grassroots dialogue and national reconciliation.
Obia (2021)	In this article, Obia addresses how social media regulation in Africa diverges from approaches in western countries. The study finds that the trend in Africa is to designate social media users as publishers and regulate them accordingly. This approach, the study suggests, reflects the politics of regulation, which negatively affects free speech.

(Continued)

TABLE 3.2: Description and main findings of the studies in the dataset (sorted by year).

III. Studies focusing on online harms	
Studies	**Description/findings**
Olaniyan and Akpojivi (2021)	The article appraises how social media regulation affects the media and democratic cultures. Those they interviewed note that fake news needs to be addressed but maintain that regulation as presently structured will harm free speech. They see no need for new regulations and instead prefers educational approaches to combatting fake news.
Fombad (2022)	The article examines the different manifestations of fake news and the attempts by African governments to combat it. The study notes that fake news can negatively impact democratic development in Africa. It argues that what is needed are partnerships at the national, regional and global levels, and the use of educational initiatives.
Garbe et al. (2023)	In this article, Garbe et al. analyse the approach that African countries use to combat fake news and hate speech, finding that African governments use legal (e.g. laws) and/or technological means (e.g. blockage). Countries with legislative constraints adopt legal means, while restrictive countries tend to use technological means.
Munoriyarwa (2023)	This book chapter explores the regulation of hate speech on social media in seven Southern African countries. The research finds that some countries have enacted news laws for hate speech, while others have included the regulation within existing laws. It calls for regional convention on social media hate speech.
IV. Studies focusing on internet governance and multistakeholderism	
Studies	**Description/findings**
Souter and Kerretts-Makau (2012)	The report discusses the environment for internet governance in Kenya. They find that internet governance participation mainly happens in Nairobi compared to the country as a whole, although there is more multistakeholder participation in Kenya than in some other African countries. Cybersecurity was identified as the most important internet governance issue facing the country.
Martin (2013)	This Ph.D. thesis investigates the functions of the East African IGF, the first regional IGF in the world. The thesis shows that the EAIGF promotes capacity building, consensus and the development of national and regional policies. Kenya is the most influential member due to its economic power. Government stakeholders are also influential, given their policymaking powers, although other stakeholders shape the goals of the forum.

(Continued)

TABLE 3.2: Description and main findings of the studies in the dataset (sorted by year).

IV. Studies focusing on internet governance and multistakeholderism	
Studies	**Description/findings**
Calandro (2015)	This discussion paper considers the involvement and participation of African countries in internet governance fora. The study notes that the need to involve African countries is presently hindered by challenges of participation at national, regional and international levels. It also establishes the importance of having African countries at these fora.
Kanjo and Jere (2015)	The conference paper considers how governance can be interwoven with technology, particularly as it relates to Africa. The study shows that Africa is a latecomer to internet governance and the regional IGFs in Africa have struggled to impact national policies. It adds that global multistakeholder structures should be made fairer and more inclusive for African countries.
Nyirenda-Jere and Biru (2015)	This report outlines the trend in the development and governance of the internet in Africa. The report notes that each of the five regions in Africa has its IGF; those in East Africa and West Africa are more advanced in terms of national coverage. It adds that the multistakeholder approach to internet governance is important for internet development on the continent.
Orji (2015)	In this conference paper, Orji investigates regional and sub-regional legal frameworks to determine whether they can provide a basis for legal assistance and cooperation among African countries. The paper finds that the AU Convention on Cyber Security and Personal Data Protection does not provide adequate mutual cooperation and that a more effective framework is required such as establishing a regional Computer Emergency Response Team.
Holden and Van Klyton (2016)	The article interrogates how African countries are represented and participate in global internet governance. The study finds that African governments have made changes to the institutional structure of national governance, but this has led to a paradox of participation, where the low ranking and weakness of African countries mean they continue to suffer under-representation in internet governance based on historical global inequities.
Calandro et al. (2016)	In this discussion paper, Calandro et al. map the evolution of multi-stakeholderism to consider how a governance process that is tailored to African realities can be developed. The study underscores the disparities between developed and developing countries in internet governance debates. For African countries, it is only by putting in place conditions for the ICT sector to thrive will continent be positioned to contribute to internet governance debates.

(Continued)

TABLE 3.2: Description and main findings of the studies in the dataset (sorted by year).

IV. Studies focusing on internet governance and multistakeholderism	
Studies	**Description/findings**
Nonnecke (2016)	In this article, Nonnecke examines the functions and impact of the East Africa IGF as the first regional IGF to be established globally. The EAIGF promotes capacity building, knowledge sharing and policy transfer in the region, but it is dominated by government players and is often seen as a talk shop. The study shows that there are inequalities among countries in the forum, with Kenya having the greatest influence.
Darch et al. (2018)	The book chapter critiques South Africa's National Integrated ICT Policy White Paper, setting it within the historical and new developments in the sector of the country. The chapter identifies a paradox, noting that South Africa criticizes the lack of multilateralism, openness, inclusivity and transparency in internet governance frameworks, even though the White Paper and other measures make the country guilty of the same.
Matsilele and Mutsvairo (2022)	This book chapter examines social media governance in South Africa, although the chapter is more related to the use of Twitter by politicians than social media governance itself. Nonetheless, the chapter calls for social media governance as a way to improve the use of the technology for public engagement purposes.
V. Studies focusing on privacy	
Studies	**Description/findings**
Borena et al. (2015)	This conference paper considers potential privacy protection mechanisms and practices for Africa. The paper finds that isolated practices are not effective for privacy protection, and that regional and global regulatory schemes are needed, along the lines of the EU model.
Abdulrauf (2020)	This book chapter discusses the extent to which data privacy is protected in South Africa based on analysis of POPIA. The chapter notes that data protection provisions have been consolidated into POPIA. The problem, however, is that the law has not come into force more than five years after it was enacted, and this has affected data protection in the country.
Alunge (2020)	Alunge's conference paper examines the ECOWAS Supplementary Data Protection Act and the AU's Convention on Cyber Security and Personal Data Protection in comparison to European standards. The paper notes that although these instruments address data protection broadly speaking (e.g. providing for Data Protection Authorities), they do not sufficiently tackle personal data security (e.g. lacking data protection by design).

(Continued)

TABLE 3.2: Description and main findings of the studies in the dataset (sorted by year).

V. Studies focusing on privacy	
Studies	**Description/findings**
Ngwenya and Ngoepe (2020)	In this article, Ngwenya and Ngoepe interrogate issues around data security, privacy and trust in consumer IoT. The article develops a framework comprising data security, data privacy and data trustworthiness, arguing that it should be adopted by regulators and apply to every digital object to protect IoT consumers.
Nyoni et al. (2020)	This article investigates the privacy risks that users are exposed to based on their use of digital technologies. The articles show that threats to data privacy mainly relate to data breaches, the use of mobile devices and user-created risks. It identifies benchmarking against international standards, effective legislation and protective measures as valuable propositions in protecting data privacy.
Bryant (2021)	The article addresses data protection in Africa, noting that the data protection landscape on the continent should be engineered to suit the particular contexts, challenges and circumstances on the continent. The article notes that Africa can draw inspiration from the GDPR, but adds that it is Eurocentric, and that an approach tailored to Africa's young and vibrant population needs to be developed, a multilateral approach that the rest of the world would have to respect.
Osakwe and Adeniran (2021)	The report interrogates the data and digital landscape in Africa, arguing for the need to strengthen the data governance frameworks on the continent. The report shows that data governance frameworks in Africa are evolving too slowly compared to the rise in the use of digital technologies, a disparity that could lead to data abuse. It also calls for uniformity in the data policy approaches of African countries.
Bronstein (2022)	Bronstein's article compares South Africa's POPIA with the EU's GDPR. The article finds that although POPIA is framed along the line of the GDPR, the former lacks many of the collaborative governance mechanisms in the latter. There is also no system of Data Protection Impact Assessments in POPIA. Hence, POPIA dilutes the accountability requirements in the GDPR and is a missed opportunity for effective data protection in South Africa.
de Veiga et al. (2022)	In this conference paper, de Veiga et al. highlight evaluation criteria for e-commerce websites that can be used to determine if they meet basic data privacy requirements. The paper provides a set of evaluation criteria, that website managers can use, structured according to POPIA principles with reference to the GDPR. It adds that POPIA specifies data privacy conditions but does not outline how they should be incorporated into websites.

studies, I began by reading their abstracts and keywords and skimming the body of relevant research entries, before carrying out in-depth analysis.

Laws or Policies Targeting Free Expression

Twenty-five of the studies are based on legal statutes or policy directives that restrict civil liberties, especially freedom of expression and, in some cases, media freedom. Based on a review of the studies' findings and recommendations, I found that government regulation of internet content, though justified on the need to combat harmful material, is worded in vague terms and is more often used as an excuse to silence dissent and free expression, leading to concerns among citizens. International law is arguably complicit in this area since it allows governments to restrict freedom of expression on national security grounds – a provision that African governments tend to exploit. Hence, there has been a consistent rise in government censorship of social media (Gumede 2016). Also relevant are the challenges that African governments face when it comes to exerting control over new media platforms (e.g. Meta or Google) based in the United States; these are challenges that make it appealing for governments to introduce statutory (e.g. laws) or technical (e.g. blocking and filtering) measures that target citizens directly. Examples include Rukundo's (2018) analysis of Uganda's Computer Misuse Act, which represents the government's move to extend its control in the offline context to the digital sphere. One study also appraises platforms' role in suppressing free speech in South Africa through content moderation, suggesting that these decisions should be subject to national judicial reviews (Sive and Price 2019).

Beyond legal/technical means and platform moderation, the studies show that African governments use social media taxes, limiting people's internet access. For instance, in Uganda, the social media tax reduced the rate of Twitter usage by 13 per cent (Boxell and Steinart-Threlkeld 2019). These taxes, sometimes introduced for revenue and debt repayment reasons (Ahmed et al. 2021), are usually not based on sound economic principles; as a result, they affect investment and productivity in the Information, Communication and Technology (ICT) sector. Even when used to target dissent, they tend to be counterproductive, given the possibility of a backlash effect (Boxell and Steinart-Threlkeld 2019), where people circumvent the taxes and find alternative means for collective action in both online and offline spaces. Social media taxes further reinforce a historical-colonial understanding of people's subjectivity to government (Bergère 2020). This colonial theme was present in other studies, highlighting the influence of Chinese technological expansion into Africa, with Bergère (2020) warning that it serves as an example of digital neo-colonialism. Digital (neo)colonialism, in this sense, is the extension of outside (typically Global North) influence on the use, application and regulation of digital media technologies in developing countries (Kwet 2019), as we see for instance in the export of the Chinese model of internet governance into Africa (Gravett 2020). Western platforms are equally complicit in this neo-colonialist act, as we see, for instance, with the introduction of Facebook's controversial Free Basics programme in Africa (Nothias 2020).

Despite the reality of internet censorship, there are fears that an unregulated internet could facilitate the spread of hacking, spam and other online harms, which refer to the production and distribution of digital content that can cause physical or psychological trauma (see World Economic Forum 2023). Therefore, what is needed is to create a balance: enacting policies designed to combat harmful content while protecting civil liberties. This would require scrutinizing government policies and the actions that internet service providers (ISPs) take to institute accountability and ensure that people are guaranteed access to the internet as a right. Some scholars like Gumede (2016) suggest that this scrutiny should be done by supranational bodies such as the African Union (AU) and the United Nations. Still, there are instruments such as the African Charter on Human and People's Rights, which restrictive national policies contravene, as Ayalew (2020) demonstrates – indicating that these regional and international instruments tend to have little bearing on national governments. Perhaps, this is why Hwang et al. (2016) recommend that the AU and other regional bodies in Africa should be reformed and that monitoring and watchdog organizations be created so they can collectively serve as a check on national governments.

Internet Shutdown

Studies that explore internet shutdowns are closely related to the previous discussion on laws or policies that target free expression since shutdowns also limit internet access and negatively affect freedom of expression. Nonetheless, I have separated them because of the considerable attention scholars have given to internet shutdowns in Africa from 2017 (and particularly from 2019), which means that it has grown into a field of scholarship in its own right. This includes a call to study the spectrum of shutdowns on the continent, which comprises the duration, breadth, depth, speed and frequency of shutdowns (Marchant and Stremlau 2019). The scholarship began with studies on the shutdown ordered by the Hosni Mubarak regime in Egypt during the Arab Spring, with Gerbaudo (2013) concluding that the shutdown was counterproductive, further fanning the flames of that revolution. It implies a correlation between internet shutdowns and greater protest mobilizations (Rydzak et al. 2020). In Ethiopia, Ayalew (2019) observes that the government uses narratives such as 'war on terror' and the need for 'economic development' as justification for shutdowns, even though they do not meet international rule of law principles. Also, in the Southern Africa region, governments do not have the power to order shutdowns (Southern Africa Litigation 2019), a case different from the Egyptian context where the legal framework enables and legitimizes internet censorship (Open Technology Fund 2019).

Shutdowns are typically more likely if leaders have had extended stays in office and when elections are imminent (Mwanzia et al. 2021). These leaders have facilitated the 'Big Man' syndrome in African politics – strongmen who have the power to shut down the internet (Mpofu 2023). Hence, people tend to view shutdowns as a power game that highlights governments' ulterior motives (Chari 2023; Akinyetun and Ebonine 2022). Shutdowns are also tied to political economic considerations since owners of ISPs (including foreign owners) find that they have to comply with shutdown directives if they have any hope of operating within the markets of concern (Freyburg and Garbe 2018). The examples that Freyburg and Garbe (2018) give include the requests issued to ISPs by the Republic of Congo and Uganda to shut down media websites or social media sites during election periods. Other ISP owners have fears of political harassment, victimization and even imprisonment. Nevertheless, by complying, these owners become enablers rather than resistors of internet shutdowns (Mare 2020). Together with policy actions such as internet filtering and blocking, shutdowns can be described as digital authoritarianism (see Mare 2020). Fano (2020), for instance, shows that 16 out of 25 African countries have policies on digital authoritarianism, highlighting the relationship between China's soft power and digital authoritarianism in Africa. There are also indications that African governments are moving from blunt shutdowns to more advanced technical tactics. This includes the use of slow internet shutdowns in Tanzania, for instance (Parks and Thompson 2020); a slow shutdown is a situation where laws are progressively enacted to systematically reduce online interaction and entrench government control over the information ecosystem.

Other studies consider the opposition people mount against shutdowns (Madenga 2020) through VPN circumvention tactics, for instance (Okunoye 2020). We see this in the use of VPN by Zimbabweans to evade internet shutdown in their country during nationwide protests in 2019.[1] However, despite the opposition to shutdowns, there remains a need for a broader debate on the relevance of shutdowns which can be useful for protecting human rights and security (Marchant and Stremlau 2019); creating a space for this debate will be crucial.

Online Harms

The research in this area primarily considers legal and other measures that African governments have introduced to combat online harms such as fake news, hate speech and cybercrime. Regarding cybercrime, studies show that approximately

23 African countries have cybercrime laws targeting fake news, laws which contravene international principles (Salau 2020). Consequently, discussions on cybersecurity governance point to the need for a balance between cyber regulation and freedom of expression (Turianskyi 2018). Turianskyi (2018) also highlights the unequal relationship between weak Global South countries and powerful private actors regarding internet regulation, an area that needs further exploration. Cybercrime also relates to cyber-terrorism, harm for which multilateral cooperation is needed (Ogunlana 2019). Van Vuuren et al. (2012), on their part, examine cybersecurity in South Africa and propose an approach for effective cybersecurity governance based on the Cyber Security Awareness Toolkit (CyberSAT). Other studies examine approaches to hate speech control and concerns of the general populace. Kiai (2015), for instance, shows that bloggers prefer sensitization and literacy approaches to the use of laws, and Delelegn (2021) observes that a multilayered approach built on trust, dialogue and national reconciliation is essential.

Concerning fake news, Abdullateef (2021) examines perceptions of Nigeria's Internet Falsehood Bill and finds that people do not trust the government's position on the legislation. This is not surprising since most misinformation laws on the continent do not target misinformation (Cunliffe-Jones et al. 2021). These laws tend to relate to legal censorship measures that governments adopt when facing legislative constraints; other governments without similar constraints use technical means (Garbe et al. 2023). Obia (2021) also shows that social media regulation reflects the politics of regulation where users are designated and regulated as publishers – the basis for an unworkable legal framework. Again, the remedy to this, studies suggest, is the need for balance. Furthermore, Sugow (2019) shows that balance in the law can be achieved if regulation only targets obvious or extreme cases like disinformation, while other less stringent measures (e.g. awareness initiatives) are used for less harmful information disorders. This underscores the importance that scholars attach to approaches combining content regulation and digital literacy, as we see in other studies (Mutua and Yanqui 2020; Olaniyan and Akpojivi 2021). Rutenberg and Sugow (2020) also highlight the need for regulation that targets platform design, not content. However, I note that they do not consider the power dynamics that underline the uncertainty regarding whether African governments can dictate how (western) platforms are designed. This is important because without this consideration, the assumption is that African countries can exert influence on foreign-based platforms, which further increasing the potential for stakeholders to overlook other approaches where African government can contribute to digital policy agenda in a collective framework. Examples include a multistakeholder approach such as a regional convention on social media hate speech (Munoriyarwa 2023), partnerships at the national, regional and global levels (Fombad 2022) or UN mediation in cases where online hate speech has led to significant offline harms (De Gregorio and Stremlau 2021). This multistakeholder approach is what I consider next.

Internet Governance and Multi-Stakeholderism

Studies here primarily focus on the development and activities of the various Internet Governance Forum (IGF) bodies as a multistakeholder arrangement in Africa. There is an IGF for the continent as a whole, and all five regions equally have their separate IGFs, although they have struggled to influence national policies (Kanjo and Jere 2015). Nyirenda-Jere and Biru (2015) observe that the IGFs in East and West Africa are the most advanced in national coverage. This is particularly so for the East Africa IGF, the world's first regional IGF (Martin 2013). Martin (2013) adds that the East Africa IGF does its work of promoting consensus. However, it also reflects other issues of unequal representation, given that Kenya is the most influential member (see also Nonnecke 2016). Government stakeholders are also more influential than others. Even within Kenya, the indication is that participation in the Kenyan IGF mainly happens in Nairobi, the capital, neglecting other areas in the country (Souter and Kerretts-Makau 2012). Darch et al. (2018) also find that South Africa's National Integrated ICT Policy White Paper omits multilateralism, openness, inclusivity and transparency, even though the country criticizes global internet governance frameworks for lacking the same.

What this implies is that concerns of under-representation that African scholars have with global multi-stakeholderism also find expression within similar structures on the continent. We see, for instance, that Africa has been described as a latecomer in global internet governance fora (Kanjo and Jere 2015), lacking the ability to effectively participate in shaping the agenda (Calandro 2015). Holden and Van Klyton (2016) conceptualize the unequal representation of African countries as the paradox of participation, where Africa continues to suffer under-representation as a continuation of the legacy of historical global inequities. Calandro et al. (2016) also underscore the disparities between developed and developing countries in internet governance conversations, noting that it is only by growing its ICT sector that the continent can be positioned to influence these debates. By implication, local examples reflect global inequities.

Data Privacy

The last subject area that I discuss is privacy, and there are only ten research items here, the least of all. It should be noted, however, that I did not include studies on privacy that I found during the forward and backward search phase. This was so that I could manage the final count, which would have been unwieldy if

I had included studies on privacy (see methodology section). In general, there is an indication that data privacy relates closely to multi-stakeholderism. Osakwe and Adeniran (2021), for instance, see the need for uniformity in African countries' data policy approaches since this will lead to benefits from greater economic integration and lessons learned following previous regional efforts. However, it is unclear how this will work if individual governments have separate policies. Borena et al. (2015) further note that separate national policies are ineffective for privacy protection and that regional or global approaches are needed, tailored according to the cooperation in the European Union.

The practice of following European standards is also noticeable in Alunge (2020), which compares the ECOWAS Supplementary Data Protection Act and the AU's Convention on Cyber Security and Personal Data Protection to European principles. Bronstein (2022) also compares South Africa's Protection of Personal Information Act (POPIA) with Europe's General Data Protection Regulation (GDPR), noting that POPIA does not have collaborative governance measures and the Data Protection Impact Assessments system in the GDPR. What I find, therefore, is that scholars working in this area tend to use European standards and frameworks as a benchmark to assess Africa's data privacy instruments. I note that this points to evidence of postcolonialism, reflected in the way that African stakeholders see western approaches as examples to follow, even though there are contextual peculiarities that make African experiences different from what obtains elsewhere.

Byrant (2021) is one of the few studies that see the underlying postcolonial undertone. The study notes that even though lessons can be drawn from the GDPR, African countries should be wary of its Eurocentric nature, precisely because of the need for Africa to develop its data protection framework to suit its context and challenges (Bryant 2021). One approach to this might be to consider Ngwenya and Ngoepe's (2020) framework, which comprises data security, privacy and trustworthiness. Overall, the research on data protection reflects the power imbalances that Africa faces, given that countries on the continent are attempting to regulate the use of technologies that are largely owned by western corporations and that come with pre-set norms drawn from standards and principles in other regions of the world.

Discussion and Conclusion

In writing this chapter, I set out to provide an overarching synthesis of the research published on digital media regulation in Africa up until May 2023. By so doing, I have laid out the research landscape and set the stage for the book in showing that digital media regulation in Africa revolves around state-citizen distrust, broad application of regulatory policy, censorship, political self-interest, digital authoritarianism, regulatory power dynamics, lack of broad-based participation locally and internationally and a search for digital sovereignty. My objective was to identify the timeline of research in the area, the types of publications, the regions they focus on and the methodologies they employ. I was also interested in the subject areas that the studies consider and their findings. To achieve this, I systematically reviewed 87 studies drawn from academic databases and backward searches (the search yielded 157 studies, from which 70 were removed based on specified inclusion and exclusion criteria). My findings revealed that the first item was published in 2011 and that it was in 2015 that scholars began to show interest in the area, an interest that became more pronounced in 2019 and peaked in 2020. I also found that slightly above half (51.7 per cent) of the studies were journal articles; the remaining were reports, book chapters, conference papers, Master's dissertations, policy briefs, discussion papers and one Ph.D. thesis in that order. The findings further show that 39 studies considered either the broader African or Sub-Saharan African context; apart from these, most of the studies (eighteen each) focused on Eastern and Southern African regions. In terms of national counts, the majority of the studies consider South Africa and then Nigeria. This implies the potential gap in areas outside of Eastern and Southern Africa, South Africa and Nigeria. Even if we account for the fact that this chapter is based on English-language publications, there is still reason to believe that research has not captured a fuller picture of the regulatory landscape across Africa.

Regarding methodology, I found that nearly two-thirds, or 56 studies, had no methodological section, even though most of these studies included a note on the method in their respective abstracts or introductions – an accepted practice. Overall, I found that policy analysis based on legal interpretation was the most used method – 56.7 per cent, or 38 studies, included policy analysis, whether in a standalone or triangulated format. On subject areas, I divided the studies into five categories: laws or policies targeting free expression, internet shutdown, online harms, internet governance/multi-stakeholderism and data privacy. I found that most of the studies centre around internet censorship and restrictions that limit civil liberties based on vaguely worded legal instruments justified by governments on altruistic grounds, even though people generally feel that they are designed to silence dissent and freedom of expression. Internet shutdowns, on their part, represent overt censorship. One thing that is crucial here is the political economy of shutdowns, which highlights ownership concerns as it relates to ISPs (Freyburg and Garbe 2018; Mare 2020), indicating that African governments will always have the power to implement shutdowns as long as ISPs operate under local laws. The reverse is the seeming lack of power that African governments have when dealing with western platforms and powerful private actors (Turianskyi 2018). More studies are needed to explore how this is tied to the dependence that African governments face when it comes to Global North platforms and governments. Some studies are now exploring Chinese influence and technological expansion into Africa as a form of digital neo-colonialism (Gravett 2020; Fano 2020; Elega et al. 2023), which is helpful. However, more is required to comprehensively understand the geopolitical balance of power dynamics and how this affects the kind of regulation that African governments (can potentially) implement. What level of importance should we attach to the relation of dependence? Is digital neo-colonialism the appropriate conceptualization? How can we develop tools, ideas and approaches that define Africa's place in the global governance of the internet in light of existing regulations on the continent?

These are preliminary questions that will likely prompt a deeper study of the issues of concern, particularly in areas around multi-stakeholderism. And some studies describe multi-stakeholderism as the key to the challenge of internet content regulation on the continent (Nyirenda-Jere and Biru 2015; Fombad 2022), while other studies have highlighted the inequalities that exist in multistakeholder arrangements both within Africa (Martin 2013) and in the wider global context (Calandro 2015; Holden and Van Klyton 2016). The only study that perhaps considers how African countries can reverse the inequality trend is Calandro et al. (2016), which notes the importance of developing the ICT sector in Africa. This suggests the need for research that examines global multistakeholder frameworks and what is needed to secure a collegiate system, one where Global South countries contribute to shaping the agenda. Also important are considerations of how regional multistakeholder bodies can become more effective in influencing national regulations on the continent.

In the broader sense, studies need to explore alternative solutions to the challenge of digital media regulation. These studies will also need to consider the regulation of 'newer' forms of technology such as the Internet of Things and general-purpose artificial intelligence. Scholars should examine what Africa can do to influence the regulation of these technologies, whether in a unilateral or multilateral set-up. This is important in ensuring that regulation in Africa is not just reactive, as we see in data privacy research, where the EU's GDPR has effectively become a benchmark for Africa. Moreover, if unilateral approaches are to be considered, scholars will need to explore further the concept of balance (Kakungulu-Mayambala and Rukundo 2019; Delelegn 2021; Nakaayi 2023). For instance, how can African countries enact regulations addressing the challenges associated with internet usage while protecting civil liberties? There is little to suggest that this balance can be achieved in Africa, given that governments on the continent still widely engage in digital authoritarianism and censorship practices. Remedying the situation will require a change in policy in favour of building state-citizen trust, encouraging broad participation in national governance efforts, and upholding national security above regime interest.

Balance also suggests that scholars need to de-emphasize the focus on binary contraptions where digital media regulations are either seen as good or bad. For instance, there is a need for a broader conversation on the usefulness of restrictive tools such as internet shutdowns, as Marchant and Stremlau (2019) observe. This points to the relevance of a more nuanced approach to researching the regulation of digital media technologies in Africa, an approach that goes beyond analysing regulatory policies into developing new concepts and frameworks that address the issues that the continent faces in the global scheme of things. Relevant here are the innovative principles that research can contribute to shape a global multi-stakeholder protocol that is inclusive of all voices (including Global South voices) to address the relation of dependence, systemic in dealing with the deep-rooted issues of digital governance, and flexible enough to flow with changes in the tech ecosystem. African stakeholders should be at the forefront in canvassing for such a protocol.

NOTE

1. See https://qz.com/africa/1528663/zimbabwe-intnerent-shutdown-leads-to-vpn-use. Accessed 4 May 2023.

REFERENCES

Abdullateef, Mohammed (2021), 'Regulating social media in Nigeria: A quantitative perception study', *Political Science*, 2:1, pp. 52–77.

Abdulrauf, Lukman (2020), 'Data protection in the internet: South Africa', in D. M. Vicente and S. D. Casimiro (eds), *Data Protection in the Internet*, Cham: Springer, pp. 349–70.

Abraha, Halefom (2017), 'Examining approaches to internet regulation in Ethiopia', *Information and Communications Technology Law*, 26:3, pp. 293–311.

Ahmed, Shamira, Chinembiri, Tapiwa and Govan-Vassen, Naila (2021), 'COVID-19 exposes the contradictions of social media taxes in Africa', *Research ICT Africa*, https://www.africaportal.org/publications/covid-19-exposes-contradictions-social-media-taxes-africa/. Accessed 15 May 2023.

Akinyetun, Tope and Ebonine, Victor (2022), 'The challenge of democratisation in Africa: From digital democracy to digital authoritarianism', in E. Alaverdov and M. W. Bari (eds), *Regulating Human Rights, Social Security, and Socio-Economic Structures in a Global Perspective*, Hershey: IGI Global, pp. 250–69.

Alunge, Rogers (2020), 'Africa's multilateral legal framework on personal data security: What prospects for the digital environment?' in R. Zitouni, M. Agueh, P. Houngue and H. Soude (eds), *e-Infrastructure and e-Services for Developing Countries*, Porto-Novo, pp. 38–58, https://doi.org/10.1007/978-3-030-41593-8_4.

Asiedu, Michael (2022), *Digital Censorship and Africa's Democratic Future*, Electoral Institute for Sustainable Democracy in Africa, https://www.eisa.org/wp-content/uploads/2023/05/policy-brief-2022-gipps-digital-censorship-africas-democratic-future-eisa.pdf. Accessed 13 May 2023.

Ayalew, Yohannes (2019), 'The internet shutdown muzzle(s) freedom of expression in Ethiopia: Competing narratives', *Information and Communications Technology Law*, 28:2, pp. 208–24.

Ayalew, Yohannes (2020), 'Assessing the limitations to freedom of expression on the internet in Ethiopia against the African Charter on Human and Peoples' Rights', *African Human Rights Law Journal*, 20:1, pp. 315–45.

Ayalew, Yohannes (2021), 'From digital authoritarianism to platforms' Leviathan power: Freedom of expression in the digital age under siege in Africa', *Mizan Law Review*, 15:2, pp. 455–92.

Bergère, Clovis (2020), 'Internet shutdowns in Africa | "Don't tax my megabytes": Digital infrastructure and the regulation of citizenship in Africa', *International Journal of Communication*, 14, pp. 4309–26.

Bitso, Constance (2014), 'Internet censorship in South Africa: A brief exposé of negative and positive trends', *South African Journal of Library and Information Science*, 80:1, pp. 41–51.

Boateng, Akwasi (2023), 'Social media usage and digital rights restrictions in the Republic of Chad', in F. A. Kperogi (ed.), *Digital Dissidence and Social Media Censorship in Africa*, London: Routledge, pp. 197–208.

Borena, Berhanu, Belanger, France and Egigu, Dejene (2015), 'Information privacy protection practices in Africa: A review through the lens of critical social theory', 48th Hawaii International Conference on System Sciences, Kauai, Hawaii, 5–8 January.

Boxell, Levi and Steinert-Threlkeld, Zachary (2019), 'Taxing dissent: The impact of a social media tax in Uganda', *arXiv*, pp. 1–28. https://arxiv.org/pdf/1909.04107. Accessed 24 June 2025.

Bronstein, Victoria (2022), 'Prioritising command-and-control over collaborative governance: The role of the information regulator under the Protection of Personal Information Act', *Potchefstroom Electronic Law Journal*, 25, pp. 1–41, https://doi.org/10.17159/1727-3781/2022/v25i0a11661.

Bryant, Justin (2021), 'Africa in the information age: Challenges, opportunities, and strategies for data protection and digital rights', *Stanford Technology Law Review*, 24:2, pp. 389–439.

Calandro, Enrico (2015), 'Stakeholders' involvement and participation in the internet governance ecosystem: An African perspective', Internet Policy Observatory, https://repository.upenn.edu/internetpolicyobservatory/17. Accessed 16 May 2023.

Calandro, Enrico, Gillwald, Alison and Zingales, Nicolo (2016), 'Mapping multistakeholderism in internet governance: Implications for Africa', Research ICT Africa, https://www.researchictafrica.net/publications/Evidence_for_ICT_Policy_Action/Discussion_paper_-_Mapping_Multistakeholderism_in_Internet_Governance_-_Implications_for_Africa.pdf. Accessed 10 May 2023.

Chari, Tendai (2023), 'Between state interests and citizen digital rights: Making sense of internet shutdowns in Zimbabwe', in F. A. Kperogi (ed.), *Digital Dissidence and Social Media Censorship in Africa*, London: Routledge, pp. 76–97.

Cross, Charlotte (2019), 'Cybercrime and the policing of politics in Tanzania', in M. Dwyer and T. Molony (eds), *Social Media and Politics in Africa: Democracy, Censorship and Security*, London: Zed Books, pp. 195–213.

Cunliffe-Jones, Peter, Diagne, Assane, Finlay, Alan and Schiffrin, Anya (2021), 'Bad law: Legal and regulatory responses to misinformation in Sub-Saharan Africa 2016–2020', CAMRI Policy Briefs and Reports, https://www.uwestminsterpress.co.uk/site/chapters/m/10.16997/book53.b/. Accessed 17 May 2023.

Darch, Colin, Adams, Rachel and Ke, Yu (2018), 'Deconstructing the paradoxes of South Africa's emerging discourse and framework on ICTs and internet governance', in D. Opperman (ed.), *Internet Governance in the Global South: Theory, History, and Contemporary Debates*, Sao Paulo: Earthscan, pp. 277–300.

De Gregorio, Giovanni and Stremlau, Nicole (2021), 'Platform governance at the periphery: Moderation, shutdowns and intervention', in J. Bayer, B. Holznagel, P. Korpisaari and L. Woods (eds), *Perspectives on Platform Regulation: Concepts and Models of Social Media Governance Across the Globe*, Baden-Baden: Nomos Verlagsgesellschaft mbH and Co, pp. 433–50.

Delelegn, Misganaw (2021), 'Hate speech regulation in Ethiopia: Lessons to be learned from other jurisdictions', Master's dissertation, Amhara: Bahir Dar University.

de Veiga, Adéle, Ochola, Elisha, Mujinga, Mathias and Mwim, Emilia (2022), 'Investigating data privacy evaluation criteria and requirements for e-commerce websites', Advanced Research in Technologies, Information, Innovation and Sustainability: Second International Conference, ARTIIS 2022, Santiago de Compostela, Spain, 12–15 September.

Elega, Adeola, Mohammed, Abdullateef and Oloyede, Felix (2023), '"The fall of a dry leaf is a warning to the green ones": Exploring the Twitter ban and the impending dangers of data politics, algorithmic governance, and mass surveillance in Nigeria', *First Monday*, 28:4, pp. 1–15.

Fano, Emma (2020), 'Digital authoritarianism in Sub-Saharan Africa: Internet control techniques and censorship', Master's dissertation, Erfurt: University of Erfurt.

Fombad, Charles (2022), 'Democracy and fake news in Africa', *Journal of International and Comparative Law*, 9:1, pp. 131–54.

Freyburg, Tina and Garbe, Lisa (2018), 'Blocking the bottleneck: Internet shutdowns and ownership at election times in Sub-Saharan Africa', *International Journal of Communication*, 12, pp. 3896–3916.

Gambiza, Grace (2020), 'Fake news and social media regulation in Zimbabwe: A case study of the 2019 National #Shutdown', Master's dissertation, Johannesburg: University of Johannesburg.

Garbe, Lisa, Selvik, Lisa-Marie and Lemaire, Pauline (2023), 'How African countries respond to fake news and hate speech', *Information, Communication & Society*, 26:1, pp. 86–103, https://doi.org/10.1080/1369118X.2021.1994623.

Gerbaudo, Paolo (2013), 'The "kill switch" as "suicide switch": Mobilising side effects of Mubarak's communication blackout', *Westminster Papers in Communication and Culture*, 9:2, pp. 25–46.

Goldstein, Eric (1999), *The Internet in the Mideast and North Africa: Free Expression and Censorship*, New York: Human Rights Watch, https://searchworks.stanford.edu/view/4299909. Accessed 14 May 2023.

Gravett, Willem (2020), 'Digital neo-colonialism: The Chinese model of internet sovereignty in Africa', *African Human Rights Law Journal*, 20:1, pp. 125–46.

Gumede, William (2016), 'Rise in censorship of the Internet and social media in Africa', *Journal of African Media Studies*, 8:3, pp. 413–21.

Holden, Kerry and Van Klyton, Aaron (2016), 'Exploring the tensions and incongruities of internet governance in Africa', *Government Information Quarterly*, 33:4, pp. 736–45.

Houissa, Ali (2020), 'The internet predicament in the Middle East and North Africa: Access and censorship', *Journal of Librarianship and Information Science*, 32:2, pp. 56–63.

Hwang, Katherine, Gerson, Ben, Laing, Nyasha, Harrison, David, Lindahl, Danielle, Allen, Hawa, Nims, Tyler, Jackson, Marissa and Ouattara, Sondah (2016), 'The right to freedom of expression on the internet as it applies to social media in Africa', *New York City Bar*, https://www2.nycbar.org/pdf/report/uploads/20073028-FreedomofExpressionontheInternetAfrican312016.pdf. Accessed 16 May 2023.

International Commission of Jurists (ICJ) (2021), *Regulation of Communications Surveillance and Access to Internet in Selected African States*, Geneva: International Commission of Jurists, https://www.kas.de/documents/275350/0/Report-on-Regulation-of-Communications-Surveillance-and-Access-to-Internet-in-Selected-African-States.pdf/66dbd47d-4d7d-2779-a595-a34e9f93cfbb?t=1639140695434. Accessed 16 May 2023.

John, Ubena (2020), 'The bolts and nuts of online content regulation in Tanzania', *Information and Communications Technology Law*, 29:1, pp. 45–65.

Kakungulu-Mayambala, Ronald and Rukundo, Solomon (2019), 'Digital activism and free expression in Uganda', *African Human Rights Law Journal*, 19, pp. 167–92.

Kalemera, Ashnah, Kapiyo, Victor, Kimumwe, Paul, Nalwoga, Lillian, Nankufa, Juliet, Wanyama, Edrine and Wakabi, Wairagala (2020), *State of Internet Freedom in Chad 2019: Mapping Trends in Government Internet Controls, 1999–2019*, Kampala: CIPESA, https://cipesa.org/wp-content/files/State-of-Internet-Freedom-in-Chad-2019.pdf. Accessed 16 May 2023.

Kanjo, Chipo and Jere, Towela (2015), 'On bringing governance into technology: Case of internet governance and implications for Africa', 2015 IST-Africa Conference, Lilongwe, Malawi, 6–8 May, https://10.1109/ISTAFRICA.2015.7190589.

Kiai, Nyaruai (2015), 'Factors affecting hate speech control for peace building in Kenyan social media: A case of Kenyan bloggers', Master's dissertation, Nairobi: University of Nairobi.

Kwet, Michael (2019), 'Digital colonialism: US empire and the new imperialism in the Global South', *Race & Class*, 60:4, pp. 2–26.

Madenga, Florence (2020), 'From transparency to opacity: Storytelling in Zimbabwe under state surveillance and the internet shutdown', *Information, Communication & Society*, 24:3, pp. 400–21.

Marchant, Eleanor and Stremlau, Nicole (2019), *Africa's Internet Shutdowns: A Report on the Johannesburg Workshop*, European Research Council, https://pcmlp.socleg.ox.ac.uk/wp-content/uploads/2019/10/Internet-Shutdown-Workshop-Report-171019.pdf. Accessed 16 May 2023.

Marchant, Eleanor and Stremlau, Nicole (2020a), 'The changing landscape of internet shutdowns in Africa: Introduction', *International Journal of Communication*, 14, pp. 4216–23.

Marchant, Eleanor and Stremlau, Nicole (2020b), 'A spectrum of shutdowns: Reframing internet shutdowns from Africa', *International Journal of Communication*, 14, pp. 4327–42.

Mare, Admire (2020), 'State-ordered internet shutdowns and digital authoritarianism in Zimbabwe', *International Journal of Communication*, 14, pp. 4244–63.

Martin, Brandie (2013), 'Capacity building and collaborative policymaking: A case study of the East Africa Internet Governance Forum', Ph.D. thesis, Pennsylvania: The Pennsylvania State University.

Matsilele, Trust and Mutsvairo, Bruce (2022), 'Understanding the dynamics of social media governance in South Africa', in S. A. Ganter and H. Badr (eds), *Media Governance: A Cosmopolitan Critique*, Cham: Springer International Publishing, pp. 231–60.

Moses, John, Targema, Tordue and Ishaku, Jesse (2022), 'Tale of an ill-fated scapegoat: National security and the struggle for state regulation of social media in Nigeria', *Journal of Digital Media & Policy*, pp. 1–19.

Mpofu, Shepherd (2023), 'His excellency, the internet and outraged citizens: An analysis of the big man syndrome and internet shutdowns in Africa', in F. A. Kperogi (ed.), *Digital Dissidence and Social Media Censorship in Africa*, London: Routledge, pp. 37–57.

Mthimkhulu, Zongile (2011), 'Regulating freedom?: An examination of the discourse on internet regulation and freedom of expression in South Africa', Master's dissertation, Johannesburg: University of the Witwatersrand.

Munoriyarwa, Allen (2023), 'Mapping social media hate speech regulations in Southern Africa: A regional comparative analysis', in B. Di Fátima (ed.), *Hate Speech on Social Media: A Global Approach*, LabCom Books & EdiPUCE, pp. 203–26.

Mutua, Sylvia and Yanqiu, Zhang (2020), 'Regulating online content in East Africa: Potential challenges and possible solutions', *Journal of African Media Studies*, 12:3, pp. 319–34, https://doi.org/10.1386/jams_00027.

Mwanzia, Sigi, Kapiyo, Victor and Madung, Odanga (2021), *Study on Internet Shutdown in Africa, 2021*, African Internet Rights Alliance, https://aira.africa/wp-content/uploads/2022/04/STUDY-ON-INTERNET-SHUTDOWNS-IN-AFRICA-2021.pdf. Accessed 15 May 2023.

Nakaayi, Anna (2023), 'Case studies on anti-social media laws in African countries', in F. A. Kperogi (ed.), *Digital Dissidence and Social Media Censorship in Africa*, London: Routledge, pp. 242–66.

Ngwenya, Mfanasibili and Ngoepe, Mpho (2020), 'A framework for data security, privacy, and trust in "consumer internet of things" assemblages in South Africa', *Security and Privacy*, 3:5, pp. 1–10.

Nkrumah, Bright (2018), 'Words that wound: Rethinking online hate speech in South Africa', *Alternation*, 23, pp. 108–33.

Nonnecke, Brandie (2016), 'The transformative effects of multistakeholderism in internet governance: A case study of the East Africa Internet Governance Forum', *Telecommunications Policy*, 40:4, pp. 343–52.

Nothias, Toussaint (2020), 'Access granted: Facebook's free basics in Africa', *Media, Culture and Society*, 42:3, pp. 329–48, https://doi.org/10.1177/0163443719890530.

Nyirenda-Jere, Towela and Biru, Tesfaye (2015), *Internet Development and Internet Governance in Africa*, Internet Society, https://www.internetsociety.org/wp-content/uploads/2017/08/InternetInAfrica-2015070820Final.pdf. Accessed 15 May 2023.

Nyoni, Phil, Velempini, Mthulisi and Mavetera, Nehemiah (2020), 'Emerging internet technologies and the regulation of user privacy', *The African Journal of Information Systems*, 13:1, pp. 1–32.

Obia, Vincent (2021), 'Are social media users publishers?: Alternative regulation of social media in selected African countries', *Makings*, 2:1, pp. 1–13.

Obia, Vincent (2023), 'Regulatory annexation: Extending broadcast media regulation to social media and internet content', *Communication Law and Policy*, 28:2, pp. 99–123.

Ogunlana, Sunday (2019), 'Halting Boko Haram/Islamic State's West Africa Province propaganda in cyberspace with cybersecurity technologies', *Journal of Strategic Security*, 12:1, pp. 72–106, https://doi.org/10.5038/1944-0472.12.1.1707.

Okunoye, Babatunde (2020), *Censored Continent: Understanding the Use of Tools During Internet Censorship in Africa: Cameroon, Nigeria, Uganda and Zimbabwe as Case Studies*, Open Technology Fund, https://research.torproject.org/techreports/icfp-censored-continent-2020-07-31.pdf. Accessed 15 May 2023.

Olaniyan, Akintola and Akpojivi, Ufuoma (2021), 'Transforming communication, social media, counter-hegemony and the struggle for the soul of Nigeria', *Information, Communication & Society*, 24:3, pp. 422–37, https://doi.org/10.1080/1369118X.2020.1804983.

Olukolu, Rasul, Ogwezzy-Ndisika, Abigail, Faustino, Babatunde and Oloruntoba, Faith (2019), 'Social media regulation and challenges of communication in an evolving Nigerian society', *University of Baltimore Journal of Media Law and Ethics*, 7:1–2, pp. 68–84.

Open Technology Fund (2019), *Digital Authoritarianism in Egypt: Digital Expression Arrests 2011–2019*, OTF, https://public.opentech.fund/documents/EgyptReportV06.pdf. Accessed 15 May 2023.

Orji, Uchenna (2015), 'Multilateral legal responses to cyber security in Africa: Any hope for effective international cooperation?' in M. Maybaum and A. M. Osula and L. Lindström (eds), 7th International Conference on Cyber Conflict: Architectures in Cyberspace, Tallinn, Estonia, pp. 105–18.

Osakwe, Sone and Adeniran, Adedeji (2021), *Strengthening Data Governance in Africa*, Centre for the Study of the Economies of Africa, https://www.africaportal.org/publications/strengthening-data-governance-africa/. Accessed 13 May 2023).

Parks, Lisa and Thompson, Rachel (2020), 'The slow shutdown: Information and internet regulation in Tanzania from 2010 to 2018 and impacts on online content creators', *International Journal of Communication*, 14, pp. 4288–4308.

Petticrew, Mark and Roberts, Helen (2006), *Systematic Reviews in the Social Sciences: A Practical Guide*, Oxford: Blackwell Publishing.

Powell, CH and Schonwetter, Tobias (2019), 'Africa, the internet and human rights', in M. Susi (ed.), *Human Rights, Digital Society and the Law*, London: Routledge, pp. 319–36.

Reinard, John and Ortiz, Sandra (2005), 'Communication law and policy: The state of research and theory', *Journal of Communication*, 55:3, pp. 594–631.

Rukundo, Solomon (2018), '"My president is a pair of buttocks": The limits of online freedom of expression in Uganda', *International Journal of Law and Information Technology*, 26:3, pp. 252–71.

Rutenberg, Isaac and Sugow, Abdulmalik (2020), 'Regulation of the social media in electoral democracies: A case of Kenya', *SOAS Law Journal*, 7:1, pp. 301–61.

Rydzak, Jan, Karanja, Moses and Opiyo, Nicholas (2020), 'Dissent does not die in darkness: Network shutdowns and collective action in African countries', *International Journal of Communication*, 14, pp. 4264–87.

Salau, Aaron (2020), 'Social media and the prohibition of "false news": Can the free speech jurisprudence of the African Commission on Human and Peoples' Rights provide a litmus test?' *African Human Rights Yearbook*, 4, pp. 231–54.

Santas, Tsegyu and Inobemhe, Kevin (2021), 'Social media regulation in a democratic Nigeria: Challenges and implication', *Media & Communication Currents*, 5:1, pp. 71–88.

Selnes, Florence (2021), 'Internet restrictions in Uganda: Examining their impact on journalism', *Information, Communication & Society*, 24:3, pp. 490–506.

Sive, Daniel and Price, Alistair (2019), 'Regulating expression on social media', *South African Law Journal*, 136:1, pp. 51–83.

Souter, David and Kerretts-Makau, Monica (2012), *Internet Governance in Kenya: An Assessment for the Internet Society*, ICT Development Associates Ltd., https://www.researchictafrica.net/multistake/Souter_Kerretts-Makau_2012_-_Internet_governance_in_Kenya_-_an_assessment_for_the_Internet_Society.pdf. Accessed 15 May 2023.

Southern Africa Litigation Centre (2019), *Navigating Litigation During Internet Shutdowns in Southern Africa*, Southern Africa Litigation Centre and Media Institute of Southern Africa, https://www.southernafricalitigationcentre.org/wp-content/uploads/2019/08/SALC-Internet-Shutdown-Guide-FINAL.pdf. Accessed 15 May 2023.

Stork, Christoph and Esselaar, Steve (2019), *Regulatory and Tax Treatment of OTTs in Africa*, Mozilla and African Union, https://blog.mozilla.org/netpolicy/files/2019/11/Regulatory-Treatment-of-OTTs-in-Africa-1.pdf. Accessed 16 May 2023.

Sugow, Abdulmalik (2019), 'The right to be wrong: Examining the (im)possibilities of regulating fake news while preserving the freedom of expression in Kenya', *Strathmore Law Review*, 4:1, pp. 19–46.

Turianskyi, Yarik (2018), *Balancing Cyber Security and Internet Freedom in Africa*, South African Institute of International Affairs, https://saiia.org.za/wp-content/uploads/2018/02/Occasional-Paper-275.pdf. Accessed 14 May 2023.

Van Vuuren, Jansen, Phahlamohlaka, Jackie and Leenen, Louise (2012), 'Governance of cybersecurity in South Africa', Proceedings of the 11th European Conference on Information Warfare and Security, Laval, France, 5–6 July.

Vareba, Anthony, Nwinaene, Vivian-Peace and Theophilus, Singto (2017), 'Internet censorship and freedom of expression in Nigeria', *International Journal of Media Journalism and Mass Communication*, 3:2, pp. 25–30.

World Economic Forum (2023), *Toolkit for Digital Safety Design Interventions and Innovations: Typology of Online Harms*, Geneva: World Economic Forum, https://www3.weforum.org/docs/WEF_Typology_of_Online_Harms_2023.pdf. Accessed 28 September 2023.

Xiao, Yu and Watson, Maria (2019), 'Guidance on conducting a systematic literature review', *Journal of Planning Education and Research*, 39:1, pp. 93–112.

PART 2

STATE POLICY APPROACHES AND REGULATORY CHALLENGES

4

Cybersecurity Laws, Digital Media Spaces and Media Freedoms in Zambia

Ndawana Youngson, Joanne Knowles and Elastus Mambwe

Introduction: Digital Journalism Redefining Journalism

The introduction of cybersecurity laws in Zambia came on the back foot of an increasingly intolerant political environment that has seen worrying trends of a declining democratic culture. Since the mid-2000s, successive events affected the democratic space in general (Cheeseman and Klaas 2018), but more within the media space (Goldring and Wahman 2016; Roberts et al. 2021), threatening to reverse the gains that the country had recorded since the reinstitution of democracy at the turn of the last decade of the twentieth century. Increasing state overreach that affected mainstream media operators coincided with the emergence of a vibrant online media tradition which seemed to evade traditional modes of regulatory control. With the fast-paced nature of this emergent media sector, the state was seen to be playing catch-up. Traditional regulatory laws and mechanisms were not sufficient to cover this potentially more effective digital media sector. This is because it presents immense opportunities for journalists and citizens alike to have quicker access to a variety of information and the ability to share this information more widely and quickly. Around the same period, the nation and the region at large had been consumed in the debates surrounding regulatory models between state-sponsored and self-regulatory. With these many debates and focal areas, the discussion surrounding the regulation of digital media therefore raised significant apprehension as most professional journalists, scholars and citizens felt the state intended to gag the sector and not promote its growth and promote a democratic culture of transparency, participation, promotion of debate and exchange of opinions among various stakeholders. This study therefore analyses some of the implications of this law on press freedom, focusing on digital journalism and new media.

Digital and new media have evolved over the past decade to redefine journalism profoundly. This is both in the professional values and ethics of the trade and the tools at the disposal of professional journalists. With the internet as the main platform and carrier of digital and new media content, a lot of the work that goes on in this space including creating and managing content and its dissemination carries with it technical as well as social elements. Kperogi, for example, notes that:

> Technological and philosophical foundations have been pivotal to the growth, mass appeal, and universal acceptance of social media networks: they are free, require no special skills to use, create opportunities for prosumption (i.e., the simultaneous production and consumption of content), are devolved and non-hierarchical, are alterable sometimes immediately, and are perpetually evolving.
>
> (Kperogi 2022: 3)

This study demonstrates how state actors carve out their role in ensuring that digital journalism and social media are placed within the continuum of journalism for purposes of legislation and regulating their operations. Several studies elsewhere show that it is a frequent practice in most political systems to attempt to control digital and social media influence using different tactics. For example, Stoycheff et al. (2020: 475) argue that as access to information and communication technologies (ICTs) becomes more ubiquitous, governments around the globe will find ways of restricting, containing or monitoring how they are used. They further contend, in their multi-level analyses of 63 countries, that 'online government monitoring is negatively associated with democratization, while internet censorship exhibits no additional effect [...] theorize that suppression technologies erode democratic progress by thwarting collective action' (Stoycheff et al. 2020: 474). In autocratic jurisdictions such as Uganda, Grönlund and Wakabi (2015) reveal that expressing an opinion or siding with a political cause that is not aligned with the government opens journalists and citizens up to possible retribution and threats. These measures and government interventions are often done through legal and regulatory mechanisms.

In this chapter, we explored relevant literature and research to situate the discussion within current trends that relate to how these measures have evolved within states, especially in Zambia. We assessed the status of digital and social media operations in Zambia and related laws and regulations that have a bearing on and affect digital journalism. To achieve these goals, we interviewed a total of nine digital media journalists and other key informants including one former government minister.[1] Of the nine, two are digital and seven are digital and social media key informants who shared their views and experiences working with new media technologies, influencing and contributing to the formulation of policy and legislation on matters that have a direct bearing on digital journalism in a pseudo-democracy like Zambia (Branch and Cheeseman 2008; Goldring and Wahman 2016). The Minister interviewed was key to informing the research on government thinking during the formulation of the cybersecurity and crimes that remain contentious. We also analyze key provisions of The Cyber Security and Cyber Crimes (CCS) Act (2021) and related policy documents. The CCS law was enacted at the height of increased media intolerance by the former ruling party, the Patriotic Front (PF) in Zambia. With this historical context and events occurring around the period it was enacted in April 2021, several stakeholders, from journalists to civil society actors, expressed misgivings towards the motivation of enacting such a law when Zambia was barely four months away from the general elections which elects both a president and members of parliament.

The Theory of the Public Sphere and Digital Journalism

The public sphere as a theoretical concept has evolved over several decades and speaks to how governance systems work and create spaces for the exchange of public opinions. The presence of the public sphere within digital journalism shows that the concept 'is not static, but a flexible, open and adaptable' (Dagoula 2017: 16). Early debate on this transformation of the traditional Harbermatian public sphere suggested the 'advent of online [and digital] media [w]as a second structural transformation of the public sphere' (Schäfer 2015: 2). This digital public space provides a vital platform for vigorously interrogating competing ideas. Schulz suggests that 'an intermediary system which links the base with the top of the political system (or, according to Habermas, the link between) the private and collective actors of the periphery with the political institutions in the centre' (Schulz 1997: 57). The public sphere, as it occurs within the digital space, becomes a vital, contested ground for both professional journalists and the state, as they seek to influence or undercut narratives to the greatest extent possible, in an effort to preserve and perpetuate their influence. Scholars argue that this presence of digital platforms represents the 'digital structural change [which] takes place in interconnected processes of disintermediation and re-intermediation. Digital media facilitate access to the public and contain the promise of bi-directional communication' (Seeliger and Sevignani 2022: 10). Different models of the public sphere have gained prominence in academic literature. Schulz, for example, contrasts notions of 'the discursive public (consisting mostly of individual or collective actors dominated by civil society) and the liberal public (collective actors with equal access of all, which reflects preferences of the people)' (Schulz 1997: 57). While the former is premised on Habermas' transformation of the public sphere six decades ago and his later modifications and reflections in the 1990s, the latter is anchored in political science and theories of liberal democracy.

A historical perspective of the concept and its development shows that the public sphere underwent multiple parallel transformations and deviations where large press and media organisations that were capitalist were used to manipulate the public (Soules 2007: n.pag.). Further, Habermas argues that 'the press became an institution of certain participants in the public sphere, it became the gate through which privileged private interests invaded the public sphere' (Habermas 1991: 185). It becomes clear here that when the elites realised how powerful and politically influential this space had become, they felt threatened and devised mechanisms to influence it. This is clear in contemporary times, where the state in pseudo-democracies tries to influence the narrative of political power by undercutting media ethics and professionalism for selfish gains. Our study demonstrates that these manipulations or transformations, therefore, necessitate scrutiny of the public sphere, particularly within the Zambian digital media context, to unravel these influences on digital journalism's role within emerging or fragile democracies such as Zambia.

Law and Digital Censorships in Zambia

As noted, the Zambian Cyber Security and Cyber Crimes (CSCC) Act has had an unsettling effect on the exercise of freedom of expression, press freedom and right to privacy in Zambia. This law came against the backdrop of repressive measures against mainstream media by the former ruling party, the PF. Several mainstream media outlets were either shut down, such as in the case of *The Post* newspaper in 2016 and Prime Television in 2020, or suspended, as in the case of Komboni Radio, Itezhi Tezhi Radio, etc. (Ndawana et al. 2021: 2–3). These mainstream media outlets were suspended or shut down using laws such as the Independent Broadcasting Act no. 26 of 2010 and IBA Act no. 18 of 2017 where they were accused of breaching their licencing conditions in the case of broadcast media or outright state assault as was the case for the newspaper which had accrued significant tax arrears. Similarly, when the Cyber Security Act was passed, observers deemed it as a tool that would be used to target digital media players. This is a view similar to what other research shows exists in other jurisdictions. For instance, Mare observes that since the 'Internet relies on a hierarchical physical infrastructure, [this] provides governments, regulatory authorities and telecommunications companies with control opportunities' (Mare 2020: 13). This law was therefore viewed by many stakeholders, including scholars, press freedom advocacy groups and legal experts, to be targeted at new media and digital media spaces where professional journalists have been thriving in the last decade or so, and the platforms where citizens have turned to for current affairs, news and expression of public opinion on many national debates.

From the literature reviewed, we observed that these trends are not new in the region as other countries such as Zimbabwe (Mare 2020) and Uganda (Abrahamsen and Bareebe 2021) have experienced similar episodes of impediments to the exercise of rights and freedoms among digital journalists and citizens alike. As we discuss in the next subtexts, this is impacting the practice of the profession within Zambia and elsewhere such as Ethiopia and Uganda (Gumede 2016: 416–18). These trends have been widespread and have harmed how digital journalism is practised in affected countries. With the enactment of laws that legalize these practices, many governments have found a loophole that justifies their illegal actions under the cloak of lawfare when in fact these acts hinge on unconstitutional provisions in most cases as they fundamentally affect provisions of free expression and opinion under the Bill of Rights enshrined in many national constitutions, as derivatives of the United Nations Universal Declaration of Human Rights, especially articles 19–29 that speak to the need for freedoms of expression, association and other related fundamental human rights. Research shows that 'examples from the African continent [...] where access to digital media often rests on political interests and where compliance to human rights obligations such as access to information and freedom of expression is problematic' (Baú and Calandro 2019: 9).

In other parts of the world, these practices of censorship against digital spaces have been regarded as digital authoritarianism as we demonstrate later. A case in point is that of Pakistan which is described as a competitive authoritarian state, pointing to how democratic provisions are often disregarded (Jamil 2021). According to Jamil, these actions have been used by the government to implement measures 'such as the Internet and television channels' transmissions blockages, online threats and content censorship, imposition of stringent laws including the Prevention for Electronic Crimes Act (2016) and the Investigation for Fair Trial Act (2013), and digital surveillance of media professionals' (Jamil 2021: n.pag.). Like these provisions, the argument in Zambia has been made against the 2021 Cyber Crimes Act and related laws that continue to be challenged about their constitutional nature in the Constitutional Court of Zambia. Some of the most controversial provisions that are before the court for determination include the Act's approach to interception of communication where the government is not required to obtain a court order to listen to people's conversations (Sections 27–30), and its broad definitions of hate speech, online harassment and morally corrupting content, all of which may threaten free expression.

Importance of Digital Journalism, Freedoms and Limitations

Zambia's digital journalism and attendant technologies have exponentially increased over the last two decades. Consequently, this has caused apprehensions among state actors and others who are wary of the potential influence and widespread benefits this presents to achieving transparency in various spheres of public life, especially affecting public affairs and public offices. Public officials do not readily give in to calls for transparency and accountability as studies suggest (Cheeseman et al. 2017; Kasoma and Pitts 2017). State authorities have in turn devised measures such as infrastructure ownership and monitoring that work to limit the penetration and influence of digital journalism within society. Below, we discuss some of the principal factors that make digital journalism significant within society as well as some of the challenges that it faces because of apprehensions by other stakeholders such as the state. Broadly, we itemized one major area of the significance of digital journalism as enhancing citizen participation in democracy. We further discuss legislations and regulations, and impediments to digital journalism freedom, before casting our views on what emerging trends look like.

This growth has been influenced by the overall global shift towards digitalization and the proliferation of networked media. The use of internet broadband has continued to grow even though most Zambians are still not able to afford and make individual subscriptions (ZICTA Annual Report 2021). Much of this increase has been the result of the success of mobile broadband. Factors such as the lowered cost of access via mobile and the proliferation of cheap and easy-to-access internet-capable phones have all contributed to the inevitable rise of digital journalism practice as more people resort to using their devices to access their news (Manchishi et al. 2023). For instance, the Zambia Information and Communications Technology Authority (ZICTA) data shows Zambia had 10,357,442 mobile internet subscribers in 2021, out of a population of 18.4 million people (ZICTA 2021). However, digital rights experts such as R02-2020 suggest that this number is high because many, especially in the urban areas, have multiple SIM cards that they use to benefit the different service providers.[2] The overall prohibitive cost of broadband internet access and the lack of investment and support for universal access strategies remain some of the most crucial challenges affecting internet penetration in the country. Internet use continues to grow steadily as the demand for access increases. However, the estimated penetration rate was only about 56 per cent by 2021 (ZICTA 2021).

Together with increased internet access, social media usage has also been on the rise. The digital research data service, Kepios, estimated that there will be about 2.90 million users of social media by 2022, which is about 15.19 per cent of the population. Social media use has also become especially important to journalism practice. Numerous studies over the years have demonstrated a shift from a more individualized approach to the use of social media platforms in journalistic work to a more institutionalized approach that even has social media engagement as a pillar of the news operations of media houses (Parks and Mukherjee 2017; Calderaro

2018; Hujanen 2018; Mambwe 2019; Gondwe et al. 2021). This is not to say that all has been well. According to Pindayi (2017) and Kerunga et al. (2020), social media have been responsible for an observable decline in ethical journalism practice, among other concerns. These authors mostly attribute this to the pressure media platforms have in breaking stories first to attract readers and compete with citizen journalists at the expense of fact-checking and other ethical practices.

Citizen Participation in Democracy at a Glance

The importance of the internet to journalism practice has been elaborated by several scholars (Heinonen 1999; Atton and Mabweazara 2011, etc.). For instance, Bosch (2010: 268) has argued that the internet is a space for mediated discourse that allows for democratic participation, and more recently, Jamil (2021: 6) argues the internet has become indispensable for contemporary journalism. Importantly, the internet, with its corollaries such as the digitalized distribution of news and media, has grown as a bastion of free expression and participation for the masses. In the case of Zambia, evidence suggests an exponential proliferation of digital and social media platforms that citizens utilize in their participation in political discourses that hinge on democracy and especially electoral processes.

However, the internet's freedoms have increasingly come under threat as governments are becoming weary of the impact of the freedoms on their rule and hold on power (Lamensch 2021: n.pag.). The term 'digital authoritarianism' has emerged to describe such action by governments to curtail or crack down on internet freedoms by using both old and new repressive laws and policies. According to Bagwandeen, digital authoritarianism takes many forms such as 'online harassment, the dissemination of fake news, cyber-attacks, internet shutdowns and targeted surveillance through social media, artificial intelligence (AI) and facial recognition software' (Bagwandeen 2021: n.pag.). The acts are often associated with authoritarian or participatory authoritarian nations. However, online censorship, digital surveillance and repeated and coordinated online intimidation of those deemed to be undesirable are becoming less farfetched even in democratic regimes (Jamil 2021).

The Historicity of Legislations and Regulations of ICTs in Zambia

The legal and regulatory framework that governs or directly affects internet use and has a strong bearing on journalism practice in Zambia includes various statutes and policies. Until recently, these include the Information and Communication Technologies Act of 2009, the Electronic Communications and Transactions Act of

2009 and the moribund National ICT Policy of 2006. The two acts were enacted to respond to the rapid digitization that was taking place and the growth of digital technologies. The Zambia ICT Act no. 15 of 2009 established the regulatory regime for Zambia's ICT sector in addition to providing a framework that would facilitate access to ICTS for all Zambians. The Act established the ZICTA as the sector regulator. It gave ZICTA the powers to regulate tariffs, establish and monitor the quality of service and set rules for the protection of ICT consumer interests, among other functions.

Besides the National ICT Policy (2006), Zambia has implemented a National Child Online Protection Strategy that provides safeguards against online vulnerabilities for children and ratified the African Union Convention on Cybersecurity and Personal Data Protection, which seeks to harmonize new national cyber laws and foster multilateral cooperation in cybersecurity, cybercrime and data protection (Nkhowani 2021).

The Cyber Security and Cyber Crimes (Act No. 2 of 2021) and Digital Journalism

The CSCC was passed in April 2021 and has wide-ranging provisions, with controversial principles as evident in the ongoing legal challenges, regarding their constitutional legitimacy. In the case of *Chapter One Foundation and others* v. *The Attorney General*, the petitioners sought to have certain provisions of the CSCC Act no. 2 of 2021 removed as they were in contravention of Articles 1(1) and 2 of the Constitution of Zambia.[3] The case was, however, rumoured to have been withdrawn when the state agreed to a review of the CSCC Act with the view to amending the contentious provisions. However, Chapter One's Linda Kasonde clarified in a statement[4] that the matter had only been adjourned. We sought to understand the rationale from the state on what motivated the enactment of the cybersecurity legislation. These remarks from the former minister of Technology during the legislative process were quite revealing in aiding our understanding of why these laws ended up on Zambia's statute books. R10-2023 explain:

> Internet, unlike other things, is not owned or enjoyed by Zambians alone. It transcends borders. It is this recognition that the cyber laws are created not for the country but for internet users everywhere. Once the relevant international bodies produce frameworks for cybersecurity laws, they promulgate them through regional bodies such as the EU, AU, SADC, etc. to ensure the domestication of these laws/guidelines and standardization of laws across borders. The thinking is that if a breach happened in one country, a virus could wipe out networks and cause havoc in far-flung places because of how the Internet is interconnected and instant. It is for this reason Zambia was required to align, domesticate and implement 'best practices' in cyberspace as dictated by the international and

> regional bodies. The laws were started from international laws through the EU, and AU to the SADC and all countries were required to relook, upgrade, and meet the minimum standard in cybersecurity to lower vulnerabilities. We downloaded the templates and worked on implementing suggestions to meet the minimum requirements and provide safer cyberspace for our citizens. That is the history and background.
>
> (Personal communication with R10-2023 2023: n.pag.)[5]

The minister's argument on the enactment of the CSCC Act seems to be coming from a place of concern for cybersecurity. The language in the statement suggests that the law is a protective action for the citizenry that the government is graciously providing for its people. Further, the statement proffers that what is good for the European Union (EU) is good for Zambia and that the templates are good enough. While there is nothing wrong with both assumptions, we argue that their use as justifications does not supersede the fact that the law that was enacted in Zambia failed to meet one of the most important elements that would make them valid – consultation. The lack of consultation or the blatant ignoring of any counterpoints to the law eliminated any semblance of goodwill and good faith on the part of the Zambian government. Further, the template argument falls flat when we consider how much the Act goes against the known values the multilateral bodies espouse. We see an attempt to argue that the law is good for Zambia because it is based on templates from the EU, African Union and Southern African Development Community.

A critical analysis of the Act reveals some problematic provisions that are contentious and remain the subject of litigation in court, contesting their constitutionality by a consortium of advocacy groups within Zambia. They include Chapter One Foundation (COF), Bloggers of Zambia, Gears Initiative, People's Action for Accountability and Good Governance in Zambia and the Alliance for Community Action. These civil society organizations (CSOs) approached the High Court in Lusaka contesting that the government is violating the Constitution through the enactment of the CSCC (Musika 2021). They have argued that the new law contains provisions that threaten the right to protection of the law and the right to freedom of expression, among other constitutionally guaranteed rights (Musika 2021). The CSOs want the CSCC Act 2021 to be declared unconstitutional, with consequent repeals or amendments to contentious provisions at the very least.

These include Sections 3, 29, 38 and 59. The claimants believe that these provisions either infringe on the right to privacy of citizens or grossly infringe on the freedoms of expression by citizens and the confidentiality of journalists' work as they engage with sources in their work of gathering and disseminating information and news for public consumption.

Part I Section 3 provides for the supremacy of the Act (CSCC Act 2021: n.pag.) as follows:

> *Subject to the Constitution, where there is an inconsistency between the provisions of this Act and the provisions of any other written law relating to the regulation of cyber security, cybercrimes and digital forensics, the provisions of this Act shall prevail to the extent of the inconsistency.*

This clause implies that other provisions of the law which are in the constitution, such as freedom of expression under Article 20, can easily be overlooked or ignored in the enforcement of the provisions of this law because of this supremacy clause. In practice, this has been done by ZICTA leading to the internet shutdown on 12 August 2021, which was the presidential and parliamentary election day in Zambia. The law in its current form has provisions that infringe on various freedoms such as freedom of expression and freedom of speech. The CSCC Act of 2021 seeks to promote the responsible use of social media platforms. However, the few instances where the law has so far been applied show that this law has the potential of undermining citizens' freedoms and rights of expression in the digital space as some of the provisions below imply.

Section 29 of the CSCC (2021) Act dispenses the need to obtain a warrant for the interception of communication. This section reads as below.

> *29. (1) A law enforcement officer may intercept any communication and orally request a service provider to route duplicate signals of indirect communications specified in that request to the Central Monitoring and Coordination Centre where the law enforcement officer has reasonable grounds to believe that* [a crime has been committed].

The implications, in this case, are that this puts the interpretation and execution of the law to decide whether to arrest a citizen solely with the police. This undercuts the principle of innocent until proven guilty which undermines the fair and logical application of the rule of law and puts aside the justice system where the courts are involved in determining if there is a need or indeed if it is appropriate, in the interest of the state, to invade individuals' privacy to intercept their communication during investigations of a probable crime. This infringes, arbitrarily, this fundamental right of citizens to enjoy privacy without undue interference from the state, especially in their digital space. These are some of the provisions that police have relied on forcibly enquiring about the leaked audios of state officials without due regard to press freedom and citizens' rights to privacy as the evidence shows later.

Further, Section 38 allows service providers to monitor full-time and in real-time and to intercept communications of its subjects (CSCC Act 2021: n.pag.). The specific wording reads as follows:

> *38. (1) An electronic communication service provider shall ensure that the electronic communication service provider –*
> *(a) uses an electronic communication system that is technically capable of supporting lawful interceptions in accordance with this Act ('Cyber Security and Cyber Crimes Act, 2021 – Zambia LII');*
> *(b) installs hardware and software facilities and devices to enable the interception of communications when so required by a law enforcement officer or under a court order;*
> *(i) provides one or more interfaces from which any intercepted communication shall be transmitted to the Central Monitoring and Coordination Centre.*

This provision is problematic on many levels as we demonstrate. Firstly, it implies that internet service providers, mobile phone service providers and other similar institutions are compelled to store a record of any or all customers' activities carried out on their platforms and infrastructure without any reason or cause whatsoever. Secondly, when read together with section 29, this provision ensures that the state extends its pressure to service providers in the surveillance of citizens or journalists even where there is no reasonable or legal justification for such invasive overreach. And thirdly, the law further endangers the work of journalists and sources as the state, though its various law enforcement agencies and other security agencies, could potentially be listening in to conversations of journalists and their sources, thus compromising confidentiality.

Section 59 of the Act (2021) criminalizes the production of any objects corrupting morals. The sections read as follows:

> *59. (1) A person who commits an offence under subsection (1) is liable to imprisonment for a period not exceeding fifteen years –*
> *(a) makes, produces, or has in the person's possession any one or more obscene, drawings, paintings, pictures, images, posters, emblems, photographs, videos, or any other object tending to corrupt morals; or*
> *(b) imports, conveys, or exports, or causes to be imported conveyed or exported, any such matters or things, or in any manner whatsoever puts any of them in circulation.*

What constitutes 'corrupt morals' is undefined, leaving it to wide interpretation. Therefore, this leaves a lot of room for abuse and discretionary powers of interpreting what constitutes morals and corrupting morals. What this implies is that the state could produce charges using this provision to charge citizens or journalists on grounds that are not clear at law and therefore leave a lot of insecurities on what and what not to produce, transmit or procure materials or objects corrupting morals. Combined with other equally unfair laws still on the statute books, the cyber laws have left a chilling effect among journalists on freedom of expression and speech potentially inhibiting artistic, and journalistic, works based on undefined obscenity and corruption of morals. This inevitably leads to the stifling of information flow among citizens.

However, there have been transient developments surrounding the court case. Earlier in 2023, Minister of Justice Mulambo Haimbe proposed that the petitioners withdraw their case before the court to allow the state to review the controversial Act with the view to amend it through the parliamentary process. The COF, however, rebuffed such calls in a statement,[6] indicating that the petitioners would only withdraw the matter once the review and amendment process had been completed by drafting and tabling a satisfactory Bill before Parliament to amend the CSCC Act that conforms with constitutionally protected human rights standards.

Results and Cases in Focus; Threats Against Digital Journalism in Zambia

From interviews with journalists (see Note 1), the need for citizen participation in democracy is amplified as they realize that these acts, deliberate and through policy implementation, go a long way to consolidate the democratic gains that Zambia has scored so far in this regard. One journalist (no. 01-2022) who opted to remain anonymous observed that enacting the Cyber Security Act in 2021 has driven democratic discourse off the digital space due to citizens' fear of targeted persecution by authorities. They are 'affected [by] such as laws as the Cyber Crimes laws, among others. This makes citizens fear to share certain things online as authorities warn they can hack and detect things some people do online' (no. 01-2022 2022: n.pag.).

In the first year since the law was introduced, there were several more arrests, some of them clandestine and therefore not publicly available on record. While Zambia has made progress in repealing some of the draconian laws such as Section 69[7] on criminal defamation of the president, new laws such as these Cyber Crimes mean political opponents, critical voices and journalists are arrested for similar activities under the new set of laws. With some murky provisions that have not yet been tested before the courts, journalists and citizens alike are all too wary to avoid a conflict with such laws, especially since some provisions make sweeping conditions to avoid a clash or conflict with the law.

A case that illustrates this involved one of the opposition voices Sean Tembo. According to media reports (*Lusaka Times*, 2022: n.pag.), on 2 September 2022:

> Police, in the presence of Mr Sean Tembo's lawyer formally charged and arrested him for the offence of hate speech contrary to Section 65 of the Cyber Security and Cyber Crimes Act No. 2 of 2021 of the Laws of Zambia.[8]

This was in connection with remarks that Tembo was said to have uttered against the republican president at the time which the police adjudged could potentially be defamatory. From this, we believe that the cyber laws implemented in Zambia may be doing more harm and impeding free speech and press freedom than intended. This is what our key informants observed during interviews. The fear is that since some of the provisions of this law are not clear to understand, it becomes difficult for journalists and citizens alike, to be able to draw the lines on what is and what is not offending the law. These legal ambiguities are therefore in and of themselves as they lay legal traps that are difficult to navigate, which may result in legal jeopardy for professionals. Tembo's case, like many others, is illustrative of the perils that journalists have faced in their work since the law was enacted.

Other incidences such as the one against Petty Chanda of Kenmark Broadcasting Network Television (KBN TV) station shine the spotlight on these abuses. As media reports indicated (*allAfrica*, 2022: n.pag.):

> On January 18, [2022] privately owned Kenmark Broadcasting Network (KBN TV) aired a leaked audio conversation allegedly between Levy Ngoma, political advisor to President Hakainde Hichilema, and Joseph Akafumba, the home affairs permanent secretary, in which [the] two men were heard planning to ban the opposition Democratic Party from participating in a local by-election.[9]

Another is that involving MUVI TV journalists arrested for filming and transmitting live using digital technology, the arrest of a citizen Chilufya Tayali by the police. According to reports (R8-2023 2023: n.pag.):

> On November 13, [2022] police arrested Innocent Phiri and his camera operator Obvious Kapunda as they filmed officers preparing to arrest opposition Economic and Equity Party leader Chilufya Tayali at his home in the capital, Lusaka. [This is] according to multiple media reports, a statement by the Zambian chapter of the regional press freedom group Media Institute of Southern Africa, and a Facebook post by Phiri.[10]

A common factor in these cases and several others is how the police arbitrarily use murky provisions under this law to detain and charge journalists when in most cases these cases have either not taken off in courts of law for prosecution or have been discontinued before they are taken to court due to procedural matters or lack of prosecutable evidence or grounds. This leaves a chilling effect on journalists as they can no longer be sure of where they stand.

These cases further demonstrate another aspect, as explained by one of the respondents, that there is a peaking of unwarranted surveillance of Zambian citizens to unprecedented levels since the enactment of this law. As one respondent (R8-2023 2023: n.pag.) narrates,

> because there is a lot of interest now by the ICT sector regulator, ZICTA, working with Zambia Police who have operationalised some parts of the cybersecurity Cyber Crimes Act as well as The Data Protection Act. [However], citizens think that there is a lot of surveillance in Zambia, especially illegal surveillance.[11]

R8-2023, who belongs to a key organization focused on digital spaces and rights in Zambia, revealed that the organization has been gathering evidence from across the country showing that there are clandestine arrests of citizens for alleged crimes committed in the digital space over the last two to three years than at any other time before. These off-the-record arrests and detentions show how insidious an environment this law could exacerbate as it is currently already fragile. He narrates that these arrests go undetected by journalists or other human rights activists because often, those arrested are ordinary members of the community and therefore do not attract attention. This is all happening because there is active surveillance of citizens' activities online which are then followed up and arrests effected.

Case in Focus: *Chapter One Foundation* v. *ZICTA*

Following ZICTA's unilateral decision to shut down the internet in the aftermath of the general elections, COF Limited sued the ZICTA in the Lusaka High Court seeking an order to resume all internet services. COF argued that on 12 August ZICTA shut down the provision of internet services and communication in Zambia blacking out social media platforms such as WhatsApp, Facebook, Twitter and Instagram. This is a measure that was unprecedented in Zambia and signalled a shift from potentially harmful provisions with the Act to actions that were inimical to the enjoyment of freedoms and rights of expression. This buttressed the case that was already court-disputing the unconstitutional nature of the law. A pull-out copy of actions reported elsewhere on the continent, most notably in Uganda,[12] this action forced many citizens to turn to Virtual Private Networks (VPNs) to keep abreast with the fast-paced election process.

Thus, COF contended that ZICTA acted illegally and exceeded its powers to block the provision of internet services. COF stated that ZICTA acted on a want of authority by proceeding to make a decision that was not supported by any law ('ZICTA sued over internet shutdown – Press Reader'). It stated that the said decision is not supported by any provision of the enabling Act, the Information and Communications Technology (Amendment) Act no. 3 of 20.

Case Analysis[13]

Case Summary and Outcome

On 21 March 2022, the High Court for Zambia at Lusaka issued a consent judgment, confirming that the ZICTA would not:

> [D]o any act or make any omission outside of their legal regulatory powers and authority which may inhibit or interrupt the flow of and uninhibited access to information on all available telecommunication platforms under their control and/or regulation where the interest of consumers and their consumer and constitutional rights are threatened.

ZICTA also consented to inform the public within 36 hours of any disruptions of the reason for that interruption. Columbia Global Freedom of Expression notes that some of the information contained in this report was derived from secondary sources.

Facts

On 12 August 2021, Zambia held general elections. In the run-up to the election on 12 August local media reported that the incumbent president, Edgar Lungu, was planning to shut down access to social media 'in an effort to maintain peace and order during the voting period'. Access to internet services was curtailed during the election. The day after the election, the Zambian non-governmental organization, COF, approached the High Court, seeking a review of the decision of the ZICTA to interrupt internet access.

Decision Overview

Judge Charles Zulu signed the Court's consent judgment. The Court confirmed the parties' agreement that ZICTA would not act outside of their regulatory powers in a way that inhibited or interrupted access to information through telecommunication platforms, and if there was inhibition or interruption, ZICTA would explain within 36 hours.

Impediments to Digital Journalism Freedom

While Zambia is not an authoritarian state, its position as a country where free expression is guaranteed and protected has not been consistent. For instance, Reporters Without Borders ranked Zambia 115 out of 180 in 2021, a slight improvement from the 2020 position of 120, due to continued harassment of independent media. This ranking considers elements such as pluralism, independence of the media, legislative framework, transparency, abuses, as well as the general media freedom environment, among others. Freedom House has only described Zambia as partially free in the years. While several studies and volumes have related to journalism practice and media freedom in Zambia, very few have addressed these subjects from the perspective of digital journalism practice. Three recent studies stand out: the first study by Nkhowani (2021) is a report funded by the organization Paradigm Initiative. The report focuses on digital rights and inclusion in Zambia up to the year 2020. However, this report does not fully address digital journalism practice but is a general overview of the state of digital rights as they are enjoyed by Zambian citizens and journalists alike.

Political pressure, authorities overreach and these restrictive laws such as the cybersecurity and crimes laws, among others continue to haunt the practice of digital journalism in Zambia. Mistrust among journalists compounds these challenges as oftentimes. As one respondent explains 'mainstream media journalists tend to paint the digital media space as one that is full of propaganda, misinformation and sensationalism'. He further observes that fear and self-censorship have crept into their work within the digital space as journalists are not sure who is watching them. He narrates:

> I get to be more cautious of what I post online because I never know who is watching. I sit out of most sensitive discussions and mostly use a VPN for anything. I know of colleagues, reporters from KBN who were warned and cautioned for having access to an alleged tapped audio of a private conversation and they aired online.
>
> (no. 3-2022 2022: n.pag.)

Another respondent recounts how fellow journalists have experienced clandestine renditions for interrogations under unclear circumstances. She recounts, 'most of my Journalism friends have testified of being summoned by the police because of what they posted on social media or the article they wrote, and this was popular during the 2021 General Elections' (no. 2-2022 2022: n.pag.).

This increase in such surveillance cases has made most journalists fear being attacked or killed in case of extreme pressure from government wings. The closure of these two private institutions (*The Post* newspaper and Prime Television) was an indication that those with political power usually tend to be intolerant to criticism. Some of the voices affected by the unlawful internet shutdown expressed worry, fear and frustrations:

> I was monitoring the elections and needed to do a lot of communicating using WhatsApp as well as follow election proceedings via Twitter and Facebook. Suddenly, around midday, [the] internet shut down and I was unable to work. It was very a very frustrating experience.
>
> (Chibuta 2021: n.pag.)[14]

Another journalist working from the remote district of Lukulu in Western Province recounted how the internet shutdown affected her work:

> I was covering the August 2021 Zambian general elections, and I was required to give updates via WhatsApp until later on when I realised that my messages were not going through. I tried many VPN apps but they were not effective. Hence my work was really not enjoyable, I was also not able to follow what was happening in other areas.
>
> (Kabindama 2023: n.pag.)[15]

Conclusion

This chapter examined the potential negative impact of the Cyber Security and Cyber Crimes (CSCC) Act no. 2 of 2021 on press freedom in Zambia. The study further highlighted the implications of this law on press freedom and free expression, with a focus on digital journalism and new media. The enactment of the legislation in Zambia followed a period of government crackdowns on traditional media, raising concerns about its potential to further restrict freedom of expression, particularly online. This study used in-depth interviews with journalists and a former cabinet minister, along with Critical Discourse Analysis of reports and other relevant documents to investigate the issue at hand.

The study revealed growing anxieties surrounding the legislative implications among journalists, expressing fear of state punishments and suppression of free speech in the digital space. The events that followed the enactment of the law coupled with the PF government's history of shutting down critical media outlets all gave credence to the concerns. The study also shows how these concerns over some of the legislation's ambiguous provisions have raised inklings that it was enacted to undercut the growing importance and influence of digital journalism and new media spaces, where free expression and debate of public opinion continue to thrive among journalists and citizens. The problematic clauses and provisions include those that stipulate vague prohibitions or are ill-defined and those that directly minimize citizens' freedoms of judicial oversight in the name of surveillance and interception of communications.

Therefore, from the foregoing discussion on digital journalism, it is apparent that there are still several challenges within the justice system and culture among law enforcement agencies in the country. These challenges put journalists at significant risk of being falsely accused and charged with crimes under contentious or unconstitutional laws. It is befitting to close with a note from our research interview with the former minister who observes that 'abuse of the law is also possible by selfish individuals in government. This must be fought with all our might. Let us not weaponize the laws against citizens. It was never the intention of the cybersecurity laws' (personal communication with R10-2023 2023: n.pag.).[15]

The research contributes to ongoing conversations about journalism in the digital age, especially in countries with a known past of repressive tendencies towards freedom of expression, and free, and independent media. This relationship between democracy and digital media rights is also reflected in the study as it raises concerns on the paradox of how easily these rights and freedoms can be mutilated by democratically elected officials using democratic processes such as enacted ill-fated laws. Given the study's findings and the chapter's discussion, further research is needed to explore the law's long-term effects on media freedom in Zambia. Additionally, it would be of interest for researchers, policymakers and other stakeholders to observe and examine the evolving relationship between digital media, state regulation and democratic practices across the region and continent, especially as access to digital platforms and tools expands. Such comparative studies would provide a clearer picture of the landscape by highlighting changes and experiences in the African context.

NOTES

1. All respondents have been anonymised and coded instead with the Code **R**=Respondent followed by **NN**=Number and **YYYY**=The year the interview was carried out. Thus R00-0000. No commercial interests or otherwise are contained or infringed by the work contained herein.
2. R02-2020, personal communication, 19 April 2020.
3. Case number 2021/HP/0358 between COF Limited, Bloggers of Zambia Limited, Governance, Elections, Advocacy, Research Services (GEARS) Initiative, People's Action for Accountability and Good Governance in Zambia, Alliance for Community Action as petitioners and The Attorney General of Zambia as First respondent and Director of Public Prosecution.

4. Chapter One Press Statement on proposed amendments to the Cybersecurity and Cybercrimes Act, https://diggers.news/guest-diggers/2023/02/02/press-statement-dated-1st-february-2023-on-the-proposed-amendments-to-the-cyber-security-and-cybercrimes-act/. Accessed 21 March 2025.
5. Personal communication with R10-2023, former minister of technology and science.
6. Chapter One Press Statement on proposed amendments to the Cybersecurity and Cybercrimes Act, https://diggers.news/guest-diggers/2023/02/02/press-statement-dated-1st-february-2023-on-the-proposed-amendments-to-the-cyber-security-and-cybercrimes-act/. Accessed 21 March 2025.
7. https://ohrh.law.ox.ac.uk/you-have-the-right-to-insult-a-president-repealing-zambias-penal-code-section-69/. Accessed 20 May 2023.
8. 'Zambia Police confirm arrest and detention of opposition party leader Sean Tembo', https://www.lusakatimes.com/2022/09/02/zambia-police-confirm-the-arrest-and-detention-of-opposition-party-leader-sean-tembo/. Accessed 25 May 2023.
9. 'Police must immediately drop this gratuitous investigation into a journalist who exposed potential wrongdoing', https://allafrica.com/stories/202202040279.html. Accessed 28 May 2023.
10. 'MUVI TV journalists arrested, fined after filming Zambian police raid on politician's home', https://cpj.org/2022/11/muvi-tv-journalists-arrested-fined-after-filming-zambian-police-raid-on-politicians-home/. Accessed 26 May 2023.
11. R8-2023 – interview notes May 2023.
12. 'Internet and social media shutdowns in Uganda cannot stop growing political resistance', https://blogs.lse.ac.uk/africaatlse/2021/02/03/internet-shutdowns-uganda-museveni-political-resistance-elections-bobi-wine/. Accessed 26 May 2023.
13. https://globalfreedomofexpression.columbia.edu/cases/chapter-one-foundation-v-zambian-information-and-communications-technology-authority/. Accessed 24 April 2023.
14. https://www.accessnow.org/shutdown-in-zambia-on-election-day-how-it-affected-peoples-lives-and-wellbeing/. Accessed 13 January 2022.
15. Personal communication with R10-2023, former minister of technology and science.

REFERENCES

Abrahamsen, Rita and Bareebe, Gerald (2021), 'Uganda's fraudulent election', *Journal of Democracy*, 32:2, pp. 90–104.

Access Now (2023), 'Shutdown in Zambia on election day: How it affected people's lives and wellbeing', Access Now, https://www.accessnow.org/shutdown-in-zambia-on-election-day-how-it-affected-peopleslives-and-wellbeing/. Accessed 13 January 2022.

allAfrica (2022), 'Police must immediately drop this gratuitous investigation into a journalist who exposed potential wrongdoing', *allAfrica*, 4 February, https://allafrica.com/stories/202202040279.html. Accessed 28 May 2023.

Atton, Chris and Mabweazara, Hayes (2011), 'New media and journalism practice in Africa: An agenda for research', *Journalism*, 12:6, pp. 667–73.

Bagwandeen, Mandira (2021), 'Don't blame China for the rise of digital authoritarianism in Africa', *Africa at LSE*, https://blogs.lse.ac.uk/africaatlse/2021/09/09/dont-blame-china-for-rise-of-digital-authoritarianism-africa-surveillance-capitalism/. Accessed 9 July 2022.

Baú, Valentina and Calandro, Enrico (2019), 'Digital media and information rights', in R. Hobbs, P. Mihailidis, G. Cappello, M. Ranieri and B. Thevenin (eds), *The International Encyclopedia of Media Literacy*, Hoboken: Wiley-Blackwell, pp. 1–13.

Bosch, Tanja (2010), 'Digital journalism and online public spheres in South Africa', *Communicatio: South African Journal for Communication Theory and Research*, 36:2, pp. 265–75.

Bradshaw, Paul (2023), *The Online Journalism Handbook: Skills to Survive and Thrive in the Digital Age*, London: Routledge.

Branch, Daniel and Cheeseman, Nic (2008), 'Democratization, sequencing, and state failure in Africa: Lessons from Kenya', *African Affairs*, 108:430, pp. 1–26.

Calderaro, Andrea (2018), 'Social media and politics', in W. Outhwaite and S. Turner (eds), *The SAGE Handbook of Political Sociology*, vol. 2, London: SAGE Publications Ltd, pp. 781–95, https://doi.org/10.4135/9781526416513.

Cheeseman, Nic (2018), *Institutions and Democracy in Africa: How the Rules of the Game Shape Political Developments*, Cambridge: Cambridge University Press.

Cheeseman, Nic, Whitfield, Lindsay and Death, Carl (eds) (2017), *The African Affairs Reader: Key Texts in Politics, Development, and International Relations*, Oxford: Oxford University Press.

Chibuta, Juliet Kaira (2021), 'Shutdown in Zambia on Election Day', https://www.accessnow.org/shutdown-in-zambia-on-election-day-how-it-affected-peopleslives-and-wellbeing/. Accessed 13 January 2022.

CSCC Act (2021), 'Zambian Cyber Security and Cyber Act 2021', https://www.parliament.gov.zm/sites/default/files/documents/acts/Act%20No.%202%20of%202021The%20Cyber%20Security%20and%20Cyber%20Crimes.pdf. Accessed 10 July 2022.

Dagoula, Chrysi (2017), 'The ongoing structural transformations of the digital public sphere(s): The role of journalism', Unpublished doctoral dissertation, Sheffield: University of Sheffield. Retrieved from http://etheses.whiterose.ac.uk/18499. Accessed 24 June 2025.

Goldring, Edward and Wahman, Michael (2016), 'Democracy in reverse: The 2016 General Election in Zambia', *Africa Spectrum*, 51:3, pp. 107–21.

Gondwe, Gregory, Muchangwe, Roberta and Mwaya, Japhet Edward (2021), 'Motivations for social media use and consumption in Zambian online platforms', in P. K. Wamuyu (ed.), *Analyzing Global Social Media Consumption*, Hershey: IGI Global, pp. 204–15.

Grönlund, Åke and Wakabi, Wairagala (2015), 'Citizens' use of new media in authoritarian regimes: A case study of Uganda', *The Electronic Journal of Information Systems in Developing Countries*, 67:1, pp. 1–23.

Gumede, William (2016), 'Rise in censorship of the internet and social media in Africa', *Journal of African Media Studies*, 8:3, pp. 413–21.

Habermas, Jürgen (1991), *The Structural Transformation of the Public Sphere: An Inquiry into a Category of Bourgeois Society*, Cambridge, MA: MIT Press.

Heinonen, Ari (1999), 'Journalism in the age of the net: Changing society, changing profession', Ph.D.thesis, Tampere: University of Tampere.

Hujanen, Jaana (2018), 'Renegotiating the journalism profession in the era of social media: Journalism students from the global north and south', *Journalism & Mass Communication Educator*, 73:3, pp. 282–92.

Jamil, Sadia (2021), 'The rise of digital authoritarianism: Evolving threats to media and internet freedoms in Pakistan', *World of Media – Russian Journal of Journalism and Media Studies*, 3, pp. 5–33.

Kasoma, Twange and Pitts, Gregory (2017), 'Challenges in doing investigative reporting: A Zambian case study', *Global Investigative Journalism Conference/African Investigative Journalism*, University of Witwatersrand, Johannesburg, 16–19 November, pp. 1074–94.

Kerunga, Joseph, Evan Rowe and Gregory Gondwe (2020), 'Journalism credibility in the digital age: Examining shifts in paradigms', *SSRN Electronic Journal*, 3641943, 2 July, pp. 1–9, http://dx.doi.org/10.2139/ssrn.3641943.

Kperogi, Farooq A. (2022), 'Social media and the demotic turn in Africa's media ecology', *History Compass*, 20:2, e12711, https://doi.org/10.1111/hic3.12711.

Lamensch, Marie (2021), 'Authoritarianism has been reinvented for the digital age', *Centre for International Governance Innovation*, 9 July, https://www.cigionline.org/articles/authoritarianism-has-been-reinvented-for-the-digital-age/. Accessed 10 August 2023.

Lusaka Times (2026), 'Zambia Police confirm arrest and detention of opposition party leader Sean Tembo', *Lusaka Times*, 2 September, https://www.lusakatimes.com/2022/09/02/zambia-police-confirm-the-arrest-and-detention-of-opposition-party-leader-sean-tembo/. Accessed 25 May 2023.

Mambwe, Elastus (2019), 'Investigating the use and impact of social media in Zambian newsrooms between 2011–2013', *International Journal of Multidisciplinary Research and Development*, 6:4, pp. 30–37.

Manchishi, Kamufisa, Pindayi, Brian and Mambwe, Elastus (2023), 'Financial sustainability of social media-driven publications in Zambia: The practices, threats and opportunities at New Diggers and Kalemba', in T. Matsilele, D. Moyo and S. Mpofu (eds), *New Journalism Ecologies in East and Southern Africa: Innovations, Participatory and Newsmaking Cultures*, London: Palgrave, pp. 207–23.

Mare, A. (2020), 'Internet shutdowns in Africa: State-ordered internet shutdowns and digital authoritarianism in Zimbabwe', *International Journal of Communication*, 14, p. 20.

Musika, Chomba (2021) 'Cyber law take to ConCourt', *Zambia Daily Mail*, 2 April, http://www.daily-mail.co.zm/cyber-law-taken-to-concourt/. Accessed 11 August 2023.

Ndawana, Youngson, Knowles, Joanne and Vaughan, Christopher (2021), 'The historicity of media regulation in Zambia: Examining the proposed statutory self-regulation', *African Journalism Studies*, 42:2, pp. 59–76.

Nkhowani, Bulanda (2021), *Londa: Zambia Digital Rights and Inclusion 2020 Report*, Lagos: Paradigm Initiative.

Parks, Lisa and Mukherjee, Rahul (2017), 'From platform jumping to self-censorship: Internet freedom, social media, and circumvention practices in Zambia', *Communication and Critical/Cultural Studies*, 14:3, pp. 221–37.

Pindayi, Brain (2017), 'Social media uses and effects: The case of in Africa', in O. Nelson, B. R. Ojebuyi and A. Salawu (eds), *Impacts of the Media on African Socio-Economic Development*, Hershey: IGI Global, pp. 34–51, https://doi.org/10.4018/978-1-5225-1859-4.ch003.

Roberts, Tony, Mohamed Ali, Abrar, Karekwaivanane, George, Msonza, Natasha, Phiri, Sam, Nanfuka, Juliet, Bosch, Tanja, Oladapo, Oyewole, Ojebode, Ayo, Nyabola, Nanjala and Gagliardone, Iginio (2021), *Digital Rights in Closing Civic Space: Lessons from Ten African Countries*, Brighton: Institute of Development Studies, https://www.ids.ac.uk/publications/digital-rights-in-closing-civic-space-lessons-from-ten-african-countries/. Accessed 24 June 2025.

Schulz, Winfed (1997), 'Changes of mass media and the public sphere', *Javnost – The Public*, 4:2, pp. 57–69.

Seeliger, Martin and Sevignani, Sebastian (2022), 'A new structural transformation of the public sphere?: An introduction', *Theory, Culture & Society*, 39:4, pp. 3–16.

Shafer, Mike S. (2015), 'Digital public sphere', in M. Gianpietro, K. G. Barnhurst, K. Ikeda, R. C. Maia and H. Wessler (eds), *The International Encyclopedia of Political Communication*, London: Wiley Blackwell, pp. 322–28.

Soules, Marshall (2007), 'Jürgen Habermas and the public sphere', Media-Studies.ca, https://www.media-studies.ca/articles/habermas.htm. Accessed 9 July 2022.

Stoycheff, Elizabeth, Burgess, G. Scott and Martucci, Maria Clara (2020), 'Online censorship and digital surveillance: The relationship between suppression technologies and democratization across countries', *Information, Communication & Society*, 23:4, pp. 474–90.

The Cybersecurity and Cybercrime Act (2021), https://www.parliament.gov.zm/node/8832. Accessed 13 February 2022.

ZICTA (2021), *ZICTA Annual Report 2021: A Regulator Advancing the Nation to a Digital Society*, ZICTA website, https://www.zicta.zm/media/annual-reports. Accessed 24 June 2025.

5

Morocco's Approach to Digital Media Regulation: State Policy, Power Asymmetry, Platform Dialogue – Interview with Latifa Akharbach

Yemisi Akinbobola

YEMISI AKINBOBOLA: How would you describe Morocco's approach to regulating digital, online and social media spaces?

LATIFA AKHARBACH: Morocco's approach is primarily based on the principle that digital regulation should be designed to foster innovation and economic growth while protecting users' rights and the public interest. The Kingdom has worked to build regulatory capacity to address the multi-faceted regulatory demands imposed by the diverse dimensions of global digital platforms.

The High Authority for Audiovisual Communication (HACA), the independent administrative authority with constitutional power in charge of media regulation in Morocco, is not yet empowered by current legislation to regulate digital content. But it is heavily involved in reflection and advocacy at national and continental levels for the establishment of a regulatory model for both traditional and digital media, guaranteeing fundamental freedoms and public order in the virtual space, which interacts continuously with the real world.

HACA regularly expresses its concerns regarding the protection of users' rights to a safe digital environment that is respectful of democratic values. On a global scale, attacks on the integrity of electoral processes have become recurrent due to the instrumentalization of social networking platforms. The risks of public opinion manipulation in the global digital space are especially significant because major digital platforms have become true gatekeepers of the global information space.

We also recognize that online disinformation undermines not only trust in public and private institutions but also leads to the downgrading of democratic values within societies. As a regulator, HACA is also very concerned about the amplification of sexist discourse, stereotypes and gender violence and the many attacks on women's dignity on social media platforms.

YA: Can you point to some of the laws, policies or measures in place and the overall strategy they point towards?

LA: Morocco has established a robust legal framework that addresses various aspects of the digital sphere, combining protection, security, and the promotion of innovation. In recent years, the legal framework governing the digital economy and personal data protection has been significantly strengthened.

In addition, through key laws such as the Penal Code, which criminalizes hate speech, and the Personal Data Protection Act, Morocco strives to guarantee the security of its citizens while preserving their fundamental rights. Specific legislation also contributes to the protection of copyright and neighbouring rights, and to the fight against digital piracy through mechanisms such as 'Notice and Take Down'. Texts such as the law on the press and publishing adapt the legal framework to the realities of digital media by regulating the liability of hosts and protecting minors.

Regarding the regulation of social media platforms, no specific legal framework has yet been implemented. This issue is at the heart of a pluralistic and dynamic public debate taking place in Parliament, the media, and academic circles. The aim of this ongoing debate is to reach a social consensus on a regulatory model that protects society without curbing freedom of expression or hindering technological innovation.

Through its professional monitoring activities, HACA integrates thematic studies focusing on content disseminated via digital media. This contributes to a better understanding of how unregulated social networks function and aims to foster citizens' critical thinking concerning the informational disruptions and manipulation risks prevalent in the digital space.

YA: In what ways does the Moroccan regulatory approach align with or diverge from the broader regulatory approach across North Africa?

LA: The specificity of Morocco's experience lies in its political will to build a media regulation model that meets the highest international standards. HACA is an independent regulatory body, free from executive, legislative and judicial authority. It is adequately funded to carry out its mission independently. HACA's parity and pluralism lend its actions social and democratic credibility. Its decisions can be subject to judicial appeals. It receives complaints and requests from individual citizens as well as from civil society organizations, political parties, trade unions and human rights organizations.

Regarding Morocco's approach to digital regulation, priority is given to Pan-African action and consultation, without distinguishing between North Africa, West Africa, or other African subregions. Our continent faces major challenges in digital sovereignty and resilience to disinformation and online hate speech. This is why the establishment of inclusive and equitable global governance of the digital space is crucial. It is for this reason that HACA organized the very first session of dialogue between African media regulators and representatives of major digital platforms.

HACA believes that strengthening and updating national regulatory frameworks is essential. However, in light of the super-power of Big Tech actors, it is necessary to develop binding global mechanisms to establish robust and sustainable counterbalances against the growing techno-economic and socio-political influence of digital platforms.

YA: How do you engage with citizens and other stakeholders when drafting regulatory policies?

LA: We maintain an ongoing and open dialogue with citizens. The purpose of an independent regulator is to serve the public interest and protect users' rights. For instance, HACA offers a tele-complaint platform where citizens and civil society actors can express their grievances and expectations. The Supreme Council for Audiovisual Communication, HACA's deliberative body, consistently applies a liberal interpretation of the law. On a day-to-day basis, we try to ensure citizen regulation by aligning our decisions with the principles of human rights (freedom of expression, access to information, the fight against discrimination, protection of privacy, etc.) and democratic values (pluralism of opinion, combating hate speech, radicalization and excommunication, promoting diversity, etc.).

We also maintain constant interaction with radio and television operators, supporting them in their economic development and the enrichment of their content offering, as well as strengthening their self-regulatory mechanisms.

This includes promoting ethical best practices within their internal governance systems.

Also, HACA regularly interacts with civil society and human rights organizations, not only by handling their complaints but also by organizing workshops and interactive debates on thematic studies produced by the regulator. For example, HACA frequently organizes workshops with women's associations to address gender stereotypes in media and promote fair representation of women.

Moreover, we engage continuously with academic circles by hosting students and doctoral candidates within the institution. I also deliver regular lectures at universities across the country to promote a culture of regulation among young people and meet the needs of communication researchers.

Finally, we collaborate with other regulatory authorities, such as the National Telecommunications Regulatory Agency, to collect data on the use of information and communication technologies. We also cooperate strongly with other constitutional bodies, including the National Human Rights Council and the National Commission for the Protection of Personal Data.

YA: What regulatory challenges do policymakers in Morocco face when creating and implementing legal and policy instruments for digital or online spaces?

LA: In Morocco, as elsewhere on the African continent, building national digital sovereignty is a major challenge. For all our countries, there can be no full digital sovereignty without a secure cyberspace and a credible, competitive local cultural and information offering. This capacity to produce and distribute authentic content remains to be built up and represents an essential vector for cultural diversity, social cohesion, and regional integration. It is also essential for strengthening the continent's position in the global cultural market.

The situation is further complicated by the imbalance of resources and power between states and digital platforms, which exploit an extractive and predatory logic on digital markets. These platforms monetize personal data in an unethical way, amplify disinformation, and interfere with private and public spaces. Furthermore, most African countries face a critical shortage of essential infrastructure: As of 2025, Africa had fewer than 200 data centers, representing less than 1.5 per cent of global infrastructure.

Establishing a regulatory framework for digital content that protects Moroccan society from informational risks and disorders, while guaranteeing freedom of expression, freedom of access to information for users, and freedom of the digital market is a major challenge for Moroccan public authorities.

This work is underway in Morocco, but HACA remains highly concerned and advocates for the legal framework to be established to provide for rigorous accountability of platforms. Our observations, based on monitoring the ongoing regulatory experiences within the European Union, as well as in Australia and Canada, reveal that they have not yet delivered systemic and effective solutions to the growing risks exacerbated by rapid technological evolution and the impunity of global players.

YA: Do you see multi-stakeholderism as a solution to the global regulatory challenge? If yes, what kind of multi-stakeholder solution do you envisage? And what substantive, unique, and indigenous policy contributions can Africa and African countries like Morocco bring to the table?

LA: As President of HACA, I chaired the Network of African Communication Regulatory Authorities, which brings together 37 African regulatory bodies, for two years until November 2024. During this mandate, digital regulation was one of the main agenda items for our Pan-African network.

With the involvement and support of my fellow presidents of African media regulatory bodies, I advocated for the continent's right to participate in global negotiations with the technological giants. We have also actively been involved in UNESCO's efforts to establish guidelines promoting a trusted internet where information is regarded as a public good.

For example, in our dialogue with digital platforms, we consistently emphasize the need for strict, fair, and coherent content moderation rules. The objective is to ensure that African citizens receive the same level of online rights protection as social media users in other regions of the world. This implies that platforms must take into account the diversity of cultural, economic, and political contexts in their content moderation policies.

Africa must contribute to the establishment of international governance of the global digital space. Its voice must be heard and its perspective taken into account. Africa is the world's youngest continent, and by 2050, its population will account for a quarter of the world's total. The continent is destined to become a major digital market. Consequently, platforms need to take responsibility for this market and include in their public policies the expectations of African societies in terms of content and integrate African societal expectations into their public policies, particularly in the areas of content regulation and access to innovative technologies.

YA: What measure is Morocco taking to control emerging technologies such as artificial intelligence?

LA: Morocco is among the most proactive countries on the African continent in implementing a strategy to develop access to innovative technologies such as AI. In this regard, the very first UN resolution on Artificial Intelligence adopted, by consensus on 21 March 2024, was initiated on the joint initiative of Morocco and the United States.

Entitled 'Seizing the opportunities of safe, secure and reliable artificial intelligence systems for sustainable development', the resolution emphasizes the need for appropriate AI governance approaches that are based on international law, inclusive, and tailored to the different needs and capabilities of developed and developing countries. The resolution encourages all industry ICT players to cooperate with developing countries 'and to provide them with assistance to promote inclusive and equitable access to the benefits' of these technologies.

Furthermore, Morocco has adopted a proactive and comprehensive approach to regulating and promoting artificial intelligence. The national strategy is built on three main pillars. First is developing research centers. Morocco has established AI research hubs fostering collaboration between universities, industry, and government to ensure ethical and responsible innovation in artificial intelligence. It also hosts UNESCO's Center of Excellence. The second is enhancing educational programs. Investment in AI education includes the integration of specialized programs in universities and vocational training centers. This initiative aims to equip the workforce with the necessary digital skills. Third is the sectoral applications of AI. Morocco has targeted critical sectors for AI deployment, including healthcare (AI-assisted medical diagnostics), agriculture (smart agriculture technologies) and public services (improved administrative services through AI).

Aware of the underrepresentation of the Arabic language in AI data, Morocco has launched initiatives to contribute to advancements in Natural Language Processing (NLP), promoting greater inclusivity for Arabic-speaking populations.

Regarding regulation, Morocco advocates for developing AI systems that consider human inclusion and global diversity. For example, AI algorithms must be trained on diverse datasets to avoid algorithmic biases that perpetuate, amplify and disseminate cultural and gender stereotypes.

In summary, I believe that regulating AI should be posed not in terms of limiting its use, but in terms of controlling its use and, above all, in expanding access to the opportunities this technology offers for the global development of nations.

YA: How do you think Morocco's laws governing digital and online media will develop over the next five to ten years?

LA: To answer this question, I will be concise. Humanity now lives in an uncertain world where the rapid evolution of technology brings forth new and crucial challenges every day. No precise predictions can be made in this context. The only certainty is that, especially on our continent, we need to prepare and empower our youth to embrace active, creative and informed e-citizenship.

6

Regime Change?: Digitalization, Media Convergence and the Constraints to Reforming Ghana's Analogue-Era Regulatory System

Kobina Ano Bedu-Addo

Introduction

This chapter considers the historical factors – political and economic – that influence contemporary media and communication policymaking in Ghana and hold back the country's need to reform its analogue-era regulatory regime during the current digital era. As technological convergence in the communication sector and digitalization of technologies have resulted in the traditionally separate sectors of broadcasting, computing and telecommunications merging, it has spawned media content delivered via different digital platforms (Tambini 2001). Media audiences can now create, access and consume media content with advanced digital technologies, either offline or on numerous digital platforms. Technological advances have enabled the creation, wide circulation and multiple avenues for consuming media content, but they have also complicated the task of regulating media, which is traditionally based on specific technologies (Napoli 2001). In the United Kingdom, for example, the complexities brought about by convergence and digitalization in the country's media and communication sector resulted in the merging of previous sector-specific regulators into Ofcom, the Office of Communication (Smith 2006). According to Napoli (2001), even the Federal Communications Commission (FCC) in the United States already set up as a converged communications regulator, recognized the need to develop regulatory principles that effectively cut across traditional industry boundaries in the wake of converging technologies (Napoli 2001: 2).

In sub-Saharan Africa, following the International Telecommunication Union's (ITU) 2020 deadline for implementing the global digital switchover policy in the television industry, the evidence for structural reform of regulatory systems in the media and communication sector to accommodate the complexities in the current digital media environment is patchy (Bedu-Addo 2022). Countries such as South Africa, Tanzania and Kenya can show evidence of regulatory reform long before implementing digital switchover. From this, it is reasonable to suggest that Kenya, Tanzania and South Africa are in a better position to confront the complexities of regulating their respective broadcasting sectors, as well as the growing digital media environment. This is unlike Ghana's situation, with an experience that demonstrates regulatory inertia. Since the early 1990s, following a wave of democratic fervour that swept Africa and resulted in the return to Constitutional rule and media liberalization in Ghana, the country's media and communication regulation system has not seen reform. Policymakers have long recognized the regulatory system's inadequacies. However, concrete reform has not resulted beyond rhetoric, and despite the impact of convergence and digitalization in the communication sector, the inadequate regulatory system persists (Bedu-Addo 2022).

This chapter examines Ghana's struggle to reform its regulatory system and the factors that have sustained its antiquated analogue-based regulatory system in the new digital media and communication environment. The chapter argues that the persistence of the country's inadequate regulatory set-up is the result of the resistance of powerful state and commercial interests, whose influence in policymaking works against realizing regulatory reform, and hence the public interest, to maintain the status quo that furthers their influence and control over the sector.

The section after this introduction discusses the impact of convergence and digitalization on media and communication regulation, with the section after providing an analysis of how convergence and digitalization have resulted in regulatory reform in Kenya, Tanzania and South Africa. The section that follows then details the method and framework for the chapter. The next two sections address the establishment of Ghana's media and communication regulation system and the advocacy for its reform, respectively, while the section after analyses the reasons for the persistence of the country's regulation system in the digital media environment. The final section, highlights the main themes of discussion and concludes the chapter.

Convergence, Digitalization and Regulatory Reform

Advances in compression technology, the processing power of computers and the arrival of the internet have transformed the media and communication sector, and resulted in mergers and acquisitions in the previously separate telecommunications, computing and broadcasting industries (Collins 1998; Mansell 2016). Globally, these developments have transformed the media and communication sector, and as Picard (2020: 7–9) has observed, more actors are involved in fashioning communication policy. According to Michalis (2022), communication policy is a field of contestation that tries to address various issues simultaneously based on limited knowledge with unintended consequences, as one line of (in)action can create new or aggravate existing problems (Michalis 2022: 69). As such, policymaking in the media and communication sector reflects a constant battle by vested interests to secure and maintain their influence. Digitalization has been at the heart of convergence, as it provides a common language that makes it possible for different delivery platforms – telecommunications, broadcasting and computing – to understand each other (McQuail and Siune 1998). According to Iosifidis (2002), convergence can be understood at three interrelated levels: the technological level, the structural level and the services and markets level (Iosifidis 2002: 28). These developments have made it possible to circulate content across telephony internet and broadcast media platforms.

From the above, it becomes clear how policymaking and the regulatory requirements for the media and communication sector have become complicated and have, therefore, required new approaches to regulation (Barata 2016). The debate concerning the challenge to regulation in the context of convergence and digitalization in media and communication is not new. Scholars such as Collins (1998), Nieminen (2013), Jedrzejewski (2014), Hills and Michalis (1997) and Garcı´a-Murillo (2005) have examined the phenomenon from different perspectives and contexts. Furthermore, as Napoli (2001) has suggested, regulation has traditionally been based on sector-specific technologies (Napoli 2001: 1). However, convergence and digitalization have rendered this definitional approach based on regulatory delineations of particular technologies or forms of delivery outmoded. Moreover, as Garcı´a-Murillo (2005) has argued, inconsistencies in regulation, regulatory arbitrage and uncertainty in the market with potential court challenges have been challenges associated with separate regulatory agencies in the age of convergence (Garcı´a-Murillo 2005: 21). Hence, in the United Kingdom, for example, the consequence of convergence in the media and communications sector was the strengthening of the institutional base of regulation, with the merging of sector-specific regulators to form the Office of Communication (Ofcom) as the new regulator for the sector (Hills and Michalis 1997: 236). According to Collins (1998), this reform went ahead despite 'jurisdictional jealousies' among the country's erstwhile sector-specific regulators (Collins 1998: 385).

Michalis (2022) observes that media policy and regulation seek to address various technical, economic, social, political and cultural objectives, with regulation being the narrower instrument to achieve broad policy objectives (Michalis 2022: 67–68). Freedman (2008) has similarly argued that 'media [...] regulation points to the specific institutional mechanisms for realising [...] aims' (Freedman 2008: 13). In other words, regulatory instruments flow from stated policy goals. The cultural significance of media makes its regulation a contentious exercise (Tambini 2001: 115), which results in constant tension between the economic and sociocultural objectives in any regulatory endeavour (Napoli 2001: 17). Social objectives in regulation promote public goods such as quality and diversity of content, social inclusion and plurality of voice, which can only be partially or imperfectly addressed, left to competition alone. This accords with Hills' (2003) observation that regulation defines the public interest and balances the interests of commercial lobbies and citizens (Hills 2003: 38). Hence, to regulate necessarily requires some form of intervention in ongoing activities to serve, not just the needs of the market for reasons of technical efficiency, but also, stated public interest goals (van Cuilenburg and McQuail 2003: 201). As van Cuilenburg and McQuail (2003: 203) have also observed, communication regulation relates to two dimensions of the communications system, which Hills (2003) describes as structural and behavioural regulation. In media, structural regulation relates to questions about financing and who may broadcast, how many broadcasters there can be and where they can broadcast in the spectrum and with what power and technology, while behavioural regulation sets out the main principles by which they are expected to work (Hills 2003: 41). According to Hills (2003), a particular constraint of media regulatory agencies in Africa has concerned their financial independence and the lack of requisite human resource to run the agencies (Hills 2003: 51; see also Irion and Ledger 2013; Diop 2022). In the context of Ghana's commercialized broadcasting sector following the media's liberalization, such a situation has had the effect of rendering the media regulator weak and ineffective in its regulatory endeavour to secure the public interest.

Feintuck (2009; see also McQuail 1992), addresses the 'public interest' by arguing that it has too often meant nothing or something but is generally inadequately specified, resulting in it being vulnerable to capture or over-turning by organized interest groups (Feintuck 2009: 64; 1999). In Ghana, the public interest would be to have a regulatory system that assured the delivery of wide-ranging informational and educational media content that highlighted identity, culture as well as national interest within a commercialized digitalized media market (McQuail 1992). With the advances brought about by convergence and digitalization in the media and communication sector in the country, regulatory reform has become urgent due to the country's flourishing multichannel television market and numerous digital platforms that operate without much policy guidance and regulatory intervention.

The foregoing discussion reinforces the importance of having the requisite regulatory system in place if cultural and democratic goals in media and communication regulation are to be achieved. The analysis that follow will therefore highlight the long-established public interest for Ghana to have an effective regulatory system for its media and communication sector and demonstrate why this quest has been held back as the country continues to rely on its analogue-based regulatory system in the current digital media environment. In the next section, the experience of media and communication regulatory reform in some African countries is discussed.

Convergence and Regulatory Reform in Africa

As noted earlier, this chapter examines the reasons for the persistence of Ghana's analogue-era regulatory system in a digitalized media and communication sector. In this section, the discussion is focused on a few selected case studies from Africa that offer interesting examples of regulatory reform, since it is beyond the scope of this chapter to consider the media and communication regulation situation across Africa's 54 nations.

In the wake of convergence and digitalization in media and communications, South Africa merged its erstwhile Independent Broadcasting Authority (IBA), the regulator for the country's television market and the South African Telecommunications Regulatory Authority, the regulator for the telecommunications services sector. The new merged regulator, the Independent Communications Authority of South Africa (ICASA) was established by the Independent Communications Authority of South Africa Act (2000). Duncan and Glenn (2010) have stated that the new regulator faced questions about its independence from the government (Duncan and Glenn 2010: 54). Nevertheless, it is fair to argue that this regulatory redesign was an early recognition by South African policymakers and government of the implications of convergence and digitalization in the media and communication industry, as ICASA was given a mandate that covered both the country's telecommunications and broadcasting industries.

Similarly, Tanzania established the Tanzania Communications Regulatory Authority (TCRA) under the Tanzania Communications Regulatory Authority Act (2003). This regulatory redesign moved the country from the erstwhile Tanzania Communications Commission established in 1993, and responsible for the media and communication sector in the country. Additional legislation empowering the TCRA is the Broadcasting Services (Content) Regulations, 2005, a revision of the earlier Broadcasting Services Act, 1993 and the Electronic and Postal Communications (Digital and other Broadcasting Networks) Regulations of 2011. It is argued that the combined effect of the reformed regulatory structure and additional legislation puts Tanzania's TCRA in a stronger position to address the challenges brought about by convergence and digitalization in the country's media and communication sector.

Likewise, Kenya has also witnessed some regulatory reform in the wake of convergence and digitalization. The Communications Authority of Kenya regulates the country's media and communication sector. The original establishing Act, the Kenya Communications Act (1998), has been amended to become the Kenya Information and Communications (Amendment) Act (2011). The amended legislation strengthens the Communications Authority of Kenya to 'facilitate the development of the information and communications sector (including broadcasting, multimedia, telecommunications and postal services) and electronic commerce' in Kenya (The Kenya Information and Communications Act, preamble, 2011: n.pag.). Clearly, the new legislation was structured taking into consideration the reality of convergence and digitalization in the media and communication sector.

Even though limited, the examples provided above indicate some positive regulatory restructuring and legislative revisions that address regulatory competence, both structural and content, for the converged and digitalized media and communication sectors. Furthermore, and considering the period these regulatory redesigns occurred, it suggests an early recognition of the implications of convergence and digitalization by policymakers in those countries. This is an important outcome for the new digital communication environment, where regulators have to contend with the complexities of regulating multichannel television, the internet and the numerous digital content delivery platforms available to audiences.

As the discussion below shows, while Ghana's policymakers have long recognized the need to reform the country's regulatory system, they have repeatedly failed to take the actions needed to realize that recognition. This state of affairs explains why Ghana's analogue-era regulatory system persists in the digital media environment and works against the public interest in realizing regulatory reform in the media and communications sector.

Method

The examination in this chapter has been based on a qualitative approach consistent with an interpretative orientation, with data derived from documents and elite interviews. The interviews were conducted based on the conceptualization by Welch et al. (2002) of elite interviewing. Twenty-two actors involved in media and communication policymaking, such as regulators, legal experts, parliamentarians, media owners and journalists, were interviewed. In addition to this, and based on Scott's (1990) formulation of documents as physically embodied texts (Scott 1990: 5), various documents such as public speeches, media interviews, policy documents and legal texts were assembled. The data from documents were examined using the document analysis approach (Bowen 2009). The interview data were analysed using the thematic analytical approach to categorize themes (Braun and Clarke 2006, 2019). In both data sets, the examination yielded first-hand access to the positions of policy actors. It provided the rich interpretative schemas embedded in Ghanaian media and communication policymaking discourse.

Furthermore, the data were analysed within a combined power and historical institutionalism framework. Dahl (1957) has formulated a concept of power that rests on its visible exercise. That is, the extent of an actor's power is based on their capacity to influence the action of another actor (Dahl 1957: 202–03). The formulation of power by Bachrach and Baratz (1962) extends Dahl's formulation. As they argue, when an actor's action is confined to 'non-controversial' issues, it may reflect how a dominant actor has succeeded in preventing another actor from bringing up such controversial issues that could be detrimental to the dominant actor's interests (Bachrach and Baratz 1962: 948–49). The above formulation introduces the invisible exercise of power, similar to Lukes' conceptualization:

> If others can further my interests without my either intending or intervening to bring this about, I maintain that such cases may be among the most effective and sometimes the most insidious forms of power [...] secured through ways of averting both conflict and grievance and through the securing of consent.
>
> (Lukes 2005: 110–11)

Lukes' formulation has been applied by Freedman (2010) to examine US and UK media and communication policymaking to argue that 'inaction' or 'policy silence' may not always suggest 'doing nothing', but rather a strategic decision to promote hegemonic interests and to naturalize foundational values (Freedman 2010: 355). In other words, power is at its most potent when the interests of dominant actors become naturalized. The Ghanaian examination, argued in this chapter, demonstrates the exercise of both visible and invisible power by state and commercial interests to maintain the media and communication regulation system against the public interest.

The historical institutionalism concept (Steinmo 2008; Hay and Wincott 1998) combines with power as the analytic framework for this chapter. According to Steinmo (2008), historical institutionalism examines how structures created historically have a determining influence on current behaviour and choices (Steinmo 2008: 164). Two considerations under this concept are critical junctures and path dependence. A critical juncture is 'a period of significant change [...] hypothesised to produce different legacies' (Collier and Collier 1991: 29) while path dependence occurs when 'once [...] a country has started down a track, the costs of reversal are very high [...] [and] the entrenchments of certain institutional arrangements obstruct an easy reversal of the initial choice' (Pierson 2000: 252).

Put differently, historical events can have a determinative influence on contemporary policy choices.

The discussion below demonstrates the utility of the above in examining Ghana's experience. Ghana's transition to democratic rule in the early 1990s served as a critical juncture, during which state and commercial actors emerged in the media and communication policymaking arena. Over time, they have used their power and influence in policymaking to set regulatory reform on a path-dependent trajectory that maintains the status quo. Following Ghana's completion of its digital switchover process in 2020, the media and communication sector has expanded with multichannel television and digital platforms. In this situation, the lines that distinguish television from telecommunications and computing have become blurred as content circulates seamlessly across different delivery platforms. Yet, the regulatory system remains unchanged. The framework explains that this regulatory state of affairs is not accidental but rather the natural consequence of the nature of reconfiguration in the media and communication arena following the country's return to Constitutional rule. This explains the persistence of Ghana's analogue-based regulatory system in the converged and digitally transformed media and communication environment.

Ghana's Media and Communication Regulation System

Regarding media and communication regulation, the current structure is split between the National Media Commission (NMC) and the National Communication Authority (NCA) for the media and telecommunications sectors, respectively. These two institutions were established during the early years of Ghana's return to Constitutional democratic rule in 1993 and have become major actors in media and communication policymaking. As shown in Table 6.1, even though both institutions are state-funded, the NMC is an independent organization. In contrast, the NCA operates as a technical agency under the Ministry of Communication (MoC).

Ghana's transition to democratic rule in the early 1990s coincided with global currents of deregulation in telecommunications industries (Horwitz 1989, 2001; Picard 2020). Its domestic consequence was the liberalization of the state's post and telecommunication (P&T) monopoly with private investors invited to partner with the government in its running. Further to this, the erstwhile Transport and Communication Ministry was split into a Transport Ministry and a Ministry of Communication (now the Ministry of Communication, Digital Technology and Innovation, MoCDTI) with policy responsibility for the telecommunications sector. Given that the telecommunications sector was now liberalized, a telecommunications regulator, the NCA was established under the National Communications

TABLE 6.1: Ghana's bifurcated media and communication regulatory structure.

Institution	**National Media Commission (NMC)**	**National Communication Authority (NCA)**
Established	July 1993	December 1996
Act	Act 449, 1993/Amended Act 561 2008	Act 542, 1996/Amended Act 769 2008
Mandate	Media Regulator	Telecommunications Regulator
Funding	State Funded	State Funded/ Industry Revenue
Status	Independent	Government Technical Agency
Other Legislation	Complaints Settlement Procedure Regulations 1994 (LI1587)	Electronic Communications Regulations, 2011; L.I. 1991; Electronic Communications Regulations, 2016; L.I 2235
Policies	National Media Policy, 2000; Guidelines for Local Language Broadcasting, 2000; Broadcasting Standards 2000	

Authority Act, (1996), Act 524 (later amended by Act 769, 2008) for the telecommunications sector, and to also operate as a technical agency under the Ministry of Communication. The NCA has strong legislation backing its operations, such as the Electronic Communications Act (2008), Electronic Communications Regulations (2011), L.I. 1991 and the Electronic Communications Regulations (2016), L.I 2235. Part of the NCA's mandate covers frequency authorizations for the commercial broadcasting sector, with powers over the technical aspects of broadcasting, such as the specifications for broadcast equipment and radius ranges. However, with powers that include the revocation of broadcast frequencies, this early decision to make the NCA grant frequency authorizations has given the institution indirect but substantial influence over the development of the country's broadcasting sector, despite the NCA's consistent claim that it only plays a technical regulatory role in the broadcast sector.

In contrast, the NMC, under Article 166 of the 1992 Constitution, was designed as an independent Constitutional body to serve as the buffer between, particularly, state-owned media and government and ensure journalistic excellence. Unlike the NCA, the NMC's original establishing legislation, Act 499, 1993 (with sections later amended to Act 561 2008) was weak, despite the institution's formal role as a media regulator. The Act, among others, permits the NMC to:

> Make regulations [...] for the registration of newspapers and other publications except that the regulation shall not provide for the exercise of any direction or control over the professional functions of a person engaged in the production of newspapers or other means of mass communication.
>
> (The National Media Commission Act 1993: § 2.1.f.2)

This provision was designed to bring distance between the government and the state media to limit the government's ability to interfere in their operations, as had happened in the past under military rule. The language in the legislation is more specific on newspapers. This reflects the dominant media at the time of the legislation's passage. However, the law is vague on radio and television, and pertinent for this discussion, silent on new digital means of communication. Furthermore, published guidelines for the media by the NMC, such as the National Media Policy 2000, the Broadcasting Standards 2000 and the guidelines on Local Language Broadcasting 2000, are now outdated since many of their provisions are not applicable in the current converged digital media context. In effect, the NMC currently has no specific relevant policy guidelines designed to regulate media content, despite its formal media regulator role. This regulatory inadequacy is compounded by the lack of a broadcasting law, even though the broadcasting sector has seen the biggest growth since the media sector was liberalized under the 4th Republic 1992 Constitution (Gadzepko 2023: 1). This state of affairs illustrates Hills' (2003: 39), observation that, without legislation, a regulator works without structure, targets and accountability.

Thus, as one media policy activist commented, the NMC cannot enforce its own guidelines (even if they existed) since the absence of legal backing renders them voluntary (Ampaw 2020, in-person interview with author). The consequence of this has been broadcast media organizations pursuing their own commercial interests without any regulatory obligations for content and not paying much attention to the NMC's existing guidelines for their work. This attitude differs from the relationship broadcast media organizations have with the NCA, even though the institution is not responsible for media content.

In the context of technological convergence in the communication sector, the decision to give the NCA, rather than the NMC, the mandate to authorize broadcast frequencies gave the MoCDTI an exclusive policy remit that also covers broadcasting and digitalization and disabled the NMC's ability to formulate policy for the media sector. In that sense, the NMC was established without regulatory competence, whereby the institution would have the ability, capability and aptitude to undertake regulatory activity (Picard 2020: 32). Over time, the result has been a pattern of state dominance in media and communication policy formulation, as state-controlled institutions, such as the MoCDTI and NCA, exert more influence and control over the direction of media and communication policymaking than the NMC. Furthermore, government control over public resources, such as finances, and as sole initiator of legislation in the parliament under the 1992 Constitution has consistently benefitted agencies under its direct control than independent actors such as the NMC, and successive governments since 1992 have been happy to maintain this arrangement.

The foregoing illustrates how the NMC, from its very creation, was designed to be weak and ineffective as a media regulator, unlike the NCA. The consequence has been an NMC that does not command the authority of a media regulator among many broadcast media institutions as the NCA does. With its limited powers and lacking a specific broadcasting law to regulate the broadcasting sector, the NMC has operated more like a dispute settling Ombudsman between aggrieved citizens and media organizations, rather than as a media regulator in the real sense. In the words of a former chairman of the Commission, the NMC has resorted to 'admonitions and moral appeals' (Blay 2019: n.pag), as devices to regulate the media.

The discussion above demonstrates how state agencies under the control of the Executive have continued to exercise more power, unlike independent actors in media and communication policymaking. This can be seen in the MoCDTI's exclusive communication policy remit since the new Constitution came into force, the NCA's superior establishing and other legislation, plus the early decision to endow the organization with a broadcast frequency authorization mandate, as well as the absence of a specific broadcasting law to empower the NMC's media regulatory mandate. These should be seen as the structural constructions during Ghana's transition to democracy in the early 1990s that point to that period being the critical juncture that has resulted in 'lock-in', whereby state-controlled institutions have had a determinative policymaking influence over the trajectory of the media and communication sector's regulatory system.

Media Liberalization and the Advocacy for Regulatory Reform

The discussion above has noted how Ghana's media and communication regulatory system came to be established upon the country's return to Constitutional rule under the 4th Republic 1992 Constitution. This was after ten years of the military, Provisional National Defence Council, PNDC, government, characterized by severe media repression.

The new Constitutional environment democratized policymaking in the media and communication arena, a marked departure from the previous ten years of authoritarian military rule during the 1980s and, indeed, much of Ghana's political history, where policymaking was centralized within the government. As a result, actors such as the Ghana Independent Broadcasters Association (GIBA), the commercial broadcast lobby group, the Ghana Journalists Association (GJA), the national journalists' group and the Media Foundation for West Africa (MFWA), a non-profit civil society set-up, emerged as policy actors in the sector with the freedom to voice their policy positions on media and communication matters. The Ghanaian courts have also become influential in media and communication policymaking through case law, e.g. *The New Patriotic Party* v. *The Ghana Broadcasting Corporation* (1993); *Ghana Independent Broadcasters Association* v. *The Attorney-General and National Media Commission* (2016).

The new Constitution provided safeguards to further reduce the interfering influence of government in the media. Chapter 12, Article 162(3) of the 1992 Constitution states:

> There shall be no impediments to the establishment of private press or media; and in particular, there shall be no law requiring any person to obtain a license as a prerequisite to the establishment or operation of a newspaper, journal or other media for mass communication or information.
>
> (Constitution of the Republic of Ghana 1992: § 162.3.112)

The above section guarantees media freedom and, thus, spurred the media sector's liberalization. The result was that private ownership of broadcast media was permitted for the first time in the country's history, resulting in its rapid growth. From a handful of privately owned radio stations and no private television station in 1995, the current media landscape in the country has over 500 radio stations operating, over 100 digital television channels and growing access to online digital platforms (University of Ghana 2023: 1). The commercialization of the media sector has raised concerns about the quality and diversity of programming available to audiences. As Hills (2003) has pointed out, commercialization exacerbates the trend towards uniformity because advertisers want larger audiences and commercial broadcasters look to their audience share to sell advertising (Hills 2003: 38). In Ghana, this situation manifested primarily because of the lack of an effective regulatory system to shape the broadcasting sector's development, which over time, has also led to the strengthening of commercial broadcasters' voice in broadcasting policymaking to resist reform.

Hence, despite the plural policymaking context that followed the return to Constitutional rule, power in media and communication policymaking is concentrated in a handful of economic and political players in the policymaking arena. As such, the question of what institution best serves the public interest in such a commercialized media market has become pertinent. For example, state agencies involved in media and communication policymaking have disproportionately influenced the shape of policy. This can be seen in how the commercial broadcast media sector grew rapidly due to the NCA's frequency authorization mandate without much involvement from the independent media regulator, the NMC. Given that the NCA is controlled by the government under a Ministry, that mandate has consistently raised questions about the NCA's independence, more so when the Constitution forbade governments' direct involvement in media. And yet, this persists, explained by how Ghana's 1992 Constitution endowed enormous power within the Executive and its agencies.

Ghana's bifurcated media and communication regulation system split between the NCA and the NMC has therefore left vacuums that have been exploited by the commercial media. As noted above, the consequence of the NCA's exclusive frequency authorization mandate was the rapid growth in commercial broadcast media without a coherent broadcasting policy or an effective regulatory system (Bedu-Addo 2022: 147–48). In this context, radio and television stations have been granted frequencies without any content obligations. In addition, the NMC has been weak in establishing statutes and has lacked a broadcasting law to empower the NMC's mandate. Consequently, without clear policy guidelines on content obligations and ownership rules, as well as a broadcasting law to enforce their provisions, an unfettered broadcast media environment without regulatory obligations has developed and been entrenched by commercial broadcasters represented by GIBA, their lobby association. GIBA has used its commercial power to challenge legislative proposals in the courts or raised the spectre of state interference in media to resist efforts to introduce measures designed to curb excesses created by some broadcast media (Bedu-Addo 2022: 188–89). The lobby has consistently invoked Article 162 of the 1992 Constitution, which forbids government interference in media, as its defence. A recent demonstration of such resistance can be seen in the cases *Ghana Independent Broadcasters Association* v. *NCA and Attorney-General* (2018) and *Ghana Independent Broadcasters Association* v. *The Attorney-General and National Media Commission* (2016).

The situation discussed above illustrates how the early period of Ghana's return to Constitutional rule was the critical juncture that established state dominance in media and communication policymaking and also created the space for commercial media actors to exploit. This regulatory inadequacy has long been recognized, not just by civil society actors but by the government itself (World Bank/Government of Ghana 2005).

Given this state of affairs, especially the lack of an independent system for granting frequency authorizations, the Ghana Advocacy Steering Group for a Broadcasting Law, a civil society formation, began a campaign for regulatory reform in 2004 and presented initial draft proposals for a broadcasting law to government (Apenteng 2007). In a revised version of the proposals some years later, the group criticized the opaque broadcast licensing regime, arguing that the process is open to political manipulation and called for the passing of a broadcasting law to 'sanitize' the airwaves:

> The country does not have clear, transparent and uniformly applied legal criteria for the grant of broadcasting authorizations. This lends the process to arbitrariness and patronage. At the same time, the regulatory overview of the content of programmes is virtually non-existent. This exposes the public and children in particular to non-edifying and sometimes harmful programmes. Furthermore, some sections of the media have on occasions carried inflammatory presentations with the potential to incite one section of the society against the other.
>
> (Apenteng 2014: 3)

The final proposals submitted to the government in 2014 to pass the broadcasting law also recommended shifting the NCA's frequency authorization powers to the NMC. It is telling that after over eleven years since those proposals were submitted, successive governments have not yet introduced the bill to parliament, let alone pass it into law. Handing over the NCA's frequency authorization mandate to the NMC would mean a significant loss of policy influence and control, which would lead to the dilution of the state's influence over the sector and, therefore, not in its interests. However, by maintaining the status quo, successive governments can use their power to frustrate efforts to reform the regulatory system. When this is combined with the agency demonstrated by GIBA against what little effort has been made to reform media regulation, it shows how regulatory reform has not been an important issue simply because it has not been in the interests of those political and economic actors in the media and communication sector to make it a priority. It also demonstrates the exercise of different types of power by these economic and political interests.

Explaining the Factors Behind the Inertia in Regulatory Reform

The point to be emphasized from the foregoing is how Ghana's transition to Constitutional democratic rule was the critical juncture that democratized the media and communication policymaking space, yet retained huge powers for the Executive. Consistent with Collier and Collier's (1991) formulation of historical institutionalism, it was a period of significant change which, once established, defined the trajectory of media and communication regulation. Thus, the state has been a big beneficiary of the regulatory status quo due to how the 1992

Constitution distributed power. One media policy activist with a legal background analysed the situation this way:

> Looking at the Constitution itself, it has given too much power to government to the extent that government has its hands almost everywhere, so institutions that are supposed to be truly independent and to do independent work are not, they rather do the bidding of government.
>
> (Adow 2020: n.pag)

Hence, the retention of determinative policy power within Executive-controlled institutions under Constitutional rule has not been much different from the situation before and has effectively made state-controlled institutions like the MoCDTI and NCA monopolies in media and communication policymaking, despite the appearance of a plural policymaking context.

Furthermore, the fact that the inadequacies of the regulatory system had long been recognized but not reformed demonstrates a subtle exercise of power by governments, consistent with Lukes' (2005) analysis of power. An important demonstration of such Executive power is the fact that after over eleven years since proposals for a broadcasting law were initially submitted by civil society to the Ministry of Information, a broadcasting bill has not, as yet, been presented to the parliament for consideration. On this, a parliamentarian with experience working on communication policy stated thus:

> Bills do not just run through parliament, especially when they are not in the interests of government, and when I say interests of government I mean economic or political interests of government.
>
> (George 2020: n.pag)

Clearly, it has not been in the state's political interests to pass a broadcasting law that will make media and communication regulation more effective since this will also result in a loss of influence and control in the sector. Hence, the prolonged dithering on the broadcasting law's passage reveals the state's 'non-decision' power in policymaking (Lukes 2005; Freedman 2008). This interpretation is reflected in a comment by another media policy activist with a legal background:

> In my view I think that the government is quite happy, or governments our governments have been quite happy about this NMC more or less weaknesses, then it makes a case for why we should have the NCA which they control.
>
> (Ampaw 2020: n.pag)

As noted earlier, the inertia about media and communication regulatory reform has also been due to the resistance on the part of commercial broadcasters, represented by GIBA, to maintain the status quo since this best serves their interests. GIBA's resistance to regulatory reform has been mainly in the form of legal challenges in the courts. Article 162(4) of the 1992 Constitution forbids the government from interfering in the editorial operations of the media. On this basis, GIBA has often framed its resistance as a fight to protect the media's editorial independence from government interference. Such framing echoes with the experience in the United States, where media firms have used similar arguments under the country's First Amendment in their Constitution (Harvey 2004). On this issue, a senior GIBA official has wondered:

> Is there anything wrong with protecting our business because aside the protection of our business, it is also the protection of Ghana's democracy because when there is freedom of speech, freedom of expression, access to information, then the people are well informed, then our democracy thrives, but if it doesn't happen like that there could be any form of attack on our democracy and we feel that alone is a threat to the government itself.
>
> (Hiadzi 2020: n.pag)

By framing its resistance to regulatory reform as a fight to preserve free expression, GIBA's rhetoric taps into the deep-seated national historical trauma of media repression at the hands of military governments, in particular. What this also does is to equate media regulation to the possibility of state repression of media. In the effort to achieve policy consensus about media and communication regulatory reform, this stance has, unfortunately, combined with state dithering and indifference to either stall or extinguish any calls for reform, making it easy for the analogue-era regulatory system to persist.

Ghana's current media and communication regulation situation mirrors that of the United Kingdom during the 1990s, as analysed by Hills and Michalis (1997). However, unlike the United Kingdom, it has not resulted in the merged regulatory system that established Ofcom. Similarly, it has been unlike the experience witnessed in some South American countries like Chile, which used the implementation of the ITU's digital switchover policy to also reform media and communication regulation (García Leiva 2010). In that sense, Ghana missed yet another opportunity to construct a new regulatory system fit for the converged digital era in the country's media and communication sector. The concern this has raised is reflected in the comment by one industry actor:

> We are yet to think through the consequences and weigh the full implications of explosion in channel capacity as a result of digitalization we are yet [to] and these stakeholders have been too slow in tackling this issue.
>
> (Ashigbe 2019: n.pag)

Given the current situation, no specific policies or regulatory measures exist for the converged and digitalized media and communication sector. As a result, Ghana's regulatory system remains unreformed, as policymaking has been driven on a path-dependent trajectory fuelled by state dominance and commercial interests. This clearly has enormous implications for how the sector will be regulated in the future. Some industry actors see the requisite regulatory measures as lagging behind market transformations: 'We are ready to be able to deliver the [digital] service, is the regulator ready to regulate us?, I'm not too sure about that' (Ashigbe 2019: n.pag).

With such a vacuum created in regulation, it is argued that neither the NCA nor the NMC, as presently structured, has the capacity to adequately deal with the complexities brought about by convergence and digitalization in Ghana's media and communication sector. Ghana's completion of its digital switchover process in 2020 has resulted in an expanded multichannel television market and numerous digital platforms, in addition to an already large radio broadcasting market. And yet, there are no clear policy and regulatory guidelines to protect minors from harmful content on linear or online media; the role of public service broadcasting in this context has not been clarified; while the tendencies for media concentration have been exacerbated. These will require policy and regulatory interventions that the current architecture is not positioned to deliver. With such a clearly inadequate regulatory system, long recognized, the fact that policy actors have not seized the opportunities, such as the digital switchover process, to fashion the necessary regulatory reform demonstrates the indifference, at best, of entrenched interests in the media and communication sector. This outcome is against the public interest but clearly illustrates the stumbling blocks state and commercial interests put in place in the way of regulatory reform.

Unsurprisingly, senior figures in the regulatory set-up see nothing problematic about the current system for media and communication regulation and argue for its maintenance:

> It will be unwieldy, at least that is how the framers of the constitution imagined it, to combine this soft mandate [of the NMC's content regulation] with the hard mandate of managing say spectrum and awarding licences and authorizations [to] telecoms, broadcasting and other entities, Internet service providers, satellite companies and so on and so forth [...] from a political point of view and also considering our own history I think there is something to be said about this bifurcation because you know you don't want the entity that has the power to give and withdraw licences [have] the power to determine what is appropriate to broadcast.
>
> (Sakyi-Addo 2020: n.pag)

Clearly, this position is at odds with the US example with the FCC and in the UK's merger of sector-specific regulators into Ofcom. In Africa, South Africa's ICASA also provides another example of a merged media and communications regulator. Hence, that position downplays how convergence and digitalization have blurred the distinctions among telecommunications, computing, internet service providers and broadcasting industries. Recent comments attributed to current and former chairs of the NMC (Hawkson 2023) further highlight the difficulties in advocacy for regulatory reform in the media and communication sector. The story suggests that the chairs oppose more powers for the NMC. In the context of the long-standing advocacy for a broadcasting law and a more effective NMC, such commentary only serves to frustrate any progress made towards reform. It also offers ammunition to those opposed to empowering the NMC. Consequently, there is no sign that Ghana's media and communication regulatory system will experience reform. This is despite the visible transformations in the sector and the complications this has brought to regulation in terms of ownership rules, advertising, access to free-to-air digital channels and the viability of public service media in this digital context. Given the above viewpoints by the top hierarchies in the country's media and communication policymaking arena, the inertia about regulatory reform in Ghana is not surprising.

Conclusion

This chapter has examined the challenges in regulating Ghana's liberalized and digitalized media and communication sector. The chapter has analysed why the country's analogue-era regulatory system persists even as convergence and digitalization have transformed the sector. The examination tracked the historical factors that created the country's media and communication regulatory system, with the reconfiguration in the media and communication policymaking arena that saw the emergence of new policy actors. Despite this plural policymaking context, following the country's return to Constitutional rule, policymaking in the media and communication sector has been dominated by state interests through government-controlled institutions like the NCA. Equally, the new configuration has opened spaces for commercial actors to emerge as powerful media and communication policy actors. The chapter analysed how these sets of political and commercial interests continue to influence the shape of the regulatory system despite the transformations in the sector that warrant regulatory reform. The chapter argued that the persistence of Ghana's analogue-era regulatory system results from the exercise of power by commercial and political actors to maintain their respective interests, despite the recognized inadequacy of the country's media and communication regulatory system.

Data from elite interviews and various documents were analysed using historical institutionalism and power as frameworks. The framework has illustrated how successive governments exercised 'non-decision' policymaking power, as seen, for example, in the stalled effort to pass a broadcasting law that would have empowered the NMC to be a more effective media regulator for the digital era. Governments during Ghana's 4th Republic have simply been happy to maintain their power and have exercised indirect but powerful influence over the development of the broadcast and telecommunication industry.

In this regard, the framework has also explained why the state has and continues to invest in the institutions it controls – the NCA and MoCDTI – originating from the early decision to make the NCA, rather than the NMC, grant broadcast frequency licences, which has largely contributed to the NMC's inadequacy as a media regulator. In support of this situation has been the resistance on the part of GIBA, the commercial broadcasting lobby, to what little effort at regulatory reform there has been through legal challenges in the country's courts. Such resistance has contributed to the stalled progress and persistence of the regulatory status quo – in structure and regime – despite the digital transformations in the media and communication sector.

Even though the African cases considered in the chapter are too limited to generalize, they nonetheless offer indications about what is possible on the continent. As suggested by Sampaio-Dias et al. (2019), it remains to be seen how national legislatures and domestic courts on the continent engage with policy and regulatory legislation in the context of the ever-growing digital spaces for civic and democratic engagement in African countries. The chapter has argued that Ghana's media and communication regulatory inadequacy is not accidental but the natural consequence of how the reconfiguration of policymaking in the country during its transition to constitutional rule in the early 1990s was managed. It is evident in how Ghana's bifurcated regulatory architecture for the media and communication sector has exposed a regulatory vacuum that benefits state and commercial interests against the public interest for a better-regulated media and communication sector. As the full implications of convergence and digitalization in the media and communication sector materialize in the years ahead, Ghana's policymakers will have to confront these questions about the country's regulatory inadequacy in a converged and digitalized communication sector that continues to impair the interests of citizens. For the NMC to be an effective media regulator requires not just the passage of a broadcasting law but also a comprehensive review of its establishing legislation to make it relevant for the digital age. Ghana's government, regulators and civil society actors will have to re-energize their efforts to reform the country's regulatory system by drawing inspiration from the examples and experiences of the country's neighbours on the continent.

REFERENCES

Adow, Osei K. (2020), in-person interview with K. A. Bedu-Addo, Accra, Ghana, 15 February.

Ampaw, Akoto (2020), in-person interview with K. A. Bedu-Addo, Accra, Ghana, 11 February.

Apenteng, Berifi (2007), 'Proposals for a Broadcasting Act: Ghana Advocacy Steering Group for a Broadcasting Law', Accra, Ghana.

Apenteng, Berifi (2014), 'Revised Broadcasting Bill: Ghana Advocacy Steering Group for a Broadcasting Law', Accra, Ghana.

Ashigbe, Kenneth (2019), in-person interview with K. A. Bedu-Addo, Accra, Ghana, 19 December.

Bachrach, Peter and Baratz, Morton S. (1962), 'Two faces of power', *American Political Science Review*, 56:4, pp. 947–52, https://doi.org/10.2307/1952796.

Barata, Joan (2016), 'Challenges for audiovisual regulation', *InterMEDIA*, October, https://iicom.org. Accessed 23 November 2020.

Bedu-Addo, Kobina A. (2022), 'Power, policy, and digital switchover an analysis of communication policy making and its challenges for regulating Ghana's digital television sector', Ph.D. thesis, London: University of Westminster.

Blay, Amihere (2019), in-person interview with K. A. Bedu-Addo, Accra, Ghana, 19 December.

Bowen, Glenn A. (2009), 'Document analysis as a qualitative research method', *Qualitative Research Journal*, 9:2, pp. 27–40, https://doi.org/10.3316/QRJ0902027.

Braun, Virginia and Clarke, Victoria (2006), 'Using thematic analysis in psychology', *Qualitative Research in Psychology*, 3:2, pp. 77–101, https://doi.org/10.1191/1478088706qp063oa.

Braun, Virginia and Clarke, Victoria (2019), 'Reflecting on reflexive thematic analysis', *Qualitative Research in Sport, Exercise and Health*, 11:4, pp. 589–97, https://doi.org10.1080/2159676X.2019.1628806.

Collier, Ruth B. and Collier, David (1991), 'Critical junctures and historical legacies', in R. B. Collier and D. Collier, *The Americas*, Princeton: Princeton University Press, pp. 27–39.

Collins, Richard (1998), 'Back to the future: Digital television and convergence in the United Kingdom', *Telecommunications Policy*, 22:4/5, pp. 383–96.

Dahl, Robert (1957), 'The concept of power', *Behavioral Science*, 2:3, pp. 201–15.

Diop, Layire (2022), 'The Senegalese Council for Broadcasting Regulation: A giant with feet of clay', in W. In Mano and L. El Mkaouar (eds), *Media Ownership in Africa in the Digital Age*, Oxon: Routledge, pp. 177–90.

Duncan, Jane and Glenn, Ian (2010), 'Turning points in South African television policy and practice since 1990', in D. Moyo and W. Chuma (eds), *Media Policy in a Changing Southern Africa: Critical Reflections on Media Reform in the Global Age*, Pretoria: University of South Africa, pp. 39–72.

Electronic Communications Act (2008), Act 775. Accessed 18 July 2019.

Electronic Communications Regulations (2011), L.I 1991. Accessed 12 November 2019.

Feintuck, Mike (2009), 'Regulating media markets in the public interest: Principles beyond competition', *Journal of Media Business Studies*, 6:3, pp. 63–77, https://doi.org/10.1080/16522354.2009.11073489.

Freedman, Des (2008), *The Politics of Media Policy*, Cambridge: Polity.

Freedman, Des (2010), 'Media policy silences: The hidden face of communications decision making', *International Journal of Press/Politics*, 15:3, pp. 344–61, https://doi.org/10.1177/1940161210368292.

Gadzekpo, Audrey (2023), 'The state of the media in Ghana: An introduction', in A. Yeboah-Banin (ed.), *The State of the Ghanaian Media Report*, Accra: University of Ghana, pp. 1–7.

García Leiva, Maria T. (2010), 'The introduction of DTT in Latin America: Politics and policies', *International Journal of Digital Television*, 1:3, pp. 327–44, https://doi.org/10.1386/jdtv.1.3.327_1.

Garcı´a-Murillo, Martha (2005), 'Regulatory responses to convergence: Experiences from four countries', *INFO*, 7:1, pp. 20–40.

George, Sam (2020), in-person interview with K. A. Bedu-Addo, Accra, Ghana, 27 January.

Ghana Broadcasting Study (2005), Accra: World Bank/Government of Ghana.

Ghana Independent Broadcasters Association v. *The National Telecommunications Authority* (2018), ECT/APP/002/2017.

Harvey, Silvia (2004), 'Living with monsters: Can broadcasting regulation make a difference?' in A. Calabrese and C. Sparks (eds), *Toward a Political Economy of Culture: Capitalism and Communication in the Twenty-First Century*, Oxford: Rowman & Littlefield Publishers, Inc, pp. 194–210.

Hawkson, Ebo E. (2023), 'Experts oppose more powers for NMC', *Daily Graphic*, 15 June.

Hay, Colin and Wincott, Daniel (1998), 'Structure, agency and historical institutionalism', *Political Studies*, 46:5, pp. 951–57, https://doi.org/10.1111/1467-9248.00177.

Hiadzi, Gloria (2020), in-person interview with K. A. Bedu-Addo, Accra, Ghana, 28 January.

Hills, Jill (2003), 'Regulatory models for broadcasting in Africa', in K. Tawana (ed.), *Broadcasting Policy and Practice in Africa*, London: ARTICLE 19, pp. 34–70.

Hills, Jill and Michalis, Maria (1997), 'Technological convergence: Regulatory competition: The British case of digital television', *Policy Studies*, 18:3–4, pp. 219–37, https://doi.org/10.1080/01442879708423734.

Horwitz, Robert B. (1989), *The Irony of Regulatory Reform: Deregulation of American Telecommunications*, Oxford: Oxford University Press.

Horwitz, Robert B. (2001), *Communication and Democratic Reform in South Africa*, Cambridge: Cambridge University Press.

Iosifidis, Petros (2002), 'Digital convergence: Challenges for European regulation', *Javnost – The Public*, 9:3, pp. 27–48.

Irion, Kristina and Ledger, Michele (2013), 'Measuring independence: Approaches, limitations, and new ranking tool', in S. Wolfgang, P. Valcke and K. Irion (eds), *The Independence of the Media and Its Regulatory Agencies*, Bristol: Intellect, pp. 141–65.

Jedrzejewski, Stanislaw (2014), 'The media regulation in age of convergence', in H. Sousa, M. Pinto, J. Fidalgo, S. Jedrzejewski, E. Costa e Silva, A. Melo, L. A. Santos, S. Denicoli, M. Lameiras and M. E. Barbosa (eds), *Media Policy and Regulation: Activating Voices,*

Illuminating Silences, Minho: University of Minho, Communication and Society Research Centre, pp. 97–110.

Kenya Information and Communications Act (2011), CAP. 411. Accessed 9 November 2021.

Lukes, Steven (2005), *Power: A Radical View*, 2nd ed., New York: Palgrave Macmillan.

Mansell, Robin (2016), 'Media convergence policy issues', *Oxford Research Encyclopedia of Communication*, 22 November, https://doi.org/10.1093/acrefore/9780190228613.013.62.

McQuail, Dennis (1992), *Media Performance: Mass Communication and the Public Interest*, London: Sage Publications.

McQuail, Dennis and Siune, Karen (eds) (1998), *Media Policy: Convergence, Concentration and Commerce*, London: Sage Publications.

Michalis, Maria (2022), 'Why should we care about media policy?: Critical directions in media policy research', in P. McDonald (ed.), *The Routledge Companion to Media Industries*, London and New York: Routledge, pp. 66–75.

Napoli, Philip (2001), *Foundations of Communication Policy: Principles and Process in the Regulation of Electronic Media*, Cresskill: Hampton Press.

National Media Commission (2000), *National Media Policy*, Accra: Friedrich-Ebert-Stifung.

National Media Commission Act (1993),§ 2.1.f, p2. Accessed 16 December 2022.

New Patriotic Party v. *Ghana Broadcasting Corporation* (1993), 2 GLR 354-393.

Nieminen, Hannu (2013), 'Challenges of convergence to media regulation: From Sectoral to hybrid regulatory framework?' Summer School of Legal Informatics, Rovaniemi, Finland, 27 August.

Picard, Robert G. (2020), *Media and Communications Policy Making: Processes, Dynamics, and International Variations*, Cham: Palgrave Macmillan.

Pierson, Paul (2000), 'Increasing returns, path dependence, and the study of politics', *American Political Science Review*, 94:2, pp. 251–67.

Republic of Ghana (1992), *Constitution of the Republic of Ghana*, p. 210, https://judicial.gov.gh/index.php/the-constitution. Accessed 24 June 2025.

Sakyi-Addo, Kwaku (2020), in-person interview with K. A. Bedu-Addo, Accra, Ghana, 22 January.

Sampaio-Dias, Susana, Mabweazara, Hayes M., Townend, Judith and Osman, Idil (2019), 'Practices, policies and regulation in African journalism: Mapping a research agenda', *African Journalism Studies*, 40:3, pp. 1–9, https://doi.org/10.1080/23743670.2019.1750197.

Scott, John (1990), *A Matter of Record*, Cambridge and Oxford: Polity Press.

Smith, Paul (2006), 'The politics of UK television policy: The making of Ofcom', *Media, Culture & Society*, 28:6, pp. 929–40, https://doi.org/10.1177/0163443706068926.

Steinmo, Sven (2008), 'What is historical institutionalism?: Approaches in the social sciences', in D. Della Porta and M. Keating (eds), *Approaches in the Social Sciences*, Cambridge: Cambridge University Press, pp. 150–78.

Tambini, Damian (2001), 'Roads to digitopia', *Political Quarterly*, 72:1, pp. 114–18, https://doi.org/10.1111/1467-923X.00349.

Tanzania Communications Regulatory Authority Act (2003), No. 268. Accessed 9 February 2018.

The Independent Communications Authority of South Africa Act (2000), No. 13, https://www.icasa.org.za/legislation-and-regulations/acts/icasa-act. Accessed 14 December 2022.

The Kenya Information and Communication (Amendment) Bill (2019), https://www.parliament.go.ke/files-2019-10. Accessed 14 December 2023.

The National Media Commission Act (1993), Act 499, https://www.nmc.org.gh. Accessed 29 May 2019.

The Tanzania Communication Act (1993), No. 18, https://ictpolicyafrica.org/document. Accessed 18 July 2019.

van Cuilenburg, Jan and McQuail, Dennis (2003), 'Media policy paradigm shifts towards a new communications policy paradigm', *European Journal of Communication*, 18:2, pp. 181–207, https://doi.org/10.1177/0267323103018002002.

Welch, Catherine, Marschan-Piekkari, Rebecca, Penttinen, Heli and Tahvanainen, Marja (2002), 'Corporate elites as informants in qualitative international business research', *International Business Review*, 11, pp. 611–28.

7

Broadcast Media Regulation and Democratic Transitions in Africa: A Nigerian and South African Case Study

Yemisi Akinbobola, Vincent Obia and Trust Matsilele

Introduction

On 7 July 2021, the Nigerian broadcasting regulator, the National Broadcasting Commission (NBC), wrote a letter to all broadcasting outlets, warning them to be cautious in relaying information related to the security challenges the country was facing. The Commission asked broadcasters to work with the government by not 'glamorising the nefarious activities of insurgents' and 'advising guests and/or analysts on programmes not to polarise the citizenry with divisive rhetoric' (Oyero 2021: n.pag.). On 24 August 2021, NBC enforced this directive, issuing a 'Notice of Infraction' against Channels TV after its presenters interviewed Benue State Governor, Samuel Ortom. In particular, NBC noted that the station did not interrogate the 'inciting, divisive and unfair comments' made by the governor. For this, the presenters were invited for a meeting with the Commission (Igwe 2021: n.pag.). Such actions have been described by SERAP (2021) as gag orders that prevent broadcasters from reporting on cases of insecurity in Nigeria, which are of public interest. Examples can also be found in South Africa, where a growing intolerance for press freedom has been identified (Sparks 2011; Wasserman 2020). For instance, the governing African National Congress (ANC) around 2000 and 2001 was agitated by the role the media played in what the party characterized as 'negative, irresponsible, uninformed reporting which was sabotaging' the government's broader societal goals (Fourie 2002: n.pag.). In this chapter, we focus on state-media relations in Nigeria and South Africa, particularly given the democratic transitions that have taken place and the change they should have resulted in.

This chapter focuses on two of the most recognized post-transition African countries that underscore the so-called 'democratic wave' (see Huntington 1991; Gates et al. 2007; Gunitsky 2018) of the 1990s. This includes the end of apartheid South Africa in 1994 and Nigeria's end to military rule in 1999. For South Africa, the media post-apartheid played a unifying role between the black majority population and the white minority in what was imagined as the 'Rainbow Nation' (Barnett 1999). In Nigeria, given that the change in the political system from authoritarianism to democratic rule has lasted over two decades, we are interested in questioning whether relations between the media and the state have witnessed a similar shift. Hence, we ask:

1. What are the predominant themes in the broadcast and online broadcast policy documents in post-transition Nigeria and South Africa?
2. How do media practitioners and experts interpret these policies?
3. What implications do they have for state-media relations in both countries?

Although we consider the broader media landscape, our focus is on traditional and online broadcast media regulation and the agencies responsible for this regulation (NBC for Nigeria and ICASA for South Africa). We focus on broadcasting because of its tendency to be highly regulated. The chapter begins by outlining existing research on political economy, democratic transitions, development media and the public interest. This is followed by a consideration of the method, where policy analysis and interviews were done. In presenting our results, we show that both countries' media regulations still show signs of repression, especially in Nigeria, suggesting that the move to democracy has done little to alter state-media relations. Based on this, we argue that what exists is a situation where the approach to media regulation is dependent on the character of the political system in place and not the political system itself, whether democratic or autocratic. It shows that a democratic country can have a restrictive media system while an autocratic country can have a libertarian media system – what matters is the disposition of the ruling elite.

Political Economy, Democratic Transition and State Media Relations

Political economy and state-media relations bear close relation in the literature. Political economy is a broad field of study, ranging from institutional studies, capitalism, cultural production, activism, globalization, new media, convergence and media ownership (Mosco 2008). Mansell (2004) notes that the political economy of the media refers to structures of power and how its distribution affects the operation of the media. This power is exercised through three significant control instruments: ownership, funding and regulation. Hence, the political economy of communication 'looks specifically at how ownership, support mechanisms and government policies influence media behaviour and content' (McChesney 2000: 110). It is, therefore, closely tied to government policies and regulations and how they shape media output. This explains why although we acknowledge media ownership and funding in post-transition Africa, our focus emphasizes how power is signified within formal regulatory approaches. Indeed, government action, usually exercised through subsidies, regulation and policy, is an essential indicator of the negotiation between political power and media power, particularly as far as the state is concerned (Wasko 2005).

This presupposes a ceaseless contention over media control where the media seeks to exert its autonomy on the one hand, and the state seeks to influence editorial policy on the other hand. As Berger (1998) points out, the contention typically centres around criticisms of the government by the media. He goes on to add that notions of media power and influence in a democracy are only an illusion since the media is embedded in a 'nexus of relations' and that 'the media is usually dominated by the more powerful partners, or factions of these partners, within these relations' (Berger 1998: 605). This nexus explains the relation of subalternity between the media and the state that we refer to. To define subalternity, we draw from Spivak's (1988) work on the imperial subaltern to explain how subordinate the media was and is to the political system in pre- and post-transition Africa. Similarly, building on Spivak's work to explore state-media relations in Nigeria and South Africa, Ogunleye discusses a double subalternity, arguing that:

> Nigeria and South Africa share a colonial heritage that constructed their nation-states, and in so much as they function under this exogenous structure, their attempts at organizing themselves has been influenced by exogenous techniques that are not in symphony with their own realities. On the second level, I synthesize that this imposed construction of the nation-state has an impact on the conditions under which the media speak.
>
> (Ogunleye 2010: 92)

Transition itself, especially in the political sense, is primarily viewed from the standpoint of the third 'democratic wave' (Huntington 1991; Gates et al. 2007; Gunitsky 2018) that washed over former Soviet states and Africa between the 1980s and the 1990s. The expectation was that this period of change would lead to a new dispensation in state–media relations in places like Eastern Europe, one that mirrors liberal democratic practices in the media structures of the West, particularly the United States.

For Eastern Europe, Mangui-Pippidi (2012) shows that official repression was seen as the major issue affecting press freedom there before the waves of democratization. Given that many East European countries have since transited to democracy, she notes the need to ask why press freedom there remains low. The media still faces challenges relating to ownership control, undue political influence and media corruption (Mangui-Pippidi 2012). In essence, we see a media system that is still largely emblematic of authoritarian tendencies despite the post-Soviet transition. Sparks (2011) sees this as a feature of democratic transition, noting that political and media transitions are usually erratic. He criticizes the theory of transitology, where it is assumed that democratization follows a linear path from autocracy to full-blown liberal democracy. Instead, he argues that the process is more unpredictable than anything – there can be a transition to democracy, followed by a relapse to (quasi)autocracy, or there can be no transition at all as witnessed in some post-Soviet states. This, he says, renders the theory of transitology inadequate (Sparks 2011). Huntington (1991) buttresses this line of thinking in his reference to the 'reverse wave' – a situation where states witness regressions in democratic ideals and the number of democratic nations reduces. The suggestion, therefore, is that transitions rarely translate into press freedom, media diversity and autonomy, as we will show in this chapter. Wasserman (2020: 454), for instance, observes that, in many African countries where democracy took hold during the wave, there have been relapses into authoritarian rule, and a 'hybrid mode of governance' exists in many places. We then find that the media system and the assessment of whether it is free, compromised, or caged depend on the nature of the political system in place, as Mangui-Pippidi (2012) alludes to.

As an illustration, the state of the media in a country like apartheid South Africa reflected the socio-political struggle that found expression at the time. Also, Steenveld (2012) shows that the Truth and Reconciliation Commission's enquiry into the media found that it was regulated by more than a hundred laws, leading to considerable self-censorship. The laws effectively banned the Black press while they entrenched a White mainstream press. Black reporters were also required to reflect the establishment in their writing – they could not stray into what could be regarded as media action or activism. Hence, 'the apartheid state had defined the terms of operation of the press' (Steenveld 2012: 126), making the media reflect socio-political realities in the nation. In particular, the South African Broadcasting Commission (SABC) served as the mouthpiece of the apartheid state (Wasserman 2020). Dismantling traces of apartheid, especially the role of the public media, were some of the focal points in the lead up to the 1994 transition. Mtimde agrees observing that: 'The airwaves in South Africa were opened for the first time in history when the Independent Broadcasting Authority (IBA) was created on 30 March 1994 by an act of parliament – the IBA Act of 1993' (Mtimde 2000: 174).

With the coming of democracy in 1994, one would expect that the transition would alter the political economy of the apartheid media. The literature suggests that this optimism has not materialized, at least not entirely, since 'the relationship between the media and government [post-apartheid] has often shown signs of strain. There are increasing examples of politicians' intolerance for media criticism, but also of political interference and attempts at capturing the media agenda for political gain' (Wasserman 2020: 455).

Examples of this intolerance include the sought passage of the Protection of State Information Bill, a kind of secrecy law (Giles 2023), and there have been moves to replace self-regulation of the press with formal regulation (e.g. through MAT – the Media Appeals Tribunal). MAT has been described as showing 'a growing intolerance among the ruling political elite for media criticism' (Wasserman 2020: 457). Also, in 2010, the ruling ANC introduced a policy on media transformation, ownership and diversity. Steenveld notes that the policy 'presents a "justification" for government intervention in the sphere of the media, its main public critic' (Steenveld 2012: 130). All these have led to suggestions that South Africa is still predominantly a transitional country nearly three decades after apartheid (Wasserman 2020). This chapter shows that a similar situation exists in Nigeria, and we consider how journalists interpret and deal with the political situation the media finds itself in. Often, it is the case that the government defines the political situation in terms of the development of media thinking and the public interest.

Public Interest and Development Media Thinking

State regulation, which is the formal and informal instructions about the structure, conduct or content of the media (Mukhudwana 2022), is usually justified on the grounds of public interest – much like government policies of any kind. Conversely, journalists have always believed that they operate in the public interest (Dennis 1974), implying that less regulation and more freedom serve this purpose. The result is that 'vague and confusing meanings' have been attached to the concept of public interest (Dennis 1974: 939). This is because public interest is an abstract and normative ideal, much like love or justice – terms that mean different things to different people (Downs 1962; Iosifidis 2011). Iosifidis defines public interest as 'the collective cultural, political, social, and informational benefits to the society which serve both the democratic processes of political participation and cultural, social and economic well-being' (Iosifidis 2011: 27). This suggests that public interest serves the benefit of the generality of people, not just a minority. Downs agrees with this submission in the political sense, noting that everyone usually agrees that 'the proper function of government is to act for the greatest benefit of society, even though they may disagree widely about what actions are best for it in any given circumstances' (Downs 1962: 3).

This definitional contention has led to three major schools of thought (Glendon Schubert cited in Downs 1962). First is the rationalist school, where public interest refers to the will of the majority. Here, the goal of the public authority is to determine what this majority view is and abide by it. Second is the idealist school, where public interest entails an activity 'that is best for society according to some absolute standard of values, regardless of whether any citizens actually desire this course of action' (Downs 1962: 11). The third is the realist school, where public interest rests solely on 'the result of certain *methods* of decision-making' (Downs 1962: 11, original emphasis). In light of our discussion in this chapter, the indication is that the second school of thought is pervasive, given the way governments and journalists define the public interest. We see this in the values of press freedom that journalists are quick to latch onto and in the values of the common good that governments espouse. However, Downs, in relation to the idealist school, adds a note of warning, stating that the question is 'what standards of values is the proper one, how a person translates such values into concrete policy decisions, and what kind of relationship exists between the decision-makers and the citizenry' (Downs 1962: 14). Here, we find the connection between public interest and state-media-citizen relations – the implication being that the government rhetoric on public interest should be judged against political realities on the ground.

As previously mentioned, one way the government expresses this rhetoric is in the self-definition of its role. In other words, this is the idea that media regulation (and restriction) is always in the public interest. The second option is to construct the role of the media as an agent of national development. This is the notion that the media in third-world countries should partner with the government in facilitating developmental goals for the good of all – the public interest. An example can be found in the warning issued by the NBC, which we referred to in the introduction. Under this thinking, traditional and online broadcast media are expected to play developmental roles, especially when it comes to social change (Rodrigues 2010). Such ideas are rooted in McQuail's (1987), in his postulation, states that the media is expected to toe the national policy line. In achieving this goal, 'certain freedoms of the media and of journalists are subordinated' and 'the state has a right to intervene in, or restrict, media operations, and devices of censorship, subsidy and direct control can be justified' (McQuail 1987: 121). Indeed, one of McQuail's conditions that make for the relevance of the development media theory and that still holds today is the 'devotion of these societies [i.e., developing countries] to economic, political and social development as a primary national task, to which other institutions should submit' (McQuail 1987: 120).

On the surface, this theory can be positive when resisting cultural imperialism and stimulating national development (McQuail 1987), although it is still unclear whether the media leads or follows democratic change and societal transformation (Jebril et al. 2013). Regardless, views on development media have broadly been accepted by the African political elite. We see an example of this in post-genocide Rwanda, where journalists are required to work in conjunction with the government for development purposes (Sobel and McIntyre 2018). As such, some laws restrict how journalists refer to the genocide since the government has come up with a 'redevelopment plan' (Sobel and McIntyre 2018: 10) that the media is expected to key into. The restrictions have led to self-censorship since 'it was often difficult to determine what restrictions were put in place by the government versus self-imposed' (Sobel and McIntyre 2018: 11).

A somewhat similar situation existed in South Africa, where 'understandings of the relations between the media and democracy have been tied closely to the rhetoric of nation-building' (Barnett 1998: 553). After apartheid, the central policy question became how private broadcasting could be regulated to conform to inclusivity, development and diversity (Barnett 1998). Given this, the media is torn between defining its role either as a watchdog or as a partner that supports the government in a developmental role (Wasserman 2020). This is further compounded by the fact that it is hard to ascertain when and how the media fulfil their supporting role in development (Jebril et al. 2013). We suggest that this ambiguity means political leaders can subjectively define how and whether the media contributes to development, providing a normative justification for possible censorship policies.

Musa (1997) points to this, noting that because of development media thinking, governments in Africa have long tried to exercise control over the media for public interest purposes. However, what largely exists is the use of the media to service the interests of the private political elite, not the public interest (Musa 1997). An example that he points to is the establishment of the first African television station in Nigeria for educational purposes – a development media agenda justified on public interest grounds. Yet, he notes that 'the political class eagerly latched onto this press theory because it favoured their desire to control the media' (Musa 1997: 138). In South Africa, we find much the same scenario. Here, Sparks (2011) acknowledges that ideals of inclusivity and democratic participation have largely given way to attempts to restrict the media, especially during the Mbeki-Zuma transition. He describes the increasing repression of the media as 'an attempt to ensure the legitimacy of a remodelled elite as a whole, and to advance the interests of the dominant factions within it' (Sparks 2011: 14). Put differently, in the Zuma era, once the media became critical of the government, increasing intolerance of the media by the government became apparent (Wasserman 2020).

Hydén et al. connect this intolerance to the uncritical position of early scholarship on the role of governments in the use of the media for national development, arguing that because national development objectives had been the foci of these studies, the 'right to criticise policy or strategy were deemed as improper interferences' (Hydén et al. 2002: 8). Therefore, in the years following independence, the media in most African countries have been subjected to strict government control and often became propagandist rather than informative. Considering this, Musa (1997) notes that the democratic media theory needs to be revised to accommodate press freedom, human rights, participatory communication and alternative media. Otherwise, the likelihood is that the political elite will continue to exploit the basis of development media and public interest as a justification for the political economy of media capture long after the transition to democracy. What we, therefore, find in the literature is that media censorship and, in some cases, repression are still present in post-transition countries like Nigeria and South Africa. This censorship usually comes with the cloak of the public interest rationale and development media thinking, as governments seek to justify their control over media expression. It underscores the need to study why media censorship remains a present issue in Nigeria and South Africa, how media practitioners interpret it, and the implications for state-citizen relations, particularly as it concerns broadcasting and online broadcasting.

Method

In researching broadcast regulation and state/media relations in Nigeria and South Africa, we analysed media policy documents and conducted semi-structured interviews with media practitioners and experts. Our choice of Nigeria and South Africa was motivated by the need to present an initial overview of state-media relations in post-transition Africa. Both countries also feature as two of the most recognized African countries that transited to democracy in the 1990s. We note that the analysis should not be seen as comparative research but as a study of regulation in Nigeria and South Africa as a way of understanding the broader African context. For the policy analysis, we note that South Africa has more media policy and regulatory documents than Nigeria. This is because the laws in South Africa underwent several changes and amendments that reflect the political trajectories that have taken place since the end of apartheid in 1994. The Independent Broadcasting Authority (IBA), for example, was among the various bodies set up to facilitate the transition to democracy during the multi-party negotiations in 1993. In 2000, however, the Independent Communications Authority of South Africa (ICASA), functioning under the

ICASA Act (2000), provided for the dissolution of the IBA and the South African Telecommunication Regulation Authority (SATRA), and in 2005, the Electronic Communications Act repealed and replaced the IBA Act and the Telecommunications Act. By contrast, Nigeria has fewer legal documents, some of which were carried forward from the era of military rule, pre-1999. Overall, the documents that we reviewed are listed in Table 7.1.

We carried out a textual analysis of the policies to identify their main themes. This was to identify the regulatory emphasis in both Nigeria and South Africa. In addition to policy analysis, we also analysed the views and perspectives of media practitioners and scholars in both countries. The individuals that we interviewed have been kept anonymous for ethical and security reasons. Their designations are highlighted in Table 7.2.

Data from the policy analysis and interviews were used to address the areas of focus in the research. These areas include the independence and functionality of the media regulatory institutions, the relationship between the media and the state, and the question of control of the media in both countries, post-transition. We cover these areas in the following findings sections.

TABLE 7.1: Reviewed policy documents in Nigeria and South Africa.

Country	Policy Documents
Nigeria	Nigeria Broadcasting Code 6th edition (2019, including the 2020 Amendment that provided for online broadcasting)
Nigeria	Nigerian Broadcasting Commission Act No. 38 of 1992 (including its 1999 amendment and 2019 amendment bill)
Nigeria	The Nigerian Constitution, 1999
South Africa	South African Constitution, 1996
South Africa	The Green Papers, 1997
South Africa	Broadcasting Act 1999 and its 2002 and 2009 Amendment
South Africa	Independent Communication Authority of South Africa Act 2000 and the 2006 and 2014 amendments
South Africa	Electronic Communications Act 2005, and the 2012 and 2014 amendments

TABLE 7.2: Interviewees and their designations.

Nigeria	South Africa
Participant 1: News agency reporter	Participant 9: Media scholar
Participant 2: Media rights activist	Participant 10: Media industry researcher
Participant 3: Commissioner of Information to a state government	Participant 11: Journalist at a private broadcaster
Participant 4: Media scholar	Participant 12: Researcher at a broadcasting association
Participant 5: News executive at a public broadcaster	Participant 13: Journalist at public broad-caster
Participant 6: News editor at a private broadcaster	Participant 14: Founding Bodies Committee of Press Ombudsman
Participant 7: Journalist at a private broadcaster	Participant 16: A member of the Press Council of South Africa
Participant 8: Media scholar	Participant 17: A member of the South African National Editors' Forum
Participant 15: Online broadcasting practitioner	Participant 18: Broadcast journalist

Themes in the Policy Documents

Policy analysis of Nigerian and South African regulatory instruments revealed five themes overall: open/vague interpretation, value construction, contradictions, subtle restrictions and independence of the regulators. There were some overlaps in these themes. Some were more pronounced in the Nigerian context than in South Africa and vice versa, but they all represented an overview of both countries' regulatory and policy landscape. The themes (listed in Table 7.3) are discussed in this section, and others that follow.

Most striking in the analysis of South African media policies was how much the policies have changed to reflect the new democratic dispensation. Post-apartheid, the legislations have generally become more inclusive. For example, the Broadcasting Act of 1999 requires that, as part of the public services provided, the SABC must transmit its services in all the Republic's official languages. This is part of the development media critique that we consider subsequently. Also, in the case of South Africa, the laws in question have experienced far more fundamental changes, especially with

TABLE 7.3: Themes identified in the policy documents.

Themes
Open/vague interpretation
Value construction
Contradictions
Subtle restrictions
Independence of the regulators

the promulgation of the EC Act 2005 – and its 2012 and 2014 amendments – which was a substantial amendment of the 1993 IBA Act, and the 1999 Broadcasting Act. By contrast, the guiding policies of the NBC in Nigeria, such as the NBC Act, are still very similar to their original form under the military regime and have not undergone substantial changes. For instance, the 1999 NBC Act (which has been replaced by the National Broadcasting Act of 2004) remained largely identical to the 1992 Decree 38 enacted under the military. There is, therefore, the indication that the transition to democracy has not resulted in the regeneration of the laws governing media practices in Nigeria. This is even more so if we consider that the stipulations and sanctions in the NBC Code have been extended to online broadcasting. The 2020 Amendment to the NBC Code, for instance, makes it clear that 'contents on web/online platforms shall conform to the provision of the [NBC] Code on programming standards' (Amendment to the NBC Code: Section 2.12.7.1), with online broadcasters liable to the same sanctions as traditional broadcasters. This underscores the extent to which the broadcasting sector in Nigeria functions under a regulatory atmosphere that has its origins in autocratic rule.

On an institutional basis, there are differences in the organization of the broadcasting regulator in Nigeria and South Africa. In Nigeria, NBC is front and centre, and it is squarely concerned with the broadcasting sector. However, the ICASA in South Africa is responsible for broadcasting, telecommunications and postal regulation. As they state on their website, ICASA also,

> issues licences to telecommunications and broadcasting service providers, enforces compliance with rules and regulations, protects consumers from unfair business practices and poor-quality services, hears and decides on disputes and complaints brought against licensees, and controls and manages the effective use of radio frequency spectrum.
>
> (ICASA 2024: n.pag.)

In total, the NBC Act lists 21 responsibilities for the regulator, which includes overseeing local broadcasting and foreign and local capital investment related to broadcasting and guaranteeing the liberty and protection of broadcasting. The consequence of this relatively broad remit is that the regulator's role can become vague and open to interpretation, a central theme that we highlight. As a result, NBC can take advantage of provisions that border on social, cultural and political objectives (NBC Code 2016: Section 0.2.2) to impose wide-ranging restrictions on traditional and online broadcasting outlets. One such case was the sanction imposed on television stations for relaying social media footage on the events surrounding the Lekki Shootings in October 2020 – an action for which there was no specific basis in the books, but which was justified on the potential for a 'breakdown of law and order' (Agency Report 2020: n.pag.). This points to a situation where the Nigerian media is made subaltern (Spivak 1988) to the regulator and the state by extension. The latitude that vague provisions allow was an area that Participant 2 agreed with, suggesting that NBC may function better if given the power to regulate aspects of the industry such as frequencies and licensing.

The proposed 2019 amendment to the NBC Act further added to the objectives and functions of the Commission, specifying the regulation of digital or online broadcasting. The 2020 Amendment also contains elements of vagueness and ambiguity. The Amendment provides that online broadcasters are to be registered with NBC and are to bear liability for their content, just like traditional broadcasters. But what are the outlets that count as online broadcasters? Should online sites such as YouTube channels, podcasts and Facebook Live be seen as online broadcasting outlets? The Amendment does not specify, thus leaving room for interpretation, a situation which further widens the remit of the NBC. For South Africa, the online platforms (YouTube, podcasts, X [formerly Twitter] and Facebook) operate with carte blanche due to 'regulatory silence' around licensing. This silence has opened the space for clandestine operators, with some, building online-based social accounts around character assassination and defamation of celebrities and other public figures. Some examples of these accounts operating on X while others are on YouTube.

Also, in South Africa, the duties of ICASA are more defined, as it has only six more specific roles that cover a broader scale. In essence, ICASA's mandate is to regulate electronic communications, broadcasting and postal services in the public interest. The ICASA Act empowers ICASA to grant licenses, monitor compliance with licence terms and conditions, develop regulations, plan and manage the radio frequency spectrum and protect consumers. However, what appears to be hindering the functionality of the Authority is the continuous reduction of its independence and endless legal fights with stakeholders within the communications space. For instance, the ICASA Act was amended in 2005 and received opposition from organizations like the South African National Editors' Forum, which argued that the Minister's increased influence in the appointment process 'takes the power of selecting ICASA councillors out of the hands of Parliament, and places it in the hands of the executive, which could lead to less independence' (Gedye 2005: n.pag.). According to the 2005 ICASA Amendment Act, the Authority may make recommendations to the Minister regarding policy matters, and ICASA is obliged to consult the Minister when it comes to new regulations and must also follow directives made by the Minister. This points to the move to compromise on the independence of ICASA, another central theme that we identify. The implication is that the Authority is potentially subject to greater government control and influence. In the Broadcasting Act 1999, although the state recognizes the need for independent media, it still has a significant amount of power that it exercises through the Minister of Communication. This is similar to Nigeria's NBC, in that the Commission is obliged to give recommendations on licensing to the presidency through the office of the Minister of Information. The Minister also has considerable influence over broadcasting policy and the drafting of the NBC Code. For instance, Lai Mohammed, the then Minister of Information, was accused by the then chairman of the NBC, Ikra Bilbis, of unilaterally introducing the 2020 Amendment to the 6th NBC Code, describing it as illegal (Shibayan 2020). Regardless, the amendment is currently in force – an indication of where power lies in the regulation of broadcasting in Nigeria.

The policy on licensing is equally a pointer to the exercise of power concerning broadcasting – a way to determine who is allowed to broadcast and whose access is restricted. In Nigeria, there does not appear to be any significant restriction on ownership of broadcasting services, although certain levies on acquisition do restrain ownership. Topping the list is the power vested in the president to grant licenses, which calls into question the objectivity that the president or those delegated to carry out the task have, and second are the financial restraints. While there are no laws prohibiting broadcast ownership, the president effectively has the authority to grant or reject a licence application, not to mention the ever-increasing application fee. The implications of this in terms of the political economy of broadcasting are significant. After the Twitter ban introduced in June 2021 by the Buhari administration, licenses are now required for online broadcasting services and social media platforms.[1] We note that this widens, in no small way, the power of the government over who has access to disseminate media content. However, evidence suggests that NBC has not implemented these new licensing requirements for online broadcasters, as Participant 15 noted, perhaps because of the difficulty in applying licensing standards to outlets like YouTube channels, of which there are myriads. In the case of South Africa, licenses can only be applied for after an invitation by the Authority, as provided in Section 9(1) of the 2005

EC Act. Therefore, while private ownership is allowed, potential proprietors must wait on the ICASA for an invitation – with the accompanying implication for how the political economy of the post-apartheid media is structured. Again, the issue of licensing is limited to operators within the television and radio space considering that there has not been legislation dealing with online broadcasting. There are no existing laws that exclusively regulates online broadcasting other than the ones already in operation through the ICASA Act.

Another theme that we consider is the contradictions in the policies. This can be seen in the 2000 ICASA Act and the 1999 Broadcasting Act. Although both laws state that the ICASA is to be independent and answerable only to the Constitution, they exhibit contradictions in that they also give the Minister, and thus the state, a substantial role. The ministerial oversight has often been abused to rein in media considered as anti-transformational. We see this in the view of the media's failure to promote transformation as captured in the governing ANC's discussion document, which alleges that,

> there is a ganging up on the ANC and the movement's representatives by the media analysts, media commentators, the ultra-left and ultra-right forces. All the media outlets, including, unfortunately, the public broadcasting outlets, are dominated by the persistent attack on the NDR.
>
> (NGC 2015: 131)

These envisaged attacks have forced ANC ministers to try and rein in the media and ICASA. The Nigerian case is no different and reflects a fundamental issue in the standard-setting functions of media laws and policies. That is, should the media be left free to serve as a check on government or should it be kept on a leash to foreclose the perceived dangers of absolute press freedom? Should the media be saddled with the responsibility of contributing to national development, or should it be allowed to operate by the principles of neoliberalism? Our analysis shows that the regulations in both Nigeria and South Africa seek to capture both extremes, resulting in the realized contradictions. As an illustration, in Nigeria, the NBC Code has traditionally centred on nation-building ideals such as social and political development. However, there has been an increasing turn towards a greater neoliberal outlook as seen in the recent 2020 Amendment to the NBC Code, primarily centred on online broadcasting, competition arrangement, financial rights and exclusive content.

This is even as the 2016 NBC Code clarifies that broadcasting exists for the development of the nation and the public good. The broadcasting objectives are also expected to be in line with the directive principles of state policy (NBC Code: Section 0.2.2). Here we find the theme of value construction, as broadcasting is expected to promote accepted social norms, national identity and social justice.

Broadcasters are also to note that they exercise freedom for society's benefit. A similar principle is reiterated in the proposed 2019 amendment to the NBC Act, where as part of the news objectives, broadcasting is still primarily defined in development media terms, with the NBC required to facilitate a broadcasting industry that 'contributes to democracy, national building and development of society' (National Broadcasting Commission Act (Amendment), Bill 2019, Section 2, 1A(a)).[2] We also find a similar trend in South Africa, as we touched on earlier. On the whole, the specification of values in this manner can be found through the policies and documents that we analysed. It shows that the values specified in the policies are largely centred on development media outcomes.

Interviewee Perspectives

There was consensus among Nigerian interviewees that, although there is undoubtedly an air of freedom in the practice of journalism, not much has changed in the laws governing it. This is tied to what we noted above showing that media laws in Nigeria have not changed significantly since the transition. The main thread running through the interviews is the notion that the laws on broadcasting, particularly in Nigeria, are open to interpretation in the enforcement that the government carries out, resulting in self and state censorship of the media. For instance, the participants mentioned the over-reaching powers of NBC, where it serves as judge and jury in enforcing sanctions both for traditional and online broadcasting. They also highlighted specific laws that the government uses to constrain and control the freedom of the media. One example mentioned by Participant 8 was the state's monopoly ownership of the Nigeria Television Authority (NTA). They note that this amounts to a form of government censorship, as the NTA shoulders the responsibility of fostering national unity as outlined in the NBC Code. In South Africa, the participants generally agreed that the state had no strict control of the media; as Participant 13 stated, 'the state takes pretty much a hands-off role within the media'. However, like the Nigerian example, the state can exercise some control over the media through the Minister of Communication. Participant 16 in South Africa did not only observe that there was largely 'free' media but added that there was no need to have any extra-legal provision when it comes to online broadcasting adding that 'there are already legislations in the country, there are already voluntary regulatory mechanisms that they can join'.

Nigerian participants further revealed a lack of faith in the media regulations, and one of the main concerns was unspoken laws, i.e. fear of political intimidation over content which by law does not breach the NBC Code. Participant 2 observed that this was reflected in the 1999 amendment to the NBC Act: 'It resulted in a lot of disputes because many of the provisions were really outrageous.' This has led to the belief that the laws in place are inconsistent and should be repealed: 'There are still [media] laws in Nigeria that should not regulate the media', Participant 3 said, 'And there are still also some extra-legal controls the people believe should not be there, and even some laws that are acceptable are a bit restrictive'. This aligns with the view that even with online broadcasting, practitioners do not know when they are likely to run afoul of the regulations (Participant 15).

Other participants expressed concern that the media laws and the extent of media freedom are always dependent on the allowance given by whoever is in power. This is tied to the feeling that the government uses the public interest just as an excuse to impose restrictions on the media. We find examples with online broadcasting, where Participant 15 observed that while the NBC's stipulation on the registration of online broadcasting channels was okay, there is fear that the NBC could use the regulation for ulterior motives: 'In some countries, no matter what you're doing, you are supposed to register, even as an online publication. But the thing is, are you (the NBC) doing this [registration] to stifle the media?' (Participant 15). Participant 8 also said:

> The main problem I think we have is that, if it's in the public interest, it will be okay. But you know most of the regulations that we have in place are just for specific governments, and that is why you have some inconsistency in terms of regulation.

Participant 6, a news director, reiterated this viewpoint, pointing out that recent years have witnessed the government strengthening its hold on media output through the misinterpretation of the NBC code and other state laws:

> From time to time for the past eight years, we saw government clampdown on media houses without any reference to the [NBC] Code, and where they referred to the Code, they twisted the meanings of the provisions of the Code to suit whatever they wanted to do. For instance, with my station, where we were closed several times, one for instance for discovering the site of a crashed plane. A lot of Nigerians wondered how that became an offence, it was not provided for in the Code and all of that. Or for instance, conducting interviews where facts about government activities were exposed or clearly analysed; that's telling the truth as it is, reporting issues as they are. That didn't constitute any breach of the Code or any breach of the law in Nigeria, but of course, we came under the hammer of the government for all those kinds of things.

Related to this view of inconsistency in the application of the laws, we asked the participants to state the laws that affected them the most and that they would like to see changed. Five participants responded to this question. Four of them felt that the 1962 Official Secrets Act[3] – prohibiting the publication of stories or information considered to be in the 'national interest' – needed to be changed. We note that there is now the Freedom of Information Act of 2015, which on the surface makes the Official Secrets Act null and void. Two of the participants were concerned about how the Official Secrets Act lends itself to a capricious application by state officials, while a third, Participant 1, was particularly concerned about its effect on news content and professional practices:

> I would change it because you find that public officials don't talk with the media in Nigeria. They don't make information readily available and that's why speculation thrives a lot; they don't come clean most of the time, and the time of response to issues is too slow and short.

In addition to the notion of inconsistency, two out of the five respondents felt that the NBC Code was not independent enough and that the Code itself was unfavourable to the private broadcast media, particularly when it came to licensing, an issue which was the second most mentioned rule that participants would like to see changed. Other laws mentioned included the Constitution, the salary scale of employees of the public broadcaster, and the NTA Act. The main concern with the Constitution was the need for it to be amended to reflect a democratic environment, as Participant 2 observed:

> [The Nigerian Constitution] is likely to remain in place for a while, and while that is so, it's difficult to change the licensing regime, and that is a major problem for broadcasting freedom because it's just a question of not renewing your licence if you become too uncontrollable.

In an opposing view, Participant 5, a news executive with a public broadcaster, suggested that these laws ensure unity in the country and not engage in some form of control by the government:

> When you operate in a fair and professional manner in a very balanced manner, you go into what I can call self-regulation. You regulate yourself by yourself and know that there are certain boundaries, in the public interest. There are certain things that I'm supposed to do to ensure the unity and mutual co-existence of Nigeria as a nation, but direct control I've not witnessed it.

When we asked what laws he would like changed, they said: 'Well for Nigeria I cannot answer because I am restricted to my operation here.' They did, however, mention that there had not been much change in media laws since the transition to the civil rule: 'I cannot remember any major change of our media laws, because these things have been there, even the NBC was an establishment of the military.'

In South Africa, there was a consensus among participants working in broadcasting organizations that there is no strict control of the media by the state, and Participant 13 stated that: 'The state takes pretty much a hand-off role within the media.' Also, Participant 17 agreed with non-regulation, calling for voluntary association by media organizations to remain:

> I think I'm against any form of statutory regulation of any online content, except for those things that's already covered in legislation, whether it's online or offline, and I think online publishers should be encouraged to belong to voluntary regulatory mechanisms.

Participant 18 from South Africa supported this view:

> South Africa generally has a free press. The Broadcast Complaints Commission of South Africa is a liberal tool that keeps traditional broadcasters in check, but outside existing social media channels' policies, I don't think the SA government has any or much say over digital platforms.

Where there seems to be some form of engagement with the state is where legislation is concerned, but broadcasters generally produce news and editorials independently. Participants affiliated with the media through academia or professional associations noted that, while the state does not have complete control over the media, there is still a need for greater independent regulation. Participant 13 noted that the EC Act, which is supposedly designed to protect the public, seems to have some 'unattended consequences' for the freedom of the media. The concern was that the legislation gives leeway to pre-publication censorship and needs to be revisited.

Relationship Between the Media and the State

Overall, we have shown that the independence of both the ICASA and the NBC is lacking, or at best compromised. However, while some level of similarity exists between the two countries' regulatory bodies, our study shows that ICASA enjoys more freedom to operate in comparison to its Nigerian counterpart. What this reveals is the underlying relationship that exists between states and the media in Africa. Additionally, how freedom of expression was approached in the media laws are a potential cause for concern. This is because although freedom of expression is acknowledged in some of the South African laws, this acknowledgement was stated in a general fashion, with little or no explanation of what it entails. While the Constitution acknowledges and provides for freedom of expression, specifying a list of categories to which it applies, including press freedom, access, research and creativity, there was no real exploration of the essence of freedom of expression. The vital omission of this crucial area was a running theme through all the Acts analysed, with many of them simply referring to the principles set by the Constitution. For example, the 1999 Broadcasting Act states that: 'Freedom of expression and the journalistic, creative and programming independence of the broadcasters and independence of regulation are identified as guaranteed by the Constitution' (n.pag.). The only other mention of freedom of expression was with regard to the SABC (1999 Broadcasting Act: Section 6). The implication of this omission is the likelihood that the state–media relations in South Africa are defined by a flawed premise for freedom of expression.

Outside of this, however, there is the indication of an air of freedom in state-media relations in South Africa, given the comments by the interview participants. Participant 18 said:

> Throughout my 14-year experience as a traditional news broadcaster, [the] free press has been generally allowed to flourish in the country. The factor that now concerns me is unnamed political forces' usage of bots, for example, to sway the public with fake news misinformation online.

When participants were questioned about press freedom, most reiterated that the Constitution protected freedom of expression. In terms of restrictions, no participant said this was being encroached upon. 'There's no restriction really on the freedom of expression or the freedom of the press or freedom of speech and things like that'; Participant 12 said: 'It's just restricting in the sense that you have to meet certain language requirements, you need to meet requirements in terms of children's programming, adult content, education programming, information programming.'

In Nigeria, the state-media relationship is less optimistic, with participants describing it as operating under an atmosphere of distrust and adversarial tendencies. For one, the fact that the laws have been revisited less often (except in the case of the NBC code) indicates that the regulations do not account for the democratic transition that has taken place. This lack of renewal of the laws can be argued to indicate a restrictive socio-political environment and an attempt at paying lip service to democracy and transition, while there remains a continuation of military-era policies. Participant 15, for instance, said:

> When you see the fine that the NBC slams on [media houses], you will know that this thing is like killing a fly with a hammer [...] we still have a government that is still suffering from the carryover of the military era, and it is continuing.

When questioned about the relationship of news media/journalists with the state in terms of regulatory laws, the most frequent answers given by participants were those of fear, inconsistency in the government's approach to media policies and government interference. This fear, they said, stems from imaginary laws that do not exist on paper but that prevent journalists from reporting freely:

> There is always this kind of, you know, fear, among the journalists, even though in law, you don't have anything restricting them actually. But they get afraid of repercussions of doing things like investigative journalism and being so daring in what they report.
>
> (Participant 14)

As mentioned earlier, this vagueness in the enforcement of the NBC Code also applies to online broadcasting, where practitioners do not know when they are likely to violate it.

Participant 3, on the other hand, spoke of the government's fear of the power of the media and suggested that this contributes to the government's tendency to treat the media heavy-handedly:

> For the government, I think the greatest handicap is their fear of the media because they keep on thinking the media are too powerful to be left alone, so every government want[s] to clamp down [on] the media and control it.

This is tied to the idea of government interference when it comes to state-media relations. One participant felt that the media laws in themselves were not restrictive but that the conduct of the government in applying pressure presents the more significant problem. Another participant observed that the present state-media relationship is not in the public interest but benefits the government. Complementing this idea of public interest vs. government interest, Participant 2 warned on the extent of focus on government activities in media content:

> Sometimes governments want to be heard only about what they are doing, restraints come when you don't allow journalists to carry other information apart from

> government information. When a government insists on regulating the media to only say what the government wants it to say, it's a lot of control.

Participants in both countries further reflected on the theme of development media and how to define state–media relations. For the South African respondents, Participant 11 disagreed with the notion that news should be constructed around supporting developmental issues, as there were other ways to achieve this without involving news reporting. Participant 12, also South African, noted a need for a balancing act by the media between playing its watchdog role and supporting the government to further the development rationale. The participants generally agreed that the media should have the freedom to cover the stories they wished and be as critical as they desired. Equally, they should applaud when there was cause to do so and celebrate the country's achievements. Additionally, Participant 16 from South Africa warned that 'there are different efforts from a number of government bodies to try and stifle freedom of expression and limitations on freedom of expressions by online broadcasters and for that matter anybody who want to publish anything online'.

Non-broadcaster participants from both countries agreed that the media are generally more successful and able to achieve their objectives when they contribute to the country's development objectives. Participants 2 and 6 stated that, where the government allowed the media to work in partnership, there had been more positive accomplishments as the two parties worked towards a common goal, generally that of nation-building and training of journalists. Participant 3 suggested that the Nigerian media may consider being developmental, allowing itself to be controlled by the government to promote the developmental agenda. Considering the way the media has been used and treated in the history of both Nigeria and South Africa, it is justified to say that taking on this position would see a further deterioration of the struggle towards a democratic working environment for the media. There are also dangers of falling into the position in which the Nigerian media found itself in the early post-colonial era, where the images of development dominated the news despite the cracks that were beginning to appear in the economy (Yusuf 1988). This reaffirms the need for a clear and accurate balance between proclaiming government initiatives, critically engaging with the government according to the public's interest and educating the people on these issues.

Conclusion

In this chapter, we have looked at the role and regulatory structure of the media after democratic transitions in Africa. The study contributes to the understudied area of the role of the media in the democratization process in Sub-Saharan African countries by highlighting the impact of current media policies in Nigeria and South Africa. Our findings show that state-media relations in Nigeria and South Africa are still primarily defined by a pre-transition ethos. We captured this in the themes that found expression in both countries' various media laws and policies. The themes comprised open/vague interpretation of the policies, value construction in terms of development media or freedom of the press, contradictions in the standard-setting provisions of the laws, subtle restrictions and lack of independence of the regulators. The situation is more pronounced in Nigeria, where the legacies of military rule define the media laws. In South Africa, we recognized that there had been some changes. For instance, media policies have been constructed to reflect the new democratic order, especially as it includes those previously discriminated against during apartheid. The interview responses also show that the media system in South Africa is freer.

Given our findings, we uphold Sparks' (2011) argument on the idea of transitology. Our work shows that democratic transitions are hardly linear. Even between Nigeria and South Africa, two countries whose media system we define as subaltern and emblematic of the pre-transition state of affairs, there remain differences that reveal how divergent they are. We see this in how the regulation of broadcast licensing is structured. In Nigeria, anyone can apply for a license through the NBC to the president, who gives the final approval, and this licensing and registration requirement has been extended to online broadcasting, although it is not currently being enforced. In South Africa, potential broadcasters are required to wait on ICASA for an invitation to submit license applications. Despite how different they may seem in this way, we note that both systems bear implications for political economy considerations. For instance, we made the point in the chapter that the Nigerian system of licensing is problematic. In the discussion about political power and media power (Wasko 2005), the licensing arrangement indicates that political power is privileged, affording the state the liberty to define the parameters of access to broadcasting. There is then the possibility that those seeking broadcast licenses or license renewals will modify the tone of their content to suit the sovereign's wishes by using a public interest justification – and the danger, again, is that this can be extended to online broadcasting. Mabweazara et al. (2020: 2162) describe this as a situation where the media is 'beholding to the political leader' because the system of licensing is caught up in patronage networks aimed at solidifying the hold on power by the political and economic elite.

Political economy linkages can also be seen in the lack of independence of the regulatory bodies: ICASA and NBC. Here, we find that for both South Africa and Nigeria, the presidents through their respective ministers of information have substantial influence on ICASA and the NBC. The consequence of this is that the government effectively has power over the regulation of the broadcast industry, raising questions related to motive, restrictions and the expansion of state control. Perhaps in no other way is this more pronounced than in the development media (McQuail 1987) motive that countries like Nigeria have embraced since gaining independence. As Musa (1997) explains, this is because the political class has exploited the idea of development media and public interest. In Nigeria, for instance, national security justified on public interest grounds has been used to limit access to information (Obijiofor et al. 2017). Hence, we agree with Musa (1997) that there is a need to reconstruct the development of media rationale to make it less prone to political exploitation and to accommodate ideals such as press freedom.

Given the outcome of this research, it is pertinent to ask: what relevance does democracy have for journalism? After all, we have shown that the transition to democracy has done little or nothing in Nigeria and South Africa to cause a paradigm shift in terms of media structure, censorship and even capture. Josephi (2012) provides an answer as he shows that democracy itself may not matter to journalism. What matters in the end 'is not the political form of democracy that is essential to journalism practice but the freedom of expression and relative journalistic autonomy it affords' (Josephi 2012: 486). This means that the service of independent journalism can exist whether a country is democratic. As Josephi (2012) points out, the example of *Al-Jazeera* shows that independent media can come from a non-democratic country. Therefore, the critical ingredient in non- or quasi-democratic states is that 'journalists need the support and alliances of those who see value in such a service' (Josephi 2012: 486). In Russia, this support is provided by a faction of the political elite; in Qatar, it is provided by the sovereign (Josephi 2012).

We draw from this to argue that what matters when it comes to determining the structure of broadcasting in Africa is not the transition to democracy but the intention or motivation of the ruling elite or government. Mangui-Pippidi highlights this in stating that what determines whether a media system is corrupt is the character of the political system in place: 'Corruption of media systems can be encountered wherever one finds systemic corruption in a society' (Mangui-Pippidi 2012: 36). Therefore, what is important is not whether a system is democratic or autocratic but whether it is corrupt. As we have seen in recent years, a political system can be democratic (having features of elections, representativeness and the rule of law) and corrupt. The point is that, in theory, state intervention in the media is always present; what is variable is the political system's character and the sovereign's willingness to exploit this intervention.

An example was the Zuma era in South Africa, where media repression and intolerance became visible (Sparks 2011; Wasserman 2020). We suggest that what

South Africa witnessed then was a change in the character of the political system, which, although it remained democratic in theory, had been corrupted by the motives and intentions of the sovereign. The potential for the repression was always there; it only manifested when the sovereign chose to exploit it. Hence, we argue that in discussing media freedom and autonomy in Africa, it is the political system's character and nature that matters, not the political system itself. This explains why post-transition, the media in Nigeria and South Africa remain subaltern to the state and its apparatuses.

NOTES

1. Notice of this is contained in an advertorial released by the NBC on 10 June 2021.
2. Section 2, 1A(a), National Broadcasting Commission Act (Amendment), Bill 2019.
3. There is now the Freedom of Information Act, which was passed into law in 2011 and is meant to nullify the Official Secrets Act. Obijiofor et al. (2017) however note that government agencies still operate in secrecy, refusing at times to provide access to information.

REFERENCES

Agency Report (2020), '#EndSARS: NBC imposes N3m sanction each on AIT, Channels, Arise TV', *Premium Times*, 26 October, https://www.premiumtimesng.com/news/more-news/423162-endsars-nbc-imposes-n3m-sanction-each-on-ait-channels-arise-tv.html?tztc=1. Accessed 14 July 2024.

Barnett, Clive (1998), 'The contradictions of broadcasting reform in post-apartheid South Africa', *Review of African Political Economy*, 25:78, pp. 551–70.

Barnett, Clive (1999), 'The limits of media democratization in South Africa: Politics, privatization and regulation', *Media, Culture & Society*, 21:5, pp. 649–71.

Berger, Guy (1998), 'Media and democracy in Southern Africa', *Review of African Political Economy*, 25:78, pp. 599–610.

Dennis, Everette (1974), 'The press and the public interest: A definitional dilemma', *DePaul Law Review*, 23:3, pp. 937–60.

Downs, Anthony (1962), 'The public interest: Its meaning in a democracy', *Social Research*, 29:1, pp. 1–36.

Fourie, Pieter (2002), 'Rethinking the role of the media in South Africa', *Communicare: Journal for Communication Sciences in Southern Africa*, 21:1, pp. 17–40.

Gates, Scott, Hegre, Håvard, Jones, Mark and Strand, Håvard (2007), 'Democratic waves?: Global patterns of democratisation, 1800–2000', National Political Science Conference, Trondheim, Norway, 3–5 January.

Gedye, Lloyd (2005), 'Taking the I out of Icasa', *Mail & Guardian*, 30 September, https://mg.co.za/article/2005-09-30-taking-the-i-out-of-icasa/. Accessed 14 July 2024.

Giles, John (2023), 'Protection from State Information Bill – POSI Bill', Michalsons, 16 November, https://www.michalsons.com/blog/protection-of-state-information-bill-posi/18015. Accessed 20 June 2024.

Gunitsky, Seva (2018), 'Democratic waves in historical perspective', *Perspectives on Politics*, 16:3, pp. 634–51.

Huntington, Samuel (1991), 'Democracy's third wave', *Journal of Democracy*, 2:2, pp. 12–34.

Hydén, Goran, Leslie, Michael and Ogundimu, Folu (2002), *Media and Democracy in Africa*, New Brunswick: Transaction Publishers.

ICASA (2024), 'Our mandate', *ICasa*, https://www.icasa.org.za/pages/our-mandate. Accessed 4 June 2024.

Igwe, Ignatius (2021), 'No Channels Television anchor was arrested', *Channels*, 26 August, https://www.channelstv.com/2021/08/26/no-channels-television-anchor-was-arrested/. Accessed 13 June 2024.

Iosifidis, Petros (2011), *Global Media and Communication Policy*, London: Palgrave Macmillan.

Jebril, Nael, Stetka, Václav and Loveless, Matthew (2013), *Media and Democratisation: What Is Known About the Role of Mass Media in Transitions to Democracy*, Oxford: Reuters Institute for the Study of Journalism.

Josephi, Beate (2012), 'How much democracy does journalism need?' *Journalism*, 14:4, pp. 474–89.

Mabweazara, Hayes, Mawindi, Muneri, Taurai, Cleophas and Ndlovu, Faith (2020), 'News "media capture", relations of patronage and clientelist practices in sub-Saharan Africa: An interpretive qualitative analysis', *Journalism Studies*, 21:15, pp. 2154–75.

Mansell, Robin (2004), 'Political economy, power and new media', *New Media & Society*, 6:1, pp. 96–105.

McChesney, Robert (2000), 'The political economy of communication and the future of the field', *New Media & Society*, 22, pp. 109–16.

McQuail, Denis (1987), *Mass Communication Theory: An Introduction*, London: Sage.

Mosco, Vincent (2008), 'Current trends in the political economy of communication', *Global Media Journal*, 1:1, pp. 45–63.

Mtimde, Lumko (2000), 'Radio broadcasting in South Africa: An overview', *International Journal of Cultural Studies*, 3:2, pp. 173–79.

Mukhudwana, Rofhiwa (2022), 'The rise of peripheral actors in media regulation in South Africa: An entry of social media mob(s)', *African Journalism Studies*, 42:4, pp. 153–78.

Mungui-Pippidi, Alina (2012), 'Freedom with impartiality: The vicious circle of media capture', in P. Gross and K. Jakubowicz (eds), *Media Transformations in the Post-Communist World*, Lanham: Lexington Books, pp. 33–49.

Musa, Bala (1997), 'Uses and abuses of development media theory in sub-Saharan Africa: Critique of a quasi-descriptive/prescriptive theory', *Ecquid Novi: African Journalism Studies*, 18:1, pp. 132–47.

NGC Discussions Document (2015), *The Battle of Ideas, Media Transformation & Diversity, and Accelerating Digital Future*, https://www.anc1912.org.za/wp-content/uploads/2021/03/NGC-2015-Discussion-Document-Communications-and-Battle-of-Ideas.pdf. Accessed 4 June 2024.

Obijiofor, Levi, Murray, Richard and Singh, Shailendra (2017), 'Changes in journalism in two post-authoritarian non-Western countries', *The International Communication Gazette*, 79:4, pp. 379–99.

Ogunleye, Oluyemisi O. (2010), 'Let the subaltern speak!: Bringing African news industries into the 21st century', Ph.D. thesis, Birmingham: Birmingham City University.

Oyero, Kayode (2021), 'NBC orders TV, radio stations not to name victims, report "details" of terrorist attacks', *The Punch*, 16 July, https://punchng.com/breaking-nbc-orders-tv-radio-stations-not-to-name-victims-report-details-of-terrorist-attacks/. Accessed 13 June 2024.

Rodrigues, Usha (2010), 'The promise of a new media and development agenda', *Media International Australia*, 137:1, pp. 36–46.

SERAP (2021), 'SERAP sues Buhari, wants Court to declare gag order on reporting of terrorist attacks illegal', SERAP, 25 July, https://serap-nigeria.org/2021/07/25/serap-sues-buhari-wants-court-to-declare-gag-order-on-reporting-of-terrorist-attacks-illegal/. Accessed 23 November 2022.

Shibayan, Dyepkazah (2020), 'NBC board: Lai amended broadcasting code alone – His action is illegal', *The Cable*, 13 August, https://www.thecable.ng/nbc-board-lai-amended-broadcasting-code-alone-his-action-is-illegal/. Accessed 12 June 2024.

Sobel, Meghan and McIntyre, Karen (2018), 'The state of journalism and press freedom in postgenocide Rwanda', *Journalism & Mass Communication Quarterly*, 96:2, pp. 1–21.

Sparks, Colin (2011), 'South African media in comparative perspective', *Ecquid Novi: African Journalism Studies*, 32:2, pp. 5–19.

Spivak, Gayatri (1988), 'Can the subaltern speak?' in C. Nelson and L. Grossberg (eds), *Marxism and the Interpretation of Culture*, Urbana/Chicago: University of Illinois Press, pp. 271–313.

Steenveld, Lynette (2012), 'The pen and the sword: Media transformation and democracy after apartheid', *Ethical Space: The International Journal of Communication Ethics*, 9:2/3, pp. 125–40.

Wasko, Janet (2005), 'Studying the political economy of media and information', *Comunicação e Sociedade*, 7, pp. 25–48.

Wasserman, Herman (2020), 'The state of South African media: A space to contest democracy', *Publizistik*, 65, pp. 451–65.

Yusuf, Bilkisu (1988), 'The Nigerian media and socio-economic crisis', in M. N. Alkali (ed.), *Mass Communication in Africa: A Book of Readings*, Enugu: Delta Publications.

PART 3

DIGITAL MEDIA CENSORSHIP: FRICTIONS, TENSIONS, REACTIONS

8

Balancing Freedom with Responsibility or Simply Pandering to Political Whims: An Analysis of Kenya's 2018 Computer Misuse and Cybercrimes Act

Muthoni Esther King'ori and Maureen Syallow

Introduction

The Kenyan media is considered to be fairly independent when compared with those of other countries in Sub-Saharan Africa. This independence has been attributed to the entrenchment of media freedom in Kenya's 2010 Constitution. One of the relevant articles of the Kenyan Constitution that expressly speak about media freedom is Article 34, which guarantees 'freedom and independence of electronic, print and all other types of media' (Constitution of Kenya 2010). Limitations to this freedom are outlined in Article 33(2). These limitations include 'propaganda for war, incitement to violence, hate speech, or advocacy of hatred' (Constitution of Kenya 2010). Article 33(1) focuses on freedom of expression. This article provides that freedom of expression includes the right to 'seek, receive, or impart information or ideas' (Constitution of Kenya 2010). These freedoms have shaped media regulation debates in Kenya since the promulgation of the current Constitution in 2010.

Apart from the 2010 Constitution, there are a number of other laws that govern Kenyan media. Some are independent Acts, while others are contained in the Penal Code. Some notable laws that regulate the Kenyan media, as outlined by Media Council of Kenya (2020), are the Media Council Act, Access to Information Act, the Kenya Information and Communications Act, the Books and Newspapers Act, the Kenya Broadcasting Corporation Act, the Preservation of Public Security Act, the National Police Service Act, the Prevention of Terrorism Act, the Official

Secrets Act, the Kenya Defence Forces Act, the Defamation Act, the Computer Misuse and Cybercrimes Act, the Data Protection Act and the Copyright Act.

An interesting thing to note is that a number of these laws are related to security matters. Three of these laws are the Preservation of Public Security Act, the National Police Service Act and the Prevention of Terrorism Act. The Preservation of Public Security Act is a holdover colonial law enacted in 1960, three years before Kenya attained independence (Media Council of Kenya 2020). The law gives the president 'sweeping powers' which threaten freedoms of expression and of the media, both directly and indirectly (Media Council of Kenya 2020: 36). The National Police Service Act interferes with the freedom to access information, as the law bars police officers from divulging information deemed to be sensitive. The Prevention of Terrorism Act outlines various prohibitions against disseminating information that might incite terrorist activities. The Act further gives security agencies powers to intercept communication they believe might be used for terrorism purposes (Media Council of Kenya 2020). Other laws that are relevant to this chapter will be discussed in the section on the process that led to the enactment of the Computer Misuse and Cybercrimes Act, 2018. Experts have raised concerns about the numerous laws governing the media. For instance, the Kenya Media Sector Working Group has recommended harmonizing these laws (Moturi 2023). Mwita (2021) contends that these laws provide a challenging regulatory framework for the media. He further argues that the 'multiple legislations and policies' are aimed at curtailing media independence and the 'fundamental rights of citizens' (Mwita 2021: 33).

Based on the foregoing, the main objective of this chapter is to evaluate the intentions behind the enactment of the Computer Misuse and Cybercrimes Act. We divide this objective into two sub-objectives. First, the chapter examines stakeholders' participation in the process of enacting the law; second, it outlines the complaints that arose after the enactment of the law. To address these objectives, we analysed information from media and online news articles, journal articles, court cases and rulings on the Computer Misuse and Cybercrimes Act, 2018. The two objectives were instrumental in enabling an understanding of the various interests behind the enactment of the law. Of interest was the importance of knowing whether the enactment of the law was an effort to entrench ethics and social responsibility in the Kenyan digital space or an attempt to silence government critics.

Media Regulatory Frameworks for the Digital Space

This study adopted the normative media theoretical framework. The framework is appropriate for the research as it aids in exploring the reasoning behind the enactment of Kenya's Computer Misuse and Cybercrimes Act. Normative media theory examines how media ought to operate and the nature of their relationship with the government and society. According to the theory, media adopt 'the system and colouration of the political, economic and social environment where it operates' (Samson Owolabi 2023: 1). In addition, the theory provides a framework that helps measure media performance and gives conditions that could lead to government intervention if need be (Fourie 2017; Piontek 2016). The normative theory outlines how political systems shape media in different countries and elaborates on the media's role in championing democracy (Fourie 2017). The theory is ideal for studying how media operate in specific political systems (Baran and Davis 2015).

This study is guided by one aspect of normative theory, which is the social responsibility theory. Social responsibility is relevant as it examines how the media can uphold public interest by adopting best practices. However, the theory 'allows reasonable government media control' (Baran and Davis 2015: 80). Coe describes social responsibility as a theory that 'provides a more appropriate normative foundation for the modern media' (Coe 2021: 9). In this chapter, we consider the theory in relation to both mainstream and citizen journalists. Citizen journalists are critical in ensuring multiple voices are heard in the public sphere (Coe 2021).

Several issues that are relevant to this study emerge from the theoretical framework. One is the social and political context in which Kenya's Computer Misuse and Cybercrimes Act was enacted. Another is the performance and accountability of media practitioners and citizen journalists before and during the enactment of the law. In addition, a number of questions arise. Was the regulation necessary? What role has the law played in shaping Kenyan media into one that adheres to the values and expectations of the Kenyan citizenry? Was the regulation an attempt to exert government control on the media? A normative media framework is instrumental in helping us provide answers to the above questions concerning the Computer Misuse and Cybercrimes Act.

The questions also relate to the increased spread of fake news and hate speech via online platforms, which has continued to be a major challenge for governments, media practitioners and other stakeholders. Santuraki (2019: 143) describes hate speech as the dissemination of information to incite hatred or violence against groups of people, mainly based on race, ethnicity and religion. They define fake news as 'news items or information seemingly untrue or erroneous yet designated as realistic or accurate' (Santuraki 2019: 144). Countries around the globe have attempted to establish appropriate frameworks to deal with the two vices. However, there have been concerns that while hate speech and fake news need to be dealt with, governments may use the purported spread of the two as an excuse to introduce regulation that curbs media freedom (Santuraki 2019; Garbe et al. 2023).

Besides hate speech, another contemporary concern arising from the digital space is the increasing use of AI. Scholars note that AI regulation should focus on protecting the right to freedom of thought and opinion (Alegre 2021). Regulators are also pondering how to stop or even ban technology that manipulates the way humans think (Alegre 2021). A major concern is an ability that data and AI have to 'get inside people's minds to make inferences about how people are thinking and feeling, or to influence their thoughts and emotions to produce particular behaviours' (Alegre 2021: n.pag.). Alegre recommends reviewing existing regulations to address manipulation issues raised against AI. At the time of writing this chapter, the government has yet to amend Kenya's media regulatory framework to integrate the intricacies of AI.

Overall, a key issue in the debate that this chapter concerns itself with is the nature of regulation that should be adopted for the digital space. Some scholars have advocated for self-regulation and legally backed standards (Burri 2022). While Africa is still in the process of agreeing on frameworks that suit its unique contexts, the Global North has adopted a number of approaches. An example is the European Union, which has four approaches to regulating the digital space (Durach et al. 2020). The four are self-regulation, where the digital channels regulate themselves; co-regulation, where digital channels cooperate with stakeholders such as the government to regulate themselves; direct regulation, which involves enforcement of legal measures; and audience-centred solutions, such as fact-checking and media literacy.

Also, a debate on the regulation of online content must include social media influencers. Mahy et al. (2022) explore an online regulatory framework targeting influencers in Indonesia who use their platforms to market products and messages. The state regulation of social media platforms in Indonesia is done through the Electronic Transactions and Information Law (Mahy et al. 2022). The findings are that the law has some excessive elements, namely 'broadly defined provisions and heavy maximum criminal penalties' that may cause 'injustice that is out of proportion to any harm caused' (Mahy et al. 2022: 5890). In addition, the researchers found that besides state regulation, online users played a big part in holding influencers accountable for their ethical conduct through criticism of unbecoming behaviour.

Another area of concern in the online regulation debate is the issue of fake news and hate speech. Researchers have analysed how this issue is reported in Africa. Garbe et al. (2023) conducted research that found that governments are central actors in online content regulation in Africa. Findings from analysis of data collected from over 7000 news articles from 47 countries indicated that states that are hostile towards media are more likely to propose technological responses such as internet lockdowns, while those who value media freedom are more likely to favour legal means in tackling hate speech and fake news.

This chapter draws from and contributes to these existing studies by seeking to analyse the role of the government and other key stakeholders in the enactment of the Computer Misuse and Cybercrimes Act. Consequently, we note the importance of examining the relationship between the Kenyan government and the media. Kamau (2018) posits that the Kenyan government has continually attempted to exercise control over the country's media, given that the government has occasionally intimidated and harassed the media. The harassment has been through public castigation of media and journalists, enactment of bad laws and withholding of advertising revenue (Kamau 2018).

Scholars have analysed some of the Kenyan media laws in question. One contention has been the overlap of laws that regulate the media in Kenya (Otieno 2017). The overlap has resulted in calls for a review of the laws so that media regulation can be better coordinated (Otieno 2017). Other scholars have investigated how media houses implement accountability policies and practices and the challenges that are occasioned by the implementation process (Obuya and Ong'ondo 2019). They found that there are a number of obstacles that prevent media houses from fully implementing accountability practices. The obstacles include institutional challenges and issues caused by special interest groups (Obuya and Ong'ondo 2019).

The cited literature demonstrates that scholars have researched regulatory frameworks of online media. Some studies have examined the ethical and legal issues that arise from digital communication. Other studies have focused on the role of governments in the regulation of the digital space. While these studies have looked at regulatory frameworks for the digital space from a broad perspective, this chapter narrows down to a specific analysis of stakeholders involved in the legislative process. Our research examines the various stakeholders that were involved in the enactment process and the criticisms that arose later on. This analysis helps determine if the process was mainly government-driven to serve state interests to the exclusion of the voices of key stakeholders. The literature review uncovers a number of questions regarding Kenya's Computer Misuse and Cybercrimes Act, 2018, which we consider in this chapter. How has the Kenyan cybercrime law tackled the issue of social media influencers and citizen journalists? Is the enactment of the Computer Misuse and Cybercrimes Act an attempt by the Kenyan government to use legal means to curb hate speech and disinformation? Is the legislation an extension of government harassment of the Kenyan media?

Methodology

The study adopted a detailed qualitative content analysis approach to analyse the process that led to the enactment of the Computer Misuse and Cybercrimes

Act of 2018. Secondary data from various sources were used to address the study objectives. These include policy papers, which we reviewed to ascertain the government's objectives and perspectives underpinning the law; stakeholder submissions, which offered insights into the numerous interests from the civil society, concerned parties, and industry experts; and relevant court documents to highlight the legal challenges that followed the implementation of the law.

Qualitative content analysis was appropriate for the study as it examines 'meanings, themes and patterns that may be manifest or latent in a particular text' (Zhang and Wildemuth 2017: 318). We employed qualitative content analysis to understand the interests behind the enactment of the cybercrime law and the sentiments that emerged from the various stakeholders. The documents were selected purposively so as to provide data that responds to the study objectives. Among the documents analysed was the Computer Misuse and Cybercrimes Act, a judgement of a case filed by bloggers (*BAKE* v. *Attorney General and 3 others*, 2019), news articles and government policy papers.

Findings and Discussions

Process of Enactment – Kenya's Computer Misuse and Cybercrimes Act, 2018

We contend that before a law is enacted in any democratic country, there are key groups that should be involved in the legislative process. The involvement of these groups certifies that a wide range of perspectives have been considered and that the law is beneficial to citizens (Marleau and Montpetit 2000). In the Kenyan context, public participation is enshrined in Article 118(B)(1) of the Constitution, which states that 'parliament shall facilitate public participation and involvement in the legislative and other business of parliament and its committees' (Constitution of Kenya 2010). Article 119(1) empowers citizens to 'petition parliament to consider any matter within its authority, including to enact, amend or repeal any legislation' .

Table 8.1 indicates the stakeholders who should have been involved in the process of enacting the Computer Misuse and Cybercrimes Act.

The study findings, as shown above, indicate that key stakeholders in the process of enacting the Kenya Computer Misuse and Cybercrimes Act, 2018 were left out. This is contrary to the laid down procedure in Article 118 of the Kenyan Constitution, which requires parliament to 'facilitate public participation' in legislative processes (Constitution of Kenya 2010). The study probed further to establish those involved in the process of enacting this law. To this end, we analysed information from different publications, including the special issues of the Kenya Gazette Supplement No. 60 (Acts No. 5) published on 16 May 2018.

TABLE 8.1: Stakeholders in the legislative process.

Name	Role	Yes/No
Legislators	Propose, debate, amend, and vote on laws	Yes
Committees	Review legislation in detail, hold hearings	Yes
Executive branch	Propose and draft legislation	Yes
Legal experts	Ensure legality and clarity of laws	No
Interest groups and lobbyists	Influence legislation for specific interests	No
Civil society and advocacy groups	Represent public interest and perspectives	No
The public	Provide input through consultations	No
Academics and researchers	Offer insights and recommendations	No
Regulatory agencies	Advise on implementation and enforcement	No
Media (mainstream and social)	Inform the public and influence opinion	No
International bodies and foreign governments	Consult for international implications	No
Businesses and industry representatives	Offer industry perspective and impacts	No
Labour unions and worker representatives	Represent labour interests and conditions	No

The process of enacting Kenya's Computer Misuse and Cybercrimes Act, 2018 involved various members from different government sectors, including the Kenya Defense Forces, the National Police Service, the National Intelligence Service, the Ministry of Interior and coordination of national government, representatives from the office of the Attorney General, Director of Public Prosecutions, Communications Authority of Kenya and the Central Bank of Kenya. The Cybercrime Bill was drafted by the office of the Director of Public Prosecution and later released for deliberation by the ICT ministry (Kiai et al. 2021). Kiai et al. (2021) note that there were 'competing interests' among government agencies during deliberations on the legislation.

From the analysis, it is important to note that while the stakeholders involved played crucial roles in shaping the legislation, they do not necessarily represent a complete picture of the Kenyan public. The legislative process typically involves various stakeholders, but there was a gap in ensuring the inclusion of every individual or group within the public. The Bloggers Association of Kenya (BAKE) filed a petition at the High Court of Kenya challenging the composition of the National Computer and Cybercrimes Coordination Committee (*BAKE* v. *AG and 3 others*, 2019). In the petition, BAKE gave a breakdown of the composition of the coordination committee as: Principal Secretary, Internal Security; Principal Secretary, ICT; Attorney General; Chief of the Kenya Defense Forces; Inspector General of the National Police Service; the Director General, National Intelligence Service; Director-General, Communication Authority of Kenya; Director of Public Prosecutions; the Governor of the Central Bank; and the Director of the Committee. BAKE's contention was that the composition of the Coordination Committee lacked diversity as those in charge of the named institutions were male (*BAKE* v. *AG and 3 others*, 2019). In addition, the members of the committee were all state officials.

Part of the petition read:

> The petitioner further contends that the requirement of public participation was not satisfactorily met during the consideration of the Bill and that standing orders 130, 131 and 133 of the National Assembly standing orders are inconsistent with the constitution in so far as they allow the inclusion of clauses to a bill without public participation.
>
> (*BAKE* v. *AG and 3 others*, 2019: n.pag.)

Owing to these findings, the study established a lack of inclusion of important groups such as citizens, civil society, social media influencers and bloggers. As discussed earlier in the chapter, public participation is a right guaranteed in Article 118 of the Kenyan Constitution. The petition by the bloggers was, however, dismissed on the grounds that the petitioner had not demonstrated that the Committee had been constituted and was in violation of the provision of Article 27 of the Constitution (High Court at Nairobi, Milimani Law Courts n.d). However, the Committee was eventually set up with a membership structure wholly comprising state officers. This demonstrates the continuation of a process that shuts out major stakeholders in the enactment of the law. In order for a law to be embraced by a majority, the enactment process must include stakeholders such as government agencies, legislators, legal experts, civil society organizations, private sector representatives and academic experts who bring different perspectives, expertise and interests to the table (Marleau and Montpetit 2000). For example, the Media Council Act, 2013, which is a key law that outlines standards for the Kenyan media, is a legislation that emerged from years of consultation among key stakeholders.

In a democratic society, the involvement of various stakeholders in the legislative process is not only a matter of procedural fairness but also a cornerstone for the legitimacy and effectiveness of the law. The analysis of Kenya's Computer Misuse and Cybercrimes Act, 2018, when viewed through the lens of stakeholder involvement, presents a nuanced picture. Several key issues arise when stakeholders are inadequately involved in formulating such critical legislation. First, the law may suffer from a lack of representativeness, failing to reflect the diverse interests and concerns of the broader society. This can lead to a misalignment between the law's provisions and the real-world challenges it is meant to address. Second, insufficient stakeholder engagement can lead to a deficit in public trust and a lack of buy-in from those who are governed by the law, which is particularly problematic in areas as dynamic and rapidly evolving as cybercrime. Furthermore, the potential for unanticipated consequences increases when stakeholder expertise is not leveraged during the drafting phase. These could range from technical loopholes that cybercriminals could exploit to overly broad terms that could inadvertently stifle innovation and freedom of expression. The latter is a crucial consideration, given the vital role that digital communication plays in modern societies.

In the case of Kenya, the enactment of the Computer Misuse and Cybercrimes Act, 2018 proceeded with minimal stakeholder input. Hence, the concerns and eventual complaints that arose post-enactment are understandable and, perhaps, could have been mitigated if a more inclusive approach had been adopted. A retrospective acknowledgement of this, paired with a commitment to involve a broader array of voices in future legislative revisions, could help remedy some of the trust issues and practical challenges the current version of the law faces.

Also, while the Act may have been well-intentioned in its aim to address the real and pressing issues of cybercrime, the critical examination of its enactment process suggests that a more collaborative and transparent approach involving all relevant stakeholders could enhance the law's effectiveness and legitimacy. Engaging with technology experts, civil society groups, the private sector and the public at large in an ongoing dialogue would not only refine the existing legal framework but also ensure that it evolves in step with technological advances and societal values.

Criticisms of the Act

There were numerous criticisms from international bodies, NGOs and Civil Society Organizations after the passing of the Computer Misuse and Cybercrime Act 2018. One of the complaints was raised by the Committee to Protect Journalists (CPJ), which observed that the law would 'criminalise free speech, with journalists and bloggers likely to be among the first victims' (Committee to Protect Journalists 2018: n.pag.). The CPJ noted that some aspects of the new law that focused on curtailing speech that would hurt the 'reputation of a person' were a reintroduction of 'criminal defamation law' that had been nullified by the Kenyan High Court in 2017 (Committee to Protect Journalists 2018: n.pag.).

President Uhuru Kenyatta, despite receiving recommendations to return the bill for further revision, proceeded to sign it into law. This decision was met with disapproval from various media stakeholders. For example, the Kenya Editors Guild posted a tweet stating: 'When the public's right to know is threatened, and when the rights of free speech and free press are at risk, all of the other liberties we hold dear are endangered' (Muinde 2018: n.pag.). Reuters was concerned about the likelihood of the law being 'exploited to repress civil liberties' (Reuters Staff 2018: n.pag.). Experts felt that some aspects of the law were problematic as they put in place 'punitive measures for sharing certain information online' (Mwita 2021: 32). Some described the law as harsh because of the 'hefty fines and lengthy jail terms' (Ngirachu 2018: n.pag.). As examined above, the BAKE filed a petition at the High Court of Kenya on 29 May 2018, Petition 206 of 2019, to challenge the constitutionality of 26 sections of the Act. Some of the complaints indicated that the new law contravened the constitutional provisions on freedom of expression, freedom of opinion, freedom and security of the person, freedom of the media, right to privacy, right to property and the right to a fair hearing (*Bloggers Association of Kenya* [*BAKE*] v. *Attorney General and 3 others*; Article 19 East Africa & another [Interested Parties 2020 eKLR]).

The Law Society of Kenya (LSK) joined the efforts to declare sections of the Computer Misuse and Cybercrimes Act, 2018 as illegal. Through lawyer Waikwa Wanyoike, the LSK argued that the law would violate freedoms guaranteed in the Kenyan Constitution. The LSK was concerned that the cybercrimes law infringed on rights granted under Article 33 (Freedom of Expression), Article 34 (Freedom of the Media) and Article 35 (Freedom to Access Information). In the suit, the LSK argued that the Cybercrimes Act violated the rights of citizens to criticize and hold the government accountable. There were concerns about potential infringements on privacy rights and freedom of expression (Muendo 2018). There was an indication that certain provisions in the act are overly broad or ambiguous, potentially allowing for the abuse of power or chilling effect on legitimate online activities (Mzalendo Trust 2019). Mzalendo Trust argued that 'instead of placing more emphasis on crimes found in cyberspace and those crimes related to ICT systems, transactions and communications, the Act goes above and beyond to deal with free speech' (Mzalendo Trust 2019: 11). Media stakeholders felt that the Act provided a broad and vague definition of fake news (Mzalendo Trust 2019: 11). These concerns are related to Section 22(1) of the Act, which describes false publications as 'misleading or fictitious data' intended to 'misinform'.

Additionally, there was concern related to overreach and vagueness – individuals, lawyers and influencers across the country contended that some provisions of the

Act were overly broad, vague and lacked clear definitions, which could lead to arbitrary interpretation and application (Muendo 2018; Walubengo and Mutemi 2018). They expressed concerns that such ambiguity might result in a chilling effect on online activities and restrict the legitimate exercise of freedom of expression. For example, there is the section on Jurisdiction and Cooperation, which asserts jurisdiction over offences committed within Kenya or offences committed by Kenyan citizens regardless of the location. This encourages international cooperation in the investigation and prosecution of cybercrimes by allowing the Kenyan government to enter into agreements with other countries. How well will this be handled to avoid prosecuting the wrong victims who might be caught in identity theft issues? Considering that some stakeholders, such as international organizations like Interpol and Reporters Without Borders, were left out, does the Kenyan government have the proper mechanisms to carry out this exercise independently? These are some of the concerns that stakeholders have raised. Some follow-up issues included lack of public awareness and consultation, balancing cybersecurity and individual rights, and impact on business and innovation.

Assessing the various petitions and complaints that arose from the passing of the bill, it is evident that not all stakeholders were involved in the process of enactment. All the complaints contend that the right to seek or receive information provided under Article 35 of the Constitution of Kenya has been infringed. The plaintiffs assert that freedom of expression and the expression of views and opinions are prohibited by some sections of this law. From the thread of tweets and responses that we considered, the study establishes that most citizens in Kenya were aware of what the government was trying to do but their main complaint was that the law might work for government officials only. There is also the fear that the law will provide a cover for corrupt officials because journalists and social media users who wish to disseminate information on the same will be prevented from doing so for fear of prosecution. Due to these complaints, the High Court suspended the contested 26 sections on 30 May 2018. However, after a full hearing, the suspension was lifted on 20 February 2020 by the same court which dismissed the petition (Mwita 2021). Furthermore, the Computer Misuse and Cybercrimes Act was one of the laws temporarily declared unconstitutional by the High Court in 2021 because it was passed by the National Assembly without the Senate's input (Wanambisi and Mwangi 2021). However, this ruling was later suspended by the court to allow the two parliaments to 'regularize the laws' (Kiai et al. 2021: n.pag.).

On 7 July 2021, six civil society organizations sent a memorandum to Aden Duale, who was, at the time, the majority leader in Kenya's National Assembly, protesting some proposed amendments to the Computer Misuse and Cybercrimes Act, 2018 (Article 19 2021). Duale proposed the amendments by tabling the

Computer Misuse and Cybercrimes (Amendment) Bill, 2021 in parliament. The organizations, which asked that the bill be withdrawn in its entirety, expressed apprehension that the proposed sections were giving the government power to 'interfere with access to communication platforms and digital technologies' (Article 19 2021: n.pag.). This is as a result of the proposal to give the National Computer and Cybercrimes Coordination Committee the power to render 'websites inaccessible in the Republic of Kenya' (Article 19 2021: n.pag.). Other stakeholders have also opposed the amendment and urged parliament to await the determination of a Court of Appeal case challenging the High Court ruling that declared the Computer Misuse and Cybercrimes Act, 2018 constitutional (Access Now 2021). Gakii (2022) argues that the bill interferes with the freedoms of expression and access to information and introduces extremely exorbitant fines. These controversies that have trailed the Computer Misuse and Cybercrimes Act might have been avoided if meaningful and broad-based stakeholder involvement had taken place in the enactment of the law. By the time of publishing this chapter, the Kenyan Parliament had published a Computer Misuse and Cybercrimes Act (Amendment) Bill, 2024. One of the key proposals in the amendment bill is a provision that seeks to block Kenyans from accessing websites and applications deemed a threat to cybersecurity (Kopiyo 2024).

Conclusion

The study findings indicate that Kenya's Computer Misuse and Cybercrimes Act of 2018 is an important legislation aimed at addressing cyberspace issues such as cyberbullying, cyber terrorism, child pornography and electronic fraud, among others. However, the environment under which the law was enacted was highly politicized and hardly allowed for engaging all the relevant stakeholders. Drafters of the law appeared focused on cyber-related issues but at the same time brought in sections that seemed politically motivated with a view to curtailing media-related freedoms granted by the Constitution. Stakeholders who have challenged the law in court argue that the Act brings in sections that were nullified in other laws. For example, Sections 22 and 23 (touching on the publication of false information) appear similar to laws that have been nullified by the courts for infringing on freedom of expression.

The enactment of the Kenya Computer Misuse and Cybercrimes Act in 2018 has garnered a diverse range of responses, reflecting both commendations and concerns from different quarters. Advocates of the Act extol its virtues for safeguarding businesses and individuals both within Kenya and abroad, offering a layer of security against cyber threats. The Act is also heralded for bolstering cybersecurity measures by establishing a robust legal framework aimed at curbing cybercrimes, including online fraud, cyberbullying and hacking, which are particularly pertinent issues affecting the youth. Furthermore, the legislation's stringent penalties are seen as an effective deterrent, signalling a clear warning to would-be cyber offenders and mitigating the frequency of cybercrimes. However, the Act is not without its critics. They point to the use of broad and vague language within the Act, expressing concern that such terminology could be weaponized by government entities to undermine the autonomy of both traditional and social media, thereby stifling the media's vital role in monitoring government activities.

The debate continues with discussions around finding the right equilibrium between advancing cybersecurity and upholding individual freedoms. A delicate balance is required to ensure that while Kenya's cyberspace should be secured, this security should not come at the expense of essential liberties such as freedom of expression and the right to privacy. Given the evolving nature of technology and cyber threats, it is recommended that the Act should be consistently updated to address evolving cybercrime trends and challenges. Regular revisions can help ensure that the legislation remains relevant and effective in combating new forms of cybercrimes. In addition, government agencies and regulatory bodies should embrace the suggestion of experts that media regulation be implemented alongside media literacy (Selvi 2022). The combination of regulation and media literacy campaigns will give journalists and social media content creators skills on how to be socially responsible in the digital space (Muthoni 2017; Mutua and Zhang 2021).

REFERENCES

Access Now (2021), 'Kenya must bin its repressive Computer Misuse and Cybercrimes Bill', Access Now, 16 December, https://www.accessnow.org/press-release/kenya-must-bin-computer-misuse-and-cybercrimes-bill/. Accessed 4 April 2022.

Alegre, Susie (2021), 'Regulating around freedom in the "forum internum"', *ERA Forum*, 21, pp. 591–604, https://doi.org/10.1007/s12027-020-00633-7.

Andama v. *Director of Public Prosecution & Another* (2018), Petition No. 214 of 2018, High Court of Nairobi, http://kenyalaw.org/caselaw/cases/view/179722/. Accessed 7 April 2022.

Andare v. *Attorney General & 2 others* (2016), Petition No. 149 of 2015, High Court of Nairobi, http://kenyalaw.org/caselaw/cases/view/121033/. Accessed 14 March 2022.

Article 19 (2021), 'Kenya: Withdraw proposed amendments to cybercrimes law', *Article 19*, 7 July, https://www.article19.org/resources/kenya-withdraw-proposed-amendments-to-cybercrimes-law/. Accessed 5 April 2022.

Baran, Stanley J. and Davis, Dennis K. (2015), *Mass Communication Theory: Foundations, Ferment, and Future*, 7th ed., Boston, MA: Cengage Learning.

Brenner, Susan W. (2007), 'Cybercrime: Re-thinking crime control strategies', in Y. Jewkes (ed.), *Crime Online*, Portland: Willan Publishing, pp. 12–28.

Bloggers Association of Kenya (BAKE) v. Attorney General & 3 others; Article 19 East Africa & another (Interested Parties) (2020), Petition No. 206 of 2019, *Kenya Law*, http://kenyalaw.org/caselaw/cases/view/191276/. Accessed 22 April 2022.

Burri, Mira (2022), 'Fake news in times of pandemic and beyond: Enquiry into the rationales for regulating information platforms', in K. Mathis and A. Tor (eds), *Law and Economics of the Coronavirus Crisis: Economic Analysis of Law in European Legal Scholarship*, vol. 13, Cham: Springer, pp. 31–58, https://doi.org/10.1007/978-3-030-95876-3_2.

Coe, Peter (2021), *Media Freedom in the Age of Citizen Journalism*, Cheltenham: Edward Elgar Publishing.

Committee to Protect Journalists (2018), 'Kenya president should not sign cybercrime bill into law', *CPJ*, 10 May, https://cpj.org/2018/05/kenyan-president-should-not-sign-cybercrime-bill-i/. Accessed 22 April 2022.

Communications Authority of Kenya (n.d.), 'Cybercrime Regulations', http://www.ca.go.ke. Accessed 22 April 2022.

Constitution of Kenya (2020), Constitution of Kenya, *Kenya Law*, http://www.kenyalaw.org:8181/exist/kenyalex/actview.xql?actid=Const2010. Accessed 22 April 2022.

Durach, Flavia, Bargaoanu, Alina and Nastasiu, Catalina (2020), 'Tackling disinformation: EU regulation of the digital space', *Romanian Journal of European Affairs*, 20:1, pp. 5–20, https://papers.ssrn.com/sol3/papers.cfm?abstract_id=3650780. Accessed 8 March 2023.

Fourie, Pieter (2017), 'Normative media theory in the digital media landscape: From media ethics to ethical communication', *Communicatio*, 43:2, pp. 109–27, https://doi.org/10.1080/02500167.2017.1331927.

Gakii, Winfred (2022), 'Why parliament must not pass anti-pornography bill', *Kenya Internet Governance Forum*, 16 June, https://kigf.or.ke/why-parliament-must-not-pass-the-anti-pornography-bill/. Accessed 14 March 2023.

Garbe, Lisa, Selvik, Lisa-Marie and Lemaire, Pauline (2023), 'How African countries respond to fake news and hate speech', *Information, Communication & Society*, 26:1, pp. 86–103, https://doi.org/10.1080/1369118X.2021.1994623.

Kaigwa, Mark (2016), 'From cyber café to smartphone: Kenya's social media lens zooms in on the country and out to the world', in B. Ndemo and T. Weiss (eds), *Digital Kenya: Palgrave Studies of Entrepreneurship in Africa*, London: Palgrave Macmillan, pp. 187–217, https://doi.org/10.1057/978-1-137-57878-5_2.

Kamau, Sam (2018), 'At war: Government and media tensions in contemporary Kenya and the implications for public interest', in B. Mutsvairo and B. Karam (eds), *Perspectives on Political Communication in Africa*, London: Palgrave Macmillan, pp. 113–28, https://doi.org/10.1007/978-3-319-62057-2_7.

Kenya Information and Communications (Amendment) Act (2013), 'The Government Printer', *Kenya Law*, http://kenyalaw.org/kl/fileadmin/pdfdownloads/AmendmentActs/2013/KenyaInformationandCommunications_Amendment_Act2013.pdf. Accessed 4 March 2022.

Kiai, Mugambi, Gakii, Winfred and Mwanzi, Sigi W. (2021), 'Gagging free speech through Computer Misuse Act, Film and Stage Plays Act – Part 2', *The Star*, 27 March, https://www.the-star.co.ke/siasa/2021-03-27-gagging-free-speech-through-computer-misuse-act-and-films-and-stage-plays-act-part-2/. Accessed 15 April 2023.

Kopiyo, Victor (2024), 'Proposal to block websites and applications threatens Kenya's digital ecosystem', *KICTANet*, 3 October, https://www.kictanet.or.ke/proposal-to-block-websites-and-applications-threatens-kenyas-digital-ecosystem/. Accessed 9 October 2023.

Mahy, Petra, Winarnita, Monika and Herriman, Nicholas (2022), 'Influencing the influencers: Regulating the morality of online conduct in Indonesia', *Policy & Internet*, 14, pp. 574–96, https://doi.org/10.1002/poi3.321.

Marleau, Robert and Montpetit, Camille (2000), *House of Commons Procedure and Practice*, Ottawa: House of Commons.

Media Council of Kenya (2020), *Media Sector Legislative Review*, Nairobi, https://mediacouncil.or.ke/sites/default/files/downloads/MEDIA%20SECTOR%20LEGISLATIVE%20REVIEW%202021_1.pdf. Accessed 14 March 2023.

Moturi, Ndubi (2023), 'Deregulate media for vibrant industry, Kenya media sector working group says', *Nation*, 21 February, https://nation.africa/kenya/news/deregulate-media-for-vibrant-industry-kenya-media-sector-working-group-says-4132508. Accessed 10 April 2023.

Muendo, Mercy (2018), 'Kenya's new cybercrime law opens the door to privacy violations, censorship', *The Conversation*, 29 May, https://theconversation.com/kenyas-new-cybercrime-law-opens-the-door-to-privacy-violations-censorship-97271. Accessed 10 April 2023.

Muinde, Joel (2018), 'President Kenyatta assents to Cybercrimes Bill amid protests', *Nation*, 28 June, https://nation.africa/kenya/news/president-kenyatta-assents-to-cybercrimes-bill-amid-protests-44116. Accessed 10 April 2023.

Muraya, Joseph (2018), 'Kenya: Cyber bullies, fake news architects on notice as bill signed', *Capital FM*, 16 May, https://allafrica.com/stories/201805160270.html. Accessed 28 March 2023.

Mureithi, Muriuki (2017), 'The internet journey for Kenya: The interplay of disruptive innovation and entrepreneurship in fueling rapid growth', in B. Ndemo and T. Weiss (eds), *Digital Kenya: Palgrave Studies of Entrepreneurship in Africa*, London: Palgrave Macmillan, pp. 27–43, https://doi.org/10.1057/978-1-137-57878-5_2.

Muthoni, King'ori E. (2017), 'Exploring ethical frameworks of practice in Kenya's alternative online media platforms: A case of Kenyan news bloggers who are not mainstream journalists', Ph.D. thesis, Kenya: Daystar University.

Mutua, Sylvia and Zhang, Yanqiu (2021), 'Online content regulation policy in Kenya: Potential challenges and possible solutions', *Journal of Cyber Policy*, 6:2, pp. 177–95, https://doi.org/10.1080/23738871.2021.1916974.

Mwita, Chaacha (2021), *The Kenya Media Assessment 2021*, *Internews*, https://internews.org/wp-content/uploads/legacy/2021-03/KMAReport_Final_20210325.pdf. Accessed 10 March 2023.

Mzalendo Trust (2019), *Digital Rights in Kenya Report*, https://mzalendo.com/media/resources/DIGITAL_RIGHTS_IN_KENYA.pdf. Accessed 14 April 2023.

Ngirachu, John (2018), 'Kenya: Bad news for bloggers and fake news peddlers', *Daily Nation*, 30 April, https://allafrica.com/stories/201804300164.html. Accessed 10 May 2023.

Obuya, Jared and Ong'ondo, Charles (2019), '"Caught between a rock and a hard place": How Kenyan journalists are coping with pressure for media accountability', *African Journalism Studies*, 40:2, pp. 1–15, https://doi.org/10.1080/23743670.2019.1601118.

Ogola, George (2023), 'From advertising blackmail to physical threats, Kenya's journalists are under attack – But they must also regain public trust', *The Conversation*, 16 April, https://theconversation.com/from-advertising-blackmail-to-physical-threats-kenyas-journalists-are-under-attack-but-they-must-also-regain-public-trust-203580. Accessed 10 June 2023.

Otieno, Jaspher (2017), 'Regulation of media content in Kenya: In search of a paradigm in the era of convergence', *Saudi Journal of Humanities and Social Sciences*, 2:7, pp. 556–66, https://doi.org/10.21276/sjhss.

Piontek, Dorata (2016), 'Normative media theories: The media in the new democracies', *Przegląd Politologiczny*, 2, pp. 49–62, https://doi.org/10.14746/pp.2016.21.2.4.

Reuters Staff (2018), 'Kenya's president signs cybercrimes law opposed by media rights groups', *Reuters*, 16 May, https://www.reuters.com/article/us-kenya-lawmaking-idUSKCN1IH1KX. Accessed 15 May 2023.

Sang, Brian and Sang, Ivan (2020), 'A comparative review of cybercrime law in Kenya: Juxtaposing national legislation with international treaty standard', *International Journal of Cybercrime Research*, 10:2, pp. 100–20.

Santuraki, Suleiman Usman (2019), 'Trends in the regulation of hate speech and fake news: A threat to free speech', *Hasanuddin Law Review*, 5:2, pp. 140–58, http://dx.doi.org/10.20956/halrev.v5i2.1625.

Selvi, Murat (2022), *Regulating Digital Platforms: A Limitation to Freedom of Expression?* Istanbul: TRT World Research Centre.

Strickland, Pat and Dent, Jack (2017), 'Online harassment and cyber bullying', Briefing Paper 07967, House of Commons Library.

The Computer Misuse and Cybercrimes Act, 2018 (2018), *Kenya Law* website, http://kenyalaw.org/kl/fileadmin/pdfdownloads/Acts/ComputerMisuseandCybercrimesActNo5of2018.pdf. Accessed 14 January 2022.

The Constitution of Kenya (2010), Nairobi: The National Council of Law Reporting, https://vision2030.go.ke/wp-content/uploads/2018/05/The-Constitution-of-Kenya..pdf. Accessed 10 March 2023.

Walubengo, John and Mutemi, Mercy (2018), 'Treatment of Kenya's internet intermediaries under the Computer Misuse and Cybercrimes Act, 2018', *The African Journal of Information and Communication (AJIC)*, 21, pp. 1–19, https://doi.org/10.23962/10539/26114.

Wanambisi, Laban and Mwangi, Irene (2021), 'Appeal court reinstates 23 laws passed without senate's input', *Capital News*, 19 November, https://www.capitalfm.co.ke/news/2021/11/appeal-court-reinstates-23-laws-passed-without-senates-input/. Accessed 15 April 2022.

Zhang, Yan and Wildemuth, Barbara M. (2017), 'Qualitative analysis of content', in B. M. Wildemuth (ed.), *Applications of Social Research Methods to Questions in Information and Library Science*, 2nd ed., Santa Barbara: Libraries Unlimited, pp. 318–29.

9

Interrogating Online Journalism Regulation and Censorship in Africa – Interview with Churchill Otieno

Sulayman Bah

Churchill Otieno is a veteran digital media practitioner in Kenya. He is the president of the Africa Editors Forum and former managing editor of the Nation Media Group. In this interview, held on 18 August 2023, he shares his thoughts on the motive behind laws to regulate digital media in Africa, particularly in places like Kenya, Uganda and Tanzania. His views offer practitioner experience and perspectives on the intricacies of digital media regulation in Africa. It provides insights into how regulatory trends, challenges and practices are shaping the media landscape, especially in East Africa, outlining the need for an approach driven by self-regulation, ethical standards and user agency.

SULAYMAN BAH: How would you generally describe the digital or online media landscape in Africa? This relates broadly to the trend of regulation.

CHURCHILL OTIENO: Regulation is a big word – it means different things to different people. But a general trend that seems to be obtaining in many jurisdictions in Africa is that the regulation of online media seems to be driven by security interests, to be specific, state security interests. A lot of time, the laws and the limitations sometimes that the state imposes are informed more by fear rather than the need to enable the development and growth of online media. We have seen that in Kenya, we have seen it in Uganda, and I think a little bit in Ethiopia, where many times the state comes into that space with the main objective being to clamp down on what sometimes they see as threatening conversations, or organizing campaigns amongst their citizens that they think might jump into the offline world and translate into challenges for them, for lack of a better term, translating to governance challenges. So, their attitude, their approach seems not to be one of enabling the population of online media, but rather of trying to control the public or drive public order, so to speak.

SB: What would you say are the contemporary issues influencing digital media regulation?

CO: One thing digital technology does is the tendency to democratize. But in the offline world, social differences — or, if you like, socioeconomic classes — tend to afford different groups, differentiated access or ability to participate in civic engagements; they also seem to amplify some voices and de-emphasize others, mainly because some people are illiterate, some people do not have the platforms, or do not know how to organize themselves to be able to propel their voices beyond their immediacy. In many societies, in many communities, when we find the digital coming in and getting embraced by these people, it's been realized that when that happens, those people tend to be able to propel their voices into spaces that are ordinarily out of reach. And eventually they tend to be more aware of their rights, and therefore more able and sometimes willing to check their seats in civic and democratic engagements. So, the need to regulate digital media should of necessity be driven by a need to extend that reach so that we drive inclusion, you know, regardless of people's backgrounds. That for me would be a key one. Of course, we know, like everything in life, digital technology is fraught with many challenges, but we need to go into addressing those challenges with the overall objective to get more and more people to access and to participate meaningfully.

SB: What would you say are the salient media policies in Kenya, in particular, but also in the broader African context?

CO: We mentioned Uganda, for instance. So, what are the essential policies? Maybe Uganda is a lot more straightforward because they have a social media tax, for example. But, if for nothing else, it just increases the barrier of entry into that space so that even those who may already be included because they have access may not fully use the technology to the extent that they would want to because costs then become out of reach for some of them. We have seen in Ethiopia shutdowns, where, during periods of political contestations that sometimes are translated into security challenges, the state has tended to limit or throttle access to digital spaces. In Kenya, we have seen targeting of individuals based on what they share or how they use digital platforms. We have seen a fairly consistent campaign by the state to try and put in place customized laws that will then allow them to go after individuals.

In Kenya, we have, for instance, the Computer Misuse Law. We have what has come to be known as a KICA Act (Kenya Information and Communications Act) currently being reviewed. Many times, these laws are framed in ways that curtail the freedom of expression, for example, and sometimes even freedom of the media. In fact, the media in Kenya has been very boisterous over the years in terms of when these clauses are sneaked into these laws. The position we have held, and we continue to take, is that where some people would want to abuse their rights and end up injuring the rights of others, we already have laws that govern those and that can then build such people to do. Criminal activities offline are already governed by very stringent laws. Many times, a lot of criminal things that one might do in the online space already have comparable criminal activities in the offline world. In many instances, the Federal Court already covers such. So, when states come in with a grace of public security, in the guise of state security, to try and further limit people's ability to express themselves, many times you find that it is not a good thing. And it has happened in many African countries.

SB: What concerns you the most when it comes to how journalists navigate some of these complexities in relation to digital policies, and requirements such as social media taxation, filtering practices, and the intimidation and censorship of journalists online?

CO: Usually where you find that the state is very bullish in terms of putting in place measures to control its people's freedom in the digital space, it almost follows that that state is also very dictatorial when it comes to freedom of expression, which is very closely linked to freedom of the media. So, where you find such laws, number one, you find that the journalists operating in those spaces tend to be operating in an environment where their rights and their ability to do their work are challenging. And we see that in Uganda, where every so often we find the president lambasting independent media, sometimes he tries to put in place, policies that directly disadvantage independent media. Just a week ago, he woke up and said all public sector project must only go to government-owned media. Of course, he's now vacated that position, but you already see that. In that same environment, we have formal limitations to digital growth, with the social media tax. When you come to the media, you also find that there are very unhelpful policies that that regime then tries to push through. So, you find that the state wants to do all they can to control digital growth and digital use. We also find that they put lots of challenges in the path of journalists to be unable to do their job.

Number two is sort of on the supply side. Digital by nature, is in a constant state of change. Nothing is ever the same in the digital space, things are always moving, things are always shifting. Indeed, we seem to be currently going through the digital disrupting itself, you know, with the coming of AI and all the things that come with it. We find that the internet, as we knew it, is quickly shifting landscape. So, for that reason, it is my interest and an area of concern whether journalists are actually updating themselves fast enough, whether journalists are able to understand these shifts. So as one, they can come in a knowledgeable manner, to interpret and explain these shifts to their audiences, to their publics. But number two, whether they can then understand the space well enough so that they can ride on the opportunities that these shifts provide in terms of helping them find information, helping them understand that information, and helping them package that information in ways that will then be accessible to the populations that they serve. Critical for me, but I think if we do not do that, then we lose relevance, and if journalism loses relevance, society is poorer because the powers that be usually would like to do the stuff in darkness. It is the journalist's job to throw in some light there and to help the civic population be aware of some of those things for us to then inform whatever decisions that make up what they wrote.

SB: In what ways do you – or the journalists generally in Kenya – resist these kinds of policies, and how would you rate so far, the level of your success? And describe how that links to the attitude of the government towards you as journalists and activists.

CO: One, in mature democracies, the place of journalism is established. Society respects that, and because the ruling class knows that they owe their place to their people, they tend not to mess up journalism too much; they know ultimately, they'll get penalized by the people. Unfortunately, in growing democracies, sometimes civic awareness of the place of critical journalism or independent journalism is not that widespread. So, the ruling class always, even where they understand where journalism is coming from, [...] would like to profile journalists as threats and as competitors and as political rivals. And many times, they then are able to radicalize their constituencies against independent voices in journalism, whether it's the individuals or even media organizations. An opportunity for us is to recognize this for what it is. The ruling class, the politicians have an interest to get to power and to sustain themselves in power, and where we become the biggest threat to them, they'll probably find ways to target us. And the first step for me is to acknowledge that reality. That's the space we're working with, and we need to organize with that reality in mind. Now, what does organizing that reality in mind mean?

Number one, the best regulation of media is self-regulation. So, we must, of necessity, build amongst ourselves strong structures and strong systems that would then be able to carry self-regulation in a manner that is convincing and has the trust of the public. So that when the politicians come after us, this mechanism is able to help us stand up. But more importantly, in the natural course of journalism, errors do happen, mistakes do happen. When that happens, it should be possible to identify and acknowledge that that's a mistake, and corrective measures be taken. Sometimes those corrective measures might be punitive, where that is justified, other times, it's just a question of repairing damaged reputations. But we must, of necessity, endear processes and structures that are corrective.

The second side of that coin is that standards of ethical practice must not be obscure. There must be standards that are simple enough for the public to understand and follow, but ambitious enough for us to then help social societies grow. It would then mean that we begin to challenge ourselves as professionals in terms of how we serve the purpose that the society expects of us and how do we prepare ourselves for that assignment? Is it training? Is it schooling? Is it experience? And how do we measure that and be able to tell whether Churchill or Sulayman meet the cut in terms of playing that role, and how do we also enable peer review of ourselves? If we want to be trusted by the public, there must be ethical standards. To put it simply, we have to organize our house. It is only when we have that house organized that we can fight against the state, against a breach of freedom between us.

SB: Are there other issues of concern that you believe explain the general trend that African governments have adopted towards digital media regulation?

CO: Yes, it depends on the nation's stage in the democratization process. But [...] it might also depend on a nation's history. So, in Africa, we have some fairly weak states or what we might also want to cast as vulnerable states, mostly because there have been unfortunate events in recent history. Some of them probably [...] are coming out of strife, most of it being a war. Others probably have fallen victim to global realities that they are not organized sufficiently to be able to regain their place in. So ultimately, they end up with fairly weak internal systems. And in that kind of reality, they always see threats in anything that comes. But it also follows those certain kinds of nations, because of that same reality, have thrown out a lot of their populations into other jurisdictions. So, they tend to have a reasonable portion of the population that has probably grown in an environment that is probably freer than it is at home and are able to then organize themselves and exert their voice in a steadier manner.

And now digital is giving them what has been missing over the years, which is taking out distance as a barrier for them to reach populations back home. So today, we have our WhatsApp groups that one can participate [in] almost at an equal footing, and that is where they are in the world. We have social media that today we know can easily be deployed to organize new populations politically, and also, we have digital financial systems that enable the movement of resources from one corner of the globe to the other. So, you would see if I was a dictator in the corner of the world, and aware of these frontiers, I would say that I am likely to interpret them as battle zones, an extension of the wars that have been socialized that I'm used to. And where messaging that goes in there is messaging that is unpalatable to me, and sometimes that 'unpalatable' messaging tends to catch fire very quickly in local populations. So many of them will then see digital generally as a source of threat. And that often is what leads to shutdowns, for example, because you're saying we do not know who is good or bad in this space. Let's just shut it down or even if it is not declared as a shutdown, you find that they make it difficult for people to participate in those kinds of spaces. So somehow it still leads back to securitization because the state tends to be obsessed with that beat.

I have also seen that sometimes private interests are put historically above the public interest when it comes to managing and enabling digital systems. What I'm saying is, you know, in most cases, digital systems are deployed right, it provides traceability, and it tends to provide transparency in the management of public affairs. So, if I was an occupant of a big office and I wanted to redirect some of those public resources to my grandmother or to my home and those kinds of things, I know the risk that comes with. And many times, I want to make sure that I cover my footsteps, that anybody who comes looking in is not able to see my hand. Unfortunately, digital tends to make that less possible. And therefore, you find that even where states can afford to deploy and to promote digital systems, they tend to drag their feet in this. Because, in most instances, [...] going digital reduces chances of corruption. And the corruption and politics in Africa have become two partners in a marriage, so to speak.

SB: What can be done to deter the enactment of the kind of censorship policy that we have in Africa? And secondly, given that some form of regulation is still needed, what would you see as good regulation or best standards of practice in terms of online media regulation in Africa?

CO: You know, all rights can only be enjoyed if they are asserted. It's hardly the case that people just get their rights as they deserve. Many times, you have to fight for your rights, and you must seek to exercise them for you to be able to enjoy them. So, I think the best thing to socialize our populations is to create awareness of these realities so that the people, ultimately, would open their eyes and they're the ones who would then exert the right pressures, the right locations, so that, you know, things improve. That I hope answers question one, then the second one, I would say [is] sort of linked. But we should seek informed participation of the people so that they then set the regulatory standards that work for them.

If, for example, you look at the jurisdictions where there's what might be seen as ideal freedom of expression, where I even have the freedom to insult, you know, to throw out that word, and it's seen as my freedom of expression. And it is a common idea, but that works in those cultures; it works in those societies because they are at a certain point in time in their development trajectory. Maybe it might not work in the African space in the year 2023, but maybe it might have worked in the year 2010 or it might work in the year 2030. I think we can't impose our standards on different communities, but the key thing for me is [...] informed participation of those communities in determining how fast they want to move and what direction they want to go.

However, that comes with a huge challenge in that digital by nature breaks down national boundaries. Unfortunately, instead of breaking down those boundaries and handing whatever power to the people, it tends to break them down but hand those powers to the big tech. So, a decision is made on Facebook or Google or Twitter, and it's a decision that then affects everybody in the entire world that is active on that platform. And sometimes we know what the decision is, and we can tell what the effect or impact would be. But who knows the number of times when such decisions are made that nobody ever knows about, and we even do not know how they're affecting us. So, there's a bit of black hole, if you like, or a dark room within the big tech space. But whatever regulation we choose to go, for me, [it] would require […] a lot more transparency in terms of how those platforms are made to come together.

SB: What do you think the future is for digital media regulation in Africa, especially with regard to regulating newer technologies like artificial intelligence?

CO: It seems to me that Africa is being left behind yet again, because I'm looking at the ongoing rally around generative AI, and how the ground rules are being redrawn, raising lots of ethical questions.

But we also know that when it comes to digital, the future is shaped by what is fading. So, the fading seems to be happening not as energetically in Africa as it is happening elsewhere. It's almost clear that whatever comes out likely would be informed less by the wishes and the hopes of Africa, just purely from a participation point of view. Maybe it's because of some of our national educational strategies that perhaps have not emphasized and promoted computer technology as an area of science and an area of scholarly interest, or maybe it's in the way we manage the economies that have not enabled the propagation and flourishing of digital ecosystem or value chain, whatever the reason might be.

The net position is that we are not carrying our weight in the AI conversation. And I think it's going to present challenges for us going forward from a language perspective, from a culture perspective, from a political orientation perspective, because the ground rules are shifting and we are not pushing, we are almost not present in that conversation.

10

Senegal's Approach to Digital Media Regulation: Limited Civil Society Consultation, State Control and the Need for a Continental Approach to Governance – Interview with David Diaz-Jogeix

Sulayman Bah

David Diaz-Jogeix is the senior director of programmes at Article 19, where he has worked in several African contexts, possessing knowledge of the regulatory terrain in countries like Senegal. In this interview, which took place on 28 February 2025, David sheds light on the approach to digital media regulation in Senegal, which serves as an example for Francophone Africa. The issues touched on include freedom of expression, digital censorship, internet shutdowns, AI regulation, the importance of a continent approach to governance, the degree to which the Senegalese government consults civil society groups when drafting digital media regulatory policies and an idealistic picture of what regulation should look like in a country like Senegal.

SULAYMAN BAH: How would you describe the digital or online media regulatory landscape in Senegal?

DAVID DIAZ-JOGEIX: Well, I think that Senegal has a regulatory landscape that allows for the state to interfere in freedom of expression. And I think in that sense it is problematic. For the past years, Senegal has been synonymous with internet shutdowns, as you know, in 2021. Then in

2023, during June, July, August or recently in February 2024. I think part of the problem is the actual legislation that allows for the state to intervene in regulating expression when it does not suit the political narrative. Or when there are people actually protesting, legitimately protesting against the government for whatever the policies are. I won't go into legalities, but the 2017 Press Code allows for conditions to set up online press while considering that the Code is very restrictive as to who is a journalist. For example, to create online media or digital media, it requires that the director has ten years of professional experience, which is complete nonsense. And also, it requires the disclosure of the sources of the content, which is problematic; as you know, in terms of traditional journalism, protection of sources is important.

SB: In your view, does this tilt more towards freedom of expression or censorship?

DD-J: There are positives and there are negatives, right? I think it is very important to nuance things well, so we do not lose the analysis. I think there's a lot of positivity in terms of the diversity of online media. I think there's up to 300 online media right now in Senegal. The law, for example, does not oblige control and surveillance of information by service providers. There are certain things that are okay, like the regulation framework for the press and online media; at least there is space for self-regulation, which I think is good. However, the online press is prone to censorship, and we've seen how the authorities tend to decide to muscle all areas of communication that have hitherto escaped their control. So, we go back again to this very strict definition of journalism that is very restrictive and that excludes bloggers, it excludes citizen journalists who want to create, seek, or share information. And I think that does not match with two things: international human rights standards, but it also does not match with the common sense of the new digital societies we live in.

We have also seen how in Senegal they have used the registration. Three weeks ago, after six months of the registration process, the ministry in charge of the media sector issued a list of about 640 media registered in the country with a clear threat to those that are not meeting the standards to be sanctioned as not recognized. They have a problem of the state deciding who should be speaking or not, who should be creating a media or not. So, Senegal is in a half-half picture. In our global expression report that ranks countries in terms of freedom of expression, out of 166 countries, it ranked 74th. We have categorized Senegal as a country where freedom of expression is restricted. For the past two decades, Senegal was in the category of countries where freedom of expression is less restricted. And in the Sub-Saharan region, out of 42 countries, Senegal only ranks 14, which is quite low, and we would expect a much healthier scenario in terms of freedom of expression.

SB: On the registration point, do you mean that online media have to register with the government and then if they fall short in some way, the government can sanction them?

DD-J: Registration for the purpose of knowing who is in the media and having access to that information in order to support the media and create the right environment for the media to do their work is okay. Registration of the media for the purposes of penalizing and applying a Press Code that does not meet international standards in a manner that is arbitrary, then it might be a tool to politically censor media that do their work and by that I mean one that holds power to account. So, the registration depends on what it is for, and what the actual current legal environment is. If you start combining those things, then you start seeing tools for repression of dissent of the media, but also it affects citizens because they are not having access to the information they need to know if a government is corrupt, if a government is doing the wrong things or doing things that citizens might need to decide whether that's right or wrong.

VO: When you say media, do you mean online or social media? Or just the traditional media?

DD-J: There's a merger, right? We've seen in the last couple of decades, a merger between the traditional printed media that goes online, then you have a new digital media that is only online. And then you have different actors that are using the right to freedom of expression through different platforms, journalists or bloggers, etc. So, in the current context, applying a very restrictive definition of who is a journalist, then that is not okay, because it does not match international standards, it does not make any sense in this new digital scenario.

SB: Reflecting on what is happening in Senegal, what are some of the measures that ease or concern you when it comes to digital media regulation or freedom of expression in general?

DD-J: There's a couple of things on the positive side; one is, overall, the legal framework does refer to freedom of expression, access to information, media freedom. I think the problem is when you actually look in detail. Let's say, these grandiose statements actually do not replicate into the technicalities of it. I think there is a vibrant media industry and professionals in the country, knowing exactly what they are doing and what needs to be done in terms of how to improve professionalism and the regulatory framework. And I think there's also a consensus among different stakeholders, including the government on the importance of self-regulation of the media and proper media governance. I think that shows a high level of professional maturity around it. I think if we go back to the problems in terms of what concerns us, one is the regulatory legal framework that is not in accordance with international standards. And I think both the media and the telecom legal framework need a deep reform to align them to international standards. And we could start with the criminalization of speech which is problematic because then it can be weaponized against journalists or online activists when it does not suit the power. There's also issues that are more technical, but they are super important, like the law on electronic communications codes. It allows a regulatory authority to impose traffic management measures. So, they can reduce the speed, they can block, and this jeopardizes the net neutrality principle, which is a very important principle to make sure that the infrastructure and the flow of information remain.

SB: Are advocacy groups like yours typically invited or consulted when it comes to policymaking or legislation-crafting for digital or online media?

DD-J: I think in Senegal, both the government but also the society, they do value dialogue and the creation of consensus. I think that's a key asset of the Senegalese psyche, and I think that's actually quite important. You can see this in terms of the political governance, but also whenever things have been tense, how going back to dialogue and going back to a common denominator, it's been quite good. And I think that's something that has to be valued strongly, particularly in this global era of over-polarization. I think that's something that is truly valuable from the Senegalese society. I think we are being consulted, the answer would be yes, but there's always a but. It's the quality of the consultation that actually comes to play. There are instances where we have been properly consulted, like in the Press Code provision. Then the issue is whether the government is actually taking any of your comments or not. But that's something that is always the tradeoff between civil society and what a legitimate government is being appointed by its people decide. There's an issue there in terms of sovereignty, but also the ability to listen to what civil societies are actually saying.

And then there are situations where the consultation is very pro forma. So, we have been consulted, but it's really with very limited time. And you can see that there is no political will. There is a political will to show that civil society has been consulted, but when you actually look at the time that actually invested in that, sometimes it's less than 24 hours. Yeah. This happened to us with regard to the Access to Information Law. Therefore, that's not a serious grown-up engagement by a government with civil society around a proper process of listening, hearing your say. And then, of course, as I said, government is sovereign. They need to make their own side. But I think in terms of the quality of the consultation, it does not meet minimum standards. It's like when you talk to a friend to talk about issues, and you are actually not paying attention. And then you go into something else – then you're not talking to him. Then there are other issues where we're clearly not consulted. And this is when the government wants to pass restrictive laws. This is the case of the social media bill, which if adopted in the current context, it would create more problems for online media as it creates further obligations for content creators.

SB: Do you think this lack of consultation is a common view shared by other stakeholders you work with in Senegal?

DD-J: It's difficult to tell. I think it takes a bit of a habit for the bureaucracies, the ministries, and the first political layers of the public administration to enter into a habit, which should be transparent, and healthy. It should be professional in terms of actually presenting drafts to citizens and civil society, and receive some constructive criticism. I think the habit is not there. I think there is a responsibility from civil society that we engage professionally and constructively on these issues based on proper guiding criteria. The guiding criterion in our case is international human rights standards. When we criticize, we try to do it constructively. And it's not against the government. It's for the government to build up legislation that incorporates human rights standards because that's what matters to people ultimately. I think the habit is not there. But I think we should continue to engage with the government. There is a very clear responsibility for civil societies on how we engage, and we always engage constructively. And constructive engagement can also mean saying, 'I'm not agreeing at all with you, but I'm not agreeing with you because of this, and this is maybe a suggestion, an alternative suggestion to your text.' That's what I mean by constructive engagement.

SB: How do regulatory or censorship policies affect your work as a watchdog in Senegal? And in what ways do you resist or campaign?

DD-J: There's a couple of things. Obviously, when there is internet shutdown, general censorship measures, we are affected like everybody else. Because then you do not have access to the information or what's actually being debated. And we need to be aware of the gravity of internet shutdowns. It seems that we have grown accustomed to internet shutdowns and this is a normal reality of our lives. That's an extraordinary, massive censorship by the government. It's such a level of disproportion that it should never take place. And it affects because it literally sucks out all of the information that you need. As any other citizen, we are affected in terms of not having that, and that's where we go back to this principle of net neutrality as a principal element. There have been instances where, for example, websites have been hacked. We never established the link, whether that hack is linked to a critical work. We want to be forensic about it and be fact-based. That's not yet the case. But these things do happen.

So, how do we resist? Like an NGO, we are a think-do organization. We do law and policy work, we do legal thinking, but also we do advocacy [and] we engage with civil society and partners. And change does not take place very quickly. When dealing with social change, when dealing with government change, you need to really have a long-term vision and then specific actions. It's never a single step and then you get the result that you want. You need to build that trust and make sure that you argue your case. In that sense, we need to do proper research, making sure that what we say is based on facts and on good standards, and not whatever my opinion as a citizen is, but that it's actually a solid structure. And then engage with society, other partners, parliament, and ministries.

One of the things when we look at Senegal for the past four years is that we have had a heavy trend towards censorship. We have been really trying to build resilience, not only in terms of us as an organization but more importantly, with the partners that we work with, making sure that they are also digitally resilient against this censorship. We go back to monitoring and documentation but also keep the door open and the attitude open to engage with the government, whoever the government is, to make sure that we say what we have to say and do it in the most constructive manner. So that's a bit of our way of operating.

SB: Looking at the Senegalese landscape, what role or place does Senegal have to play in regulating AI? Also, in terms of the power that Senegal has, considering the global race for AI regulation and development.

DD-J: Senegal, as any other sovereign nation, has tools at their disposal. They have very clear frameworks around not only innovation and looking at sustainable development goals, how to use technologies for the good but also making sure that those are within a framework that respects human rights. Because there is a problem here around artificial intelligence. We know that the government of Senegal is putting in place a national strategy on artificial intelligence, which we welcome, and we will engage as constructively as always. There are a couple of issues. There's a very important regulation that has come out from the European Union on artificial intelligence. It's the first regulation or global policy in the sector that looks at artificial intelligence to make sure that there are three things. One, it is safe. Second, it is trustworthy. And then third, it respects human rights. In that sense, it's important to really look at what else is out there from Senegal and what other parts of the world are actually doing.

There is also the non-regulation from the United States, and you can see what kind of harms can actually come from that. So that's a matter, again, for the sovereign government of Senegal to think through what it is that they want. The national strategy itself, I think it's important, but it won't be enough. Thinking at the continental level, from Senegal with other African nations, and [...] thinking through what kind of global approach could be taken to the regulation of artificial intelligence would be important, and center[ing] that discussion on human rights. But then looking at the African Union or the African member states and see[ing] how do they want to position themselves *vis-à-vis* the European Union, the United States and China? How do they position themselves in that geopolitical battle we're seeing, and then use that? I think the national framework, it's important, but it's not enough. Thinking more at the continental level might be wiser in the sense of establishing the proper leverage as united nations in Africa and then represent a bigger market and therefore a bigger position of leverage on this.

SB: You mentioned the regulation in the EU; we know the EU AI Act. And with the GDPR, we've heard conversations that African countries might use the GDPR as a benchmark. With the EU AI Act, there is also a possibility that it can be seen as a benchmark that Africa should measure itself against. Do you think this is the case? And if so, what are your thoughts on it?

DD-J: We should always look at what's in the box. It's not because it comes from the European Union. It's about what's in the box – and does it actually meet international standards? The importance is not just because it's the European Union. It is, has the European Union met certain minimum international human rights standards? Then we can say this could be an interesting model for us. And let's look at this and see how this can be a source of inspiration, where from Africa, you can take your own decisions about how you look at it. I think artificial intelligence, GDPR, as you mentioned, in terms of personal data, I think there are key elements there in terms of not only freedom of expression but also our right to privacy that are quite critical. Those are important, and I think definitely, it would be worth engaging in that space.

SB: In the idealistic sense, what does your vision of appropriate digital or online media regulation in Senegal look like or should look like? Are there roles in this vision for regional players like ECOWAS or the African Union?

DD-J: I'm happy you mentioned the African Union and ECOWAS. But to begin with Senegal, I think for more appropriate regulation on digital media, the government in collaboration with professional media organizations must really work towards reducing state interference. That's the direction they should be working on. I think the state by default will not go there. I think this is where it's important to use the political opportunity of the intentions of this current government to counter that state inertia and really push back and create a reinforcement of a democratic state and a democratic society. And that goes not by words, but by pushing back against those tools that the state has. And when I advocate for this, I always say to politicians: 'Think through when you're going to be in the opposition, not now that you are in power. Create, right now that you are in power, the proper framework to make sure that there are proper checks and balances.'

The other element I would like to see is to pursue that level of professionalism in the online press. I think the more professionalism we have in online or digital media, the better we will be in a position to combat disinformation and really protect both people's dignity and privacy. But there's a couple of measures. I think a stronger self-regulation of online media will be definitely one of the areas we should be working towards. Less interference of the state, as I said. Then use the power of the state to create the right environment. For example, campaigns on media information literacy, support dialogues between the stakeholders, the digital platforms, the digital tech, and the journalists. And then create fair market competitions for the different actors. So rather than the state thinking only through the Criminal Code or the Press Code in a punitive way, I think it's the state thinking of the panoply of different measures they could actually look at to really lift up the level field. In terms of more professionalism, more fairness, and education to citizens on how to navigate the new digital world by giving them the tools. And then there are other things that are not specifically freedom of expression, but I think

Senegal is really looking into a reform of the judicial system, and I think that's really important because then we have a rule of law and a proper level field that laws are going to be adjudicated by a judiciary that is more independent. Last but not least, bring all these different discussions, technicalities, and all the rest back to human rights standards – that should be the guiding centre.

With the ECOWAS and African Union, I think I mentioned that before, in terms of some of the solutions beyond the national state. You can see that in other parts of the world, like we just said, the European Union. Countries in Europe have really put the focus on the European Union and through their representatives, ambassadors, and all the rest, making sure that at the European level, it has more political strength. I think that's where Senegal wants to really push beyond the national, and use ECOWAS and use the African Union as a regional or continental mechanism to reinforce that. I think there are a lot of allies within the African nations around this and I think in the medium to long term, it would set higher standards. It will reinforce allies on freedom of expression on the continent and it will make nations on the continent that are hesitating which way to go to lift themselves up in terms of standards. Because we've seen how in the region, we have had several military coups and some of the freedom of expression standards clearly dropping. We have also countries that do not have a military coup like Benin to drop the standards in terms of freedom of expression. So, [...] it is important to create that legal political agreement, and there are countries in Africa that are very powerful in terms of pushing for progressive human rights and freedom of expression agenda. I think Senegal is one of them. So, I think it's for a political direction of engaging with all the champions on the continent and lifting the standards up.

SB: In the realistic sense, what do you think the regulatory landscape in Senegal will resemble? Going by the trend so far, what do you think it will look like in the next five to ten years?

DD-J: I like your question in terms of realistically because you can ask for the moon. I am expecting this [Senegalese] government to really look at the political equation following the protests and the repression that led to the elections, and then this government being formed with a massive parliamentary majority. If I am not wrong, it's unprecedented, the majority that they have in parliament. So, it's to put that into what the government wants to do with that majority. My understanding is that there is a political will to reinforce the checks and balances of the Senegalese democracy. If we're talking about that, when it comes to freedom of expression, there needs to be a very serious look at the Press Code, and to really look at the legal framework and remove not only tools for censorship but reinforce the legal framework to avoid state interference. There are clauses in terms of national security, the nation under attack, health issues in which it's legitimate to limit freedom of expression. But those are very small and they should be properly protected. Because I know if we have a pandemic, we need to make sure that there is a proper reaction. But for the rest, it's to really lift out and deconstruct the tools of repression that are in the system.

So, a reform of the Press Code – I think we need a serious conversation about the audiovisual regulatory body that regulates [...] both television and media. That cannot be the state deciding. That should be an independent audiovisual regulatory body, like you have in many other countries, that is detached from the government. Then you have independent people deciding who should be given spectrums and licenses. The government is already taking the decision to go towards a reinforcement of the independence of the judiciary and going through judicial reform. Those things are not quick, but it's quite important. I think we're going to see more self-regulation of media councils, self-regulation of the press. The other element that I am convinced of is that civil society will continue to be very strong, will continue to engage critically with the government. And when I say critically, it's the constructive criticism I was referring to. And I think civil societies and all the stakeholders in the media need to engage in that direction. If we see the government hesitating, it's to continue to encourage the government to go in that direction.

SB: Broadly speaking, within the francophone countries in Africa that come from a similar colonial background, and based on your experience, do you think they have similar approaches towards digital media regulation?

DD-J: The answer is yes. And we have seen in the past two decades, if not the last decade, a severe deterioration of things. The easy answer would be for me to point to Niger, Burkina Faso and Mali, which is so obvious. But it's also about other countries that we were expecting changes, like Guinea, where there are no changes that are progressive. I refer before in terms of the severe deterioration of freedom of expression in Benin. And let's see how things will go in Cote d'Ivoire. I am saying this because of the importance of freedom of expression and a proper level field that leads to proper elections. We've seen this in Senegal, how important that is. Also, how internet shutdowns have become the norm throughout the region; that's definitely not good. The way we have seen internet shutdowns almost as normal, it's very concerning. That is why when it comes to artificial intelligence, let's look at regional mechanisms like ECOWAS or the African Union and put those standards of the Charter of the African People and Human Rights to very good use. Particularly if governments have come with a progressive reinforcement of democracy, then when they are in power, then they need to really act to see how we can engage in the African Union or ECOWAS. And then lead, because I think there's an element of political leadership at the international level that is quite critical.

11

Evasive Journalism: Circumventing the Regulation of Online Journalism in The Gambia

Sulayman Bah

Introduction

On 28 March 2007, officers of the National Intelligence Agency arrested Fatou Jaw Manneh, an exiled female Gambian journalist, on arrival at the Banjul International Airport. Manneh was eventually charged with sedition and publication of false news after accusing President Yahya Jammeh of 'tearing our beloved country to shreds' and calling him a 'bundle of terror'. The interview was first published in *The Independent Newspaper* in June 2004 and later on several websites, including AllGambian.net, in October 2005 (Faye and Camara 2008; Amnesty International 2008). On 18 August 2008, she was convicted and sentenced to four years in prison with hard labour or to pay a 250,000 Dalasi (approximately US$12,000) fine, payable the same day. Also, on 15 September 2013, another female broadcast journalist, Fatou Camara, was charged with spreading false news and false publication about the president in *Freedom Newspaper*, an online publication hosted in the United States (Samateh 2013). *The Point Newspaper* reported that Ms Camara was held incommunicado beyond the constitutional limit of 72 hours before being charged. While on bail, she absconded to the United States before the determination of her case. Such cases highlight how sedition, criminal defamation and false publication laws are being used to punish Gambian online journalists, specifically those who are in the diaspora.

For several decades, particularly under President Yahya Jammeh's rule between 1994 and 2017, The Gambia has been known for aggressively prosecuting online journalists who operate diasporic news websites. Specific websites, mainly those run by the opposition, exiled journalists and activists, are blocked in the country. The first signs of repression against online journalism were reported in 2006 when four journalists were imprisoned, two fled to exile, and *Freedom Newspaper* online was hacked by the state, revealing the names of subscribers to the website (International Federation of Journalists 2006). The tension became severe in 2013 when the government introduced the Information and Communications (Amendment) Act that forbids criticism of government officials on the internet, which carries a 15-year prison term punishment for spreading false news online.

In this chapter, I explore how this law functions and consider how journalists understand it and navigate it. To do this, I use an innovative, interdisciplinary methodology that utilizes approaches from law and cultural studies, specifically synthesizing doctrinal research alongside semi-structured interviews. The chapter seeks to contribute to academic work that investigates online media regulation such as Flew and Wilding (2020), Schäfer (2009), Skjerdal (2013) and Parks and Thompson (2020). I also consider works specific to online journalism in the Global South and the African context. While these studies demonstrate how regulation is used to restrict internet access, they rarely offer critical analyses of jurisprudence and, as Obia (2023) observes, tend to focus on western countries in Europe and the United States. In comparison, less is known about online journalism regulation in sub-Saharan African countries like The Gambia. Through interviews with Gambian journalists, I also explore how they make sense of media laws and find ways to circumvent such a repressive legal framework that is inimical to media freedom.

I show that through digital technology, Gambian journalists carefully navigate this complex political and legal environment to evade arrest, criminal prosecution and restrictions on media ownership. I suggest that these practices can be best described as evasive journalism, a form of journalistic practice that finds ways around restrictive legal frameworks to report the news.

Online Journalism and Regulation in the Global South

The evolution of online journalism can be traced back to the launch of the first web browser in 1993 (Siapera and Veglis 2012). Since then, there have been gradual developments of internet features enabling the setting up of news participatory websites and social media platforms worldwide. Allan (2012) further notes that this has led to the development of new media, ranging from blogs and forums to radicalized social media pages that directed the flow of information in the larger struggle for meaning. Atton (2004: 26) sees online journalism as an attempt to place power in the hands of those more intimately involved in those stories. This allowed internet users to communicate on a reciprocal basis, transcending nation-state boundaries (Blaug and Schwarzmantel 2000). For Foust (2017: 12), the internet has been the most significant advancement of communication since the invention of the printing press, outlining the significant role online journalism played in the growth of the internet. He further points out other advantages of the internet to journalism, including its capabilities of embracing older media (text, images, graphics, animations, audio, video, real-time delivery and a broad spectrum of other capabilities). He observes that many online journalism sites are associated with legacy media organizations such as newspapers, magazines and television stations. At the heart of technological advancement is a growing interest in regulating digital platforms, including online news media websites and social media platforms (Flew and Wilding 2020).

Internet regulation has been a contentious issue in academic debates. Scholars such as Mathiason (2009) believe it is not amenable to top-down nation-state regulation. However, there is a significant departure from this thinking as new digital legislation and regulation forms have been adopted in differing political settings. Flew and Wilding observe that although 'government control over the Internet were long associated with authoritarian governments like in China, Iran, Russia and elsewhere, it is increasingly in the liberal democracies where new forms of digital platform regulation are being developed' (Flew and Wilding 2020: 49). Broadly, online circulation of disinformation, hate speech and so-called 'fake news' by politically and ideologically motivated actors are among the reasons why governments regulate the internet. Such is the case in Thailand, where the government introduced legal liability, targeting political activists for disseminating fake news online and 'exert control over fake news content published' (Anansaringkarn and Neo 2021: 16). Similarly, in Global South, internet regulation notably covers some of these issues, but tends to target growing dissent online. For example, in Egypt, cybercrime laws are designed to target online media platforms, restricting freedom of expression (Badr 2019). Although it is believed that online journalism platforms were effective in facilitating democratic discourse and effecting political change within countries in the Global South, Schäfer (2009: 55) points out that until 2011, there was no concrete empirical evidence that supports this claim.

But in recent years, there has been a significant increase in online blogging and the use of social media platforms to exchange information, especially during periods of political uncertainty within countries in the Global South (Sarah 2012). This has forced many countries to respond to information circulating on these platforms through formal and informal means of control. For instance, in the aftermath of the Tahrir Revolution in Egypt, the authorities blocked more than 500 digital platforms. They introduced a cyber-terrorism law which tightened restrictions to the internet public sphere by incriminating Facebook groups' administrators

(Reporters Without Borders 2019). Similarly, in Zimbabwe, online publications were criminalized, blacklisted and internet shutdowns under Robert Mugabe's rule for fear of political activism that promotes regime change (Ngoshi 2021). Evident here is the use of online media platforms by African diaspora communities to challenge state media hegemony, legal restriction and repression of journalism in their respective countries of origin (Ndlovu 2019). These digital platforms have become powerful for facilitating alternative democratic participation and involvement in African countries with a political environment that does not allow the media operating inside the country to address (Ndlovu 2019).

Regarding a semi-authoritarian African country like Ethiopia, Skjerdal notes that 'the authorities have instituted numerous measures that serve to restrict rather than encourage a vibrant online sphere' (Skjerdal 2013: 89). Examples include blocking websites that promote political opposition, intimidation and legal persecution of bloggers and online journalists, and the use of an anti-terrorism law that targets explicitly online reporting. Other studies, such as Parks and Thompson (2020), discuss internet shutdown and regulation in East African countries like Tanzania, outlining a series of repressive information and internet regulation measures. Their study analyses laws on online content regulation, which led many Tanzanians to cease expressive activities on the internet. To further understand how the internet is shut down and regulated in Africa, I draw from Parks and Thompson (2020), who show three ways this is done by prohibiting, interrupting or making too costly online content creation, including blogging, alternative news production, public archiving and user-generated content. This three-way understanding of shutdown and regulation of online media makes it possible for governments to use laws to pre-empt, inhibit and criminalize certain kinds of online content to quash political dissent.

The Gambia is frequently cited as one of the African countries with strict control of access to online journalism websites, particularly those operated by the diaspora community during President Jammeh's rule (Human Rights Watch 2015; Reporters Without Borders 2014; Freedom House 2022). Reports, such as Human Rights Watch (2015), consider the use of 'false information' and 'false news' laws to repress communication across any media, including the internet, social media, telephones or even in private conversations. In terms of internet blocking, it is commonly assumed in research and reports that the former government of President Jammeh specifically targets controversial online platforms operated by exiled journalists and activists who were involved in anti-government struggles (Amnesty International 2013; Freedom House 2022). Other researchers, such as Noble (2018), have also briefly considered online media regulation in The Gambia. Beyond this, I find that there is far less critical analysis of legal frameworks of online journalism in Sub-Saharan Africa and engagement with the experiences of journalists who have to navigate these laws. My research builds on these studies by using a holistic approach, combining doctrinal legal research and interviews with journalists to understand regulation and online journalism in Global South countries like The Gambia.

Methodology

For this chapter, I used an interdisciplinary methodological approach, combining doctrinal research and interviews with journalists to study journalism and online regulation in The Gambia. Such an approach is essential for measuring the effectiveness of legal instruments for controlling media practice, particularly in Sub-Saharan African countries like The Gambia. Doctrinal research was particularly useful in exploring laws, regulations and case laws concerning journalism in The Gambia. The method is typically used by legal scholars to 'identify, analyse and synthesise the content of the law' (Hutchinson 2013: 9). It is also the method considered appropriate by scholars for a theoretical critique of the law or empirical study about the law in operation (Hutchinson 2013: 10). In this regard, as a method specifically intended for legal analysis, it is fundamental to the development of legal and communication research. Therefore, the task of employing doctrinal research in this article is not just to present the law but to facilitate an understanding of how the law relates to theory and practice. In essence, I drew on the doctrinal legal method to critically evaluate and understand how law and regulation are used to control journalism in The Gambia through empirical research.

In doing so, I looked at laws and regulations governing the operation of the media in The Gambia, both online and offline. Furthermore, examining precedents and the explanation of the application of statutes are both important aspects of the doctrinal approach (Carter 2017: 10). The starting point for doctrinal research recommended by doctrinal scholars is to gather the relevant statutes and case laws. Overall, the documents I reviewed included legislations, regulations and court judgements concerning the media and journalism in The Gambia. Drawing on my doctrinal legal research, I explore the constitutions of 1965, 1970 and 1997, the Newspaper (Amendment) Act 2004, the Information and Communications (Amendment) Act 2013 and the Criminal Code. Consultancy reports of media rights groups including Committee to Protect Journalists, Gambia Press Union, Media Sustainability Index and others that extensively documented media freedom in The Gambia were reviewed to provide contextual analysis. Other sources I consulted include law books and journals, media reports and international human rights instruments to examine the legal control of media freedom in The Gambia. In lieu of certain files being made inaccessible, I obtained media reports on incidents involving the government against journalists or the press in The Gambia to explore the context as useful sources of information for analysis.

To understand how Gambian journalists navigate these laws, I conducted 15 semi-structured interviews. These took place remotely via Microsoft Teams and also by phone. They ranged from 23 minutes in duration to over an hour. All participants were anonymized. I selected participants from the State, opposition and other privately owned news media organizations, and five were chosen from each category. This was designed to ensure broad representation of journalists from different news media organizations of diverse ownership and ideological inclination. Although some interviewees are former and current state ministers, I grouped all research participants under the broad category of journalists because they were practicing journalists; others returned to the profession when their services ended with the government. Notably, most of them were either once arrested, prosecuted or have been defendants in some of the cases discussed in this chapter. I also interviewed several journalists who have never been subjected to arrest and prosecution. Before discussing the findings from these interviews, I first discuss the legal framework for regulating online journalism in The Gambia.

Regulating Journalism from Offline to Online – A Colonial Legacy

Part of the problems confronting the regulation of journalism in The Gambia originates from the country's colonial past. To provide context, The Gambia 'maintained many legislative enactments passed by the colonial administration and enacted many other laws to support the Constitution in the governance process' (Senghore 2012: 514). I find that the colonial-era laws that succeeding Gambian governments inherited and maintained in the country's statute books served as repressive and restrictive weapons against journalists. Several Gambian journalists, such as those discussed in the introduction to this chapter, have been convicted through the use of colonial-era laws, such as sedition and criminal defamation, for criticizing the president online and offline, particularly under former President Jammeh's rule.

Among its four West African colonies, The Gambia was the last British colony to gain independence in 1965. This was preceded by the enactment of the 1964 Independence Act, making it official that on and after 18 February, Her Majesty's Government in the United Kingdom shall have no responsibility for the government of The Gambia (Independence Act 1964: 1). This meant that the British government had no further direct involvement in running the affairs of the State of The Gambia. Although The Gambia was to remain under Her Majesty's dominions, this was part of a journey towards national sovereignty. In essence, the

Independence Act marked the end of direct colonial rule, but not indirect colonial influence. This is exemplified by the type of legal framework independent Gambia adopted, taking its root from the common law of England. The common law is also understood as the unwritten law of England and includes customs, principles, judicial precedents and statutes administered by English courts or tribunals (Smith 1884). Gambian laws are generally based on modified English statutes to suit its national context (US Department of State 1990: 136). Some of these laws are still enforced in The Gambia in relation to online media offences include sedition, libel and publication of false news.

Therefore, the colonial context is also important in understanding the nature and types of current legal frameworks used in The Gambia even after independence. This is justified by the invocation of similar criminal legislations, including sedition, publication of false news and criminal libel by post-colonial African governments to jail journalists (Mbaine 2003: 4). I find that the development of repressive media legislations in The Gambia is closely tied to the country's colonial and political history. In short, the legal and regulatory framework of the media emerged out of colonial rule. Still, whereas the United Kingdom has repealed some of these old common laws, they are amended and tightened and remain in use, and they are used in countries like The Gambia. I argue that despite The Gambia gaining independence in 1965, its colonial heritage of media regulation has constantly threatened media freedom. From the first government of President Dawda Jawara's rule leading to the second government of President Yahya Jammeh's rule, journalism in The Gambia has been under immense regulatory and legislative pressure that restricts the work of journalists. It shows a pattern of rise and falls of press freedom from one rule system to another.

The legal framework of the media in The Gambia is generally considered draconian, which induces an environment of self-censorship (Noble 2018). Although the legal framework contains a set of laws that seek to protect human rights such as freedom of expression and press freedom, other subsidiary legislations repudiate the concept through criminal prosecutions and convictions of journalists for offences committed both online and offline. I now move on to look at relevant human rights laws governing the operation of the media in The Gambia to highlight the link between journalism and the protection of digital rights in regulation.

The Human Rights Framework

A human rights-based approach to online media regulation is recognized and generally accepted for the protection of rights people have offline (Beduschi 2022: 2). The Gambia did not have a codified written Constitution until 1965. This was the first step towards codifying independent Gambian laws protecting rights and freedoms, including 'freedom to hold opinions, to receive ideas and information, and to communicate ideas and information without interference' (The Gambia Independence Order 1965: 20). Although the 1965 Constitution did not explicitly provide for media freedom, it contained the right to receive and communicate ideas which is an integral part of media freedom. The 1965 Constitution also introduced a broad array of restrictions to protect defence, public safety, public order, public morality and or public health. Notably, the Independence Constitution also provided restrictions for protecting other persons' reputations, rights and freedoms, including the right to privacy, confidentiality and protection of judicial independence. This means that the Independence Constitution was anchored on a universally accepted principle that balances the right to freedom of expression and other aforementioned rights. However, despite independence, the 1965 Constitution provides for the appointment of a Governor General who shall serve as Her Majesty's representative in The Gambia. This provision suggests that an external authority has vested powers under Gambian laws, thereby making the country's independence questionable. To secure full sovereign independence status, on 24 April 1970, The Gambia adopted a new constitution with the status of a republic (Constitution of The Republic of The Gambia 1970).

The right to freedom of expression and restrictions set out in the 1965 Constitution were reproduced word by word in the 1970 Constitution. This constitution was suspended by a military junta that took over in 1994 and was replaced with decrees. Following two years of military transition rule from 1994 to 1996, The Gambia adopted its third Constitution in 1997, which also provides for the right to freedom of expression and the freedom of the press and other media. Article 25(1)(a) of the 1997 Constitution states that 'every person shall have the right to freedom of speech and expression, which shall include freedom of the press and other media'. The 1997 Constitution also recognized the social watchdog role of the media in Section 207(3):

> The press and other information media shall at all times, be free to uphold the principles, provisions and objectives of this Constitution, and the responsibility and accountability of the Government to the people of The Gambia.

The above provision suggests that the Constitution recognized the media's importance in scrutinizing the government's actions, which is an important doctrine of legal protection for media freedom. This demonstrates that despite the existence of criminal media legislation in The Gambia, it would be wrong to assume that Gambian laws had altogether ignored press freedom and freedom of expression. One could argue that this provision springs from democratic principles, which recognize the role of the media in strengthening democracy and good governance.

Arguably, the constitutional provision is also consistent with the liberalists' democratic perspective that considers the media as 'intermediaries or transmitters between democratic institutes and the public' (Raeijmaekers and Maeseele 2015: 1045). In essence, the media serves as an instrument for promoting democratic values through the dissemination of ideas between the public and national institutions.

Similarly, The Gambia is a signatory to several legally binding international treaties that guarantee and protect media freedoms. The Universal Declaration on Human Rights provides that 'everyone has the right to freedom of opinion and expression; this right includes freedom to hold opinions without interference and to seek, receive and impart information and ideas through any media and regardless of frontiers' (UDHR Article 1948). Like most United Nations Member States, The Gambia is bound by the principles of the Declaration, which is now part of the customary law of nations. The Universal Declaration of Human Rights has served as a guide and an instrument for defending the right to freedom of expression in cases involving journalists and the media globally. On 22 March 1979, The Gambia ratified the International Covenant on Civil and Political Rights. It entered into force on 22 June 1979, making it legally binding for state parties like The Gambia to protect individual's rights to freedom of expression. The Gambia is also a party to the African Charter on Human and People's Rights, an important regional treaty providing freedom of expression as set out in Article 9 of the Charter. The African Charter imposes legal obligations for protecting human rights on African States party to the treaty. This raises the question of whether this constitutional and international human rights protection, in practical terms, means the media is free to perform its watchdog role in The Gambia.

Ironically, reports suggest that in The Gambia, subsidiary legislations, including the Criminal Code, which creates offences such as false publication, sedition, libel or giving false information to a public servant, are giving primacy over constitutional protection for free speech and media freedom (Media Sustainability Index 2012: 163). As I demonstrate later in this chapter, the systematic use of these legislations and other regulations to restrict and repress freedom of expression, and media freedom over constitutional and international legal protection for these freedoms has become problematic for Gambian journalists. This confirms the claim that in Africa, the personal ambitions of rulers dominate constitutions, which prove ineffective (Jackson and Rosberg 1982: 16). In consequence, I argue that the use of secondary legislation to protect rulers from media scrutiny in a country like The Gambia becomes clear to the extent that the constitutional and international protection only exists in text, but not in practice. Also, the ambiguities and broader interpretation surrounding limitations imposed by constitutional provisions make it difficult for the media to understand its scope. This brings me to the specific legislations that govern the operation of the press in The Gambia including newspaper registration and broadcasting licensing.

Newspaper (Amendment) Act 2004

In 2004, the colonial era Newspaper Act 1944 was amended by former President Jammeh's government, which then adopted the Newspaper (Amendment) Act 2004, which provides for mandatory registration of the print media, and licensing requirements for broadcasting stations (Article 19 2012: 11). It is noted that while the 1944 Act applied to only print media, the 2004 Amendment Act was extended to include broadcasting stations (Article 19 2012: 11). Interestingly, under Section 14 of the Act, government-owned or operated media institutions are exempted from the legislation. This means the Act was specifically designed to target the private independent media. Among other things, the Act provided for restrictions on media content and penalties for violation of the law. Section 7(2)(a) of the Act sets out the press's responsibility to ensure that it is free from blasphemous, seditious or other libel and false publication criminal offences. The registration requirement introduced under the Act included a mandatory bond fee of 500,000 Gambian Dalasi (approximately £10,000) with surety or sureties that may be required and approved by the Attorney General (Newspaper Amendment Act 2004: s7.c).

Under Section 13 of the Act, failure to comply with the provisions of the Act is a punishable offence carrying a fine of up to 250,000 Dalasi (approximately £5000). It further requires licensing approvals by the minister of information, which is a politically held position under the control of the president. The Act also provides for the renewal of operational licenses every three years. Section 12 of the Act obliges newspaper printers and publishers to deliver a copy of their publications daily to the Permanent Secretary under the Ministry of Justice and Registrar-General. Article 19 (2012: 12) observes that the substantive conditions for registering a newspaper in The Gambia are incompatible with international standards. This is because Article 8 of the Declaration of Principles for Freedom of Expression in Africa states that 'any registration system for the print media shall not impose substantive restrictions on the right to freedom of expression' (African Commission on Human and Peoples' Rights 2002). This system of direct station regulation is believed to be an undesirable system for a democratic society (Ramchand 1990: 130–47). The excessive onerous conditions of newspaper registration are contrary to international standards, such as in the United States, where the print media are incorporated organizations subject to the same laws applicable to all other business entities.

Information and Communications (Amendment) Act 2013

Arguably, the Information and Communications Act 2009, which was amended in 2013, is one of the most controversial media legislations promulgated under former President Jammeh's rule to restructure, develop and regulate the information and communications sector in The Gambia. Provisions that drew the attention of journalists, scholars and NGOs since the ICA came into force are the ones on licensing and regulation of the broadcasting industry and the penalty it provides for spreading false news online (Article 19 2012; Noble 2018; European Union Election Observation Mission 2017). Experience in The Gambia shows the enforcement of this Act against journalists such as the cases discussed in the introduction of this chapter. The European Union Election Observation Mission to The Gambia (2017: 22) observed that this Act 'induces an environment of self-censorship and equips state actors, most notably the president, with a range of tools to hold a tight grip on traditional and online media outlets as well as citizens'.

The Act provides that the licensing body for radio and television is vested with a public authority, the Public Utilities Regulatory Authority. This government agency is directly accountable to the minister of information and communications, which raises concerns about potential abuse of authority and unfair assessment of licensing applications. Article 230 of the Act provides that 'the Minister, on the advice of the Authority, shall issue broadcasting licences in sufficient numbers to meet the public demand for broadcasting services'. In addition, the Act confers additional powers to the minister to renew, revoke or suspend a broadcasting license as set out under Articles 232 to 236 of said Act. This is an unlimited discretionary power in the hands of a political appointee, and the legislation does not provide for the right to appeal against his decisions. It means that owning broadcasting media solely depends on political decision-making. This is opposed to international standards, which recognize the organizational and operational autonomy of media regulatory bodies. For example, the Declaration of Principles on Freedom of Expression in Africa states that:

1. Any public authority that exercises powers in the areas of broadcast or telecommunications regulation should be independent and adequately protected against interference, particularly of a political or economic nature.
2. The appointment process for members of a regulatory body should be open and transparent, involve the participation of civil society and shall not be controlled by any particular political party.
3. Any public authority that exercises powers in the areas of broadcast or telecommunications should be formally accountable to the public through a multi-party body (African Commission on Human and Peoples' Rights 2019).

This declaration, to which The Gambia is a state party, provides the duty to adopt legislative or other measures to give effect to these provisions. Therefore, The Gambia should ensure that laws such as the ICA provide protection against government interference in broadcast media licensing. I now move on to discuss provisions of The Gambian Criminal Code, which are crucial elements of online journalism regulation, especially regarding the repression of dissent on the internet.

The Criminal Code and Journalism

The Criminal Code of The Gambia contains media offences, including false publication, sedition and criminal defamation, that profoundly impact journalism and other media activities in the country and online. These are the most common offences Gambian journalists have been contending with that place severe restrictions on freedom of expression and press freedom in The Gambia, including online publications. An example is the case of *the State* v. *Ebrima Sawaneh et al.* (2009), a significant judgement of criminal sanctions against journalists in contemporary Gambia, as six journalists were rounded up at once, prosecuted and convicted on several criminal charges for publishing an article in various newspapers and websites on the internet, critical of the president and his government. Therefore, it is the case that punishment for online journalism activities generally falls under the provisions of the criminal code. With this in mind, I find it essential to discuss the key relevant provisions of the Criminal Code.

First, Article 59 of the Criminal Code defines false publication as any statement, rumour or report which is likely to cause fear and alarm to the public or to disturb the public peace, knowing or having reason to believe that such statement, rumour or report is false. The punishment for this offence is imprisonment for a term of two years. The Criminal Code does not recognize lack of knowledge as a defence for false publication unless it is proven that reasonable measures were taken to verify the accuracy of the information. Several human rights bodies, such as Article 19 (2012), have criticized the enforcement of this provision against Gambian journalists. Among the reasons they believe that criminalizing the dissemination of false news is objectionable are:

> While journalists strive on the quality and accuracy of the information they provide, in an environment where news travels at an incredible pace, facts may be difficult to check. If journalists, or indeed bloggers and other social media users, are faced with the prospect of a prosecution for publishing false information, they are much less likely to share information, including news that is clearly in the public interest. Ultimately, therefore, false news laws can have a serious chilling effect on the free flow of information.
>
> (Article 19 2012: 17)

Also, Human Rights Watch warned that the Gambian law on false publication is 'overly broad and vague' (Human Rights Watch 2015: 63), which has been used frequently to intimidate and sometimes prosecute and imprison or fine those publishing or saying things critical of the government. They are seriously concerned that journalists, opposition members, civil servants and student leaders have been arrested and detained on charges of spreading false information.

Second, the Criminal Code also provides for various seditious offences which have been strongly criticized by human rights groups globally. This offence is one of the most serious restrictive and repressive provisions of the Criminal Code that severely affects freedom of expression and media freedom in The Gambia. Section 51 of the Criminal Code defines what a seditious intention is, including bringing hatred or contempt against the president, government and the administration of justice. Section 52 of the Criminal Code further detailed what may constitute an act of sedition. This includes uttering any seditious words, printing, publishing, selling, offering for sale, distributing or reproducing any seditious publication. It also prohibits the import of any seditious publication unless he has no reason to believe that it is seditious.

This law provides general principles of criminal liability for offences relating to the work of the media online and offline. In essence, my doctrinal analysis reveals that this law is very protective of the president and the state and attracts retributive punishments for criticizing them. For example, in March 2009, seven Gambian journalists were arrested and detained. It led to the particular case of *the State* v. *Ebrima Sawaneh et al.* (2009), where six journalists were prosecuted and convicted for several counts of sedition and criminal defamation for criticizing the president. In a joint submission to the United Nations Universal Periodic Review (2019: 5), human rights groups, including Access Now, Article 19 and Committee to Protect Journalists, argue that this law is 'designed to restrict criticism of the government and public officials, which is not a legitimate purpose for limiting the right to freedom of expression'.

Third, the Criminal Code imposes both civil and criminal defamation liability. Similar to the offences discussed above, criminal defamation is another problematic provision, which has been subjected to widespread criticisms. Section 178 of the Criminal Code provides that 'any person who, by print, writing, painting, effigy, or other sounds, unlawfully publishes any defamatory matter concerning another person with intent to defame that other person is guilty of the misdemeanour termed libel'. Furthermore, Section 179 of the Criminal Code states that 'defamatory matter is matter likely to injure the reputation of any person by exposing him to hatred, contempt or ridicule or likely to damage any person in his profession or trade by an injury to his reputation'. In The Gambia, the offence has both civil and criminal components where a victim of libellous publication can file a criminal suit in a court of law. However, the experience in The Gambia shows that libellous criminal suits are brought mainly by state authorities against media practitioners.

Contemporary scholars have pointed out that criminal defamation laws are persistently applied by many African governments to silence criticism from journalists (Herskovitz 2018; McCracken 2012). Quaqua (2017) points out that criminal defamation laws are kept as weapons against the press in Africa. For him, the law on defamation should be considered under civil matters and not criminal. He expressed concern that in enforcing criminal defamation laws, the State treats journalists as criminals when prosecuting them for criminal offences. The discussions here suggest that the national laws of The Gambia, specifically the Constitution, provide for the protection of media freedom, but subsidiary legislations severely restrict critical journalism, which creates a dilemma for Gambian journalists. I argue that the direct government regulation and criminal provisions gave the authorities sweeping censorship powers to control media freedom in The Gambia.

So far, I have considered the legal framework of the media in The Gambia, which is largely repressive and restrictive compared to independent journalism. It is compounded with legal uncertainties as it reveals a pattern of cases, including charges of sedition, criminal defamation, false news and false publication against journalists for offences committed online and in printed newspapers. Faced with the threat of criminal legislation that is inconsistent with international standards, the human rights framework has been overtaken by punitive regulatory measures. I found that the establishment of online news websites operating from the diaspora was one of the ways Gambian journalists evaded arrests and criminal punishments, and I now move on to present the findings from my interviews with 15 Gambian journalists to shed light on how they navigate such a repressive legal framework.

Navigating The Gambia's Legal Framework

This section focuses on interviews with Gambian journalists in the diaspora who established online news websites that evade and defy stringent government media regulations in The Gambia, as discussed above. This relates to the role of Africans in the diaspora, supplying news and views that contribute to shaping the democratization process of their countries (Hyden et al. 2002: 7). In this context, diaspora Gambians are not exceptional in using the internet to raise issues that could not be talked about inside The Gambia, due, in part, to a media environment where journalists are prosecuted and subject to physical attacks on themselves and their offices. As I showed in the previous section, restrictive registration requirements with high bonds for registering newspapers coupled with stringent licensing approval requirements for the broadcast media have seen dozens of online radios and websites established by exiled Gambian journalists and dissidents outside the country, to serve as alternatives to the media inside the country. My interviewees believed this was a way of challenging the government by publishing uncomfortable truths, which the media in the country dared not to do.

Prominent online news websites include *Freedom Newspaper*, *Gainako*, *Fatu Network*, *Kairo News* and *Shepherds Broadcasting Network*. Several participants identified *Freedom Newspaper* as being one of the most critical against the government – available at Freedomnewspaper.com. Also broadcasting an online radio station, the *Freedom Newspaper* was established in 2003 by an exiled Gambian journalist based in the US state of North Carolina. It provides its audience with regular news updates on The Gambia but predominantly focuses on government scandals, politicians, public officials, public institutions and state secrets. Similar to the practices of a clandestine publication, articles published on the website before the change of government in The Gambia in 2017 were mostly produced by a single known author who also runs the website. The rest of the stories were mainly written by anonymous authors who used the names Insider or The Soldier. This is not surprising as The Gambia government was very concerned about the *Freedom Newspaper*, which resulted in the hacking of the website in 2006, and names of the paper's subscribers were published in the pro-government newspaper *The Daily Observer* (Amnesty International 2008). A report by Amnesty International on this particular incident revealed that 'many people on that list were arrested, questioned, detained for several days to several weeks, and some were subjected to torture while in detention' (n.d.: n.pag.). Furthermore, it is noted that the government also 'blocked the newspaper's IP address, stating that the website was affecting security issues between Gambia and Senegal' (n.d.: n.pag.).

Most interviewees observed that because the website operates outside the country, it was free from the controlling and restrictive legal environment in The Gambia. Participant 8 considered the paper as among the few news websites 'that reports extensively on issues, not all time accurate anyway, but at least with hard news. Because media houses in the country wouldn't write those things, they are either arrested or closed down'. This indicates the significant role of the website in publishing alternative reports the local media operating inside the country would not risk. Interestingly, Participant 9 who at the time was an editor for the pro-government newspaper *The Daily Observer* in The Gambia was also an anonymous reporter for *Freedom Newspaper*. Following attempts to arrest them failed, they were declared 'wanted' by the government after the hacking of the website. According to Participant 9:

> They hacked the *Freedom Newspaper* and found all the emails I was writing to him and declared me wanted. It was a matter of escaping the laws, if I wasn't killed by

> the NIA or the Junglers. So it was a combination of both. The laws they could have used against me or the torture and suffering I would have endured. After a month I escaped, a friend of mine [...] was arrested and he died. So I escaped and wrote about all the corruptions on the *Freedom Newspaper*. After Kukoi, I was the only [...] who was declared wanted in that country. So they were putting that on TV and radio, I was traumatised and scared. I thought about suicide.

There are three points to be noted from this response. First, despite working for the pro-government *Daily Observer*, the paper with the largest circulation in The Gambia, it is quite revealing that Participant 9 would rather send information to an online newspaper operating outside the country than publishing critical reports in the *Daily Observer*. This shows that the pro-government media was tightly controlled and would not publish reports that are critical to the government. Second, it is noted that the consequences of being caught reporting for *Freedom Newspaper* might not only be imprisonment but also torture and death. Third, the mere fact of declaring a journalist wanted, like the case of Kukoi who led a rebellion to overthrow a government in The Gambia shows that the government does not take online media lightly.

Participant 4, founder of an online media platform, pointed out that they started being critical of the Gambian government when they fled into exile. According to them, the fact that they were living outside the country meant they were 'safe', and 'decided to establish the [name of organisation] to write stories on things that are happening that I could not do in The Gambia. Like I said there was dictatorship and even your family members will warn you to be careful'. They further explained that the online publication made it possible to 'go after' the regime in The Gambia. According to them, the online media publish critical 'facts' the Gambian authorities do not like. My research found that while establishing online enterprises was a strategy to avoid the repressive media laws in The Gambia, the government was also finding ways to stop or block them. Under former President Jammeh's rule, over 20 independent news and opposition websites operated by exiled journalists and activists were blocked for their criticisms of the government (Freedom House 2021). In addition, I found that the Information and Communications (Amendment) Act 2013 (Nana Law) was introduced to curb the growing dissent on the internet. As discussed earlier, the Act provides severe punishments for spreading false news online. The interview responses in the context of the Nana Law suggest the policy dimension of the government to stop journalists from running critical online publications and their sources on the ground from giving them information.

All respondents readily attributed the passing of the amendment of the Information and Communications (Amendment) Act 2013 to Nana Grey Johnson, a journalist and former minister of information and communications who tabled the Bill before the National Assembly on behalf of the government and defended its merits and principles to be considered for passage into law. Several participants observed their disappointment for a prominent journalist like Nana to 'mastermind' a law that seeks to curtail media freedom. The disappointment in Participant 8 is captured in the following words: 'You know before going further, those laws were masterminded by a former journalist. He is now a journalism lecturer at the University of The Gambia. He is the former Information Minister.' Participant 4 who was charged under the Nana Law described the law as 'unfair and too harsh'.

Again, Participant 4 notes that the law was brought in by the former information minister 'to clampdown on the online independent media'. This points to a specific individual with a background in journalism who orchestrated a law that stifles media freedom. It also suggests that expectations were high because he is from a journalism background and would be a champion of media freedom rather than being an agent to abridge this freedom. However, I argue that the minister's actions must be viewed within a broader context of a government that shows strong interest in media control. This, evidence suggests, is a government that tried to restrict the media in many ways, including through the formal application of laws and regulations and carrying out physical attacks on journalists, as I have shown in this chapter. Also, I find the use of the incorporation policy, where journalists are offered political appointments, has been yet another method of capture, particularly by former Gambian President Jammeh and even under the current President Barrow. It has been used as a strategic method of controlling journalism and legitimization.

The amendment of the Information and Communications (Amendment) Act 2013 is believed to be a result of the adversarial relationship between the government and exiled journalists, which aims to repress growing dissent on the internet (Article 19 et al. 2014: 15). This assertion is confirmed by several participants who suggest that Nana's law seeks to curtail the publication of critical stories against authorities on diasporic online news websites. The ICA provides for the punishment of online speech, including spreading false news about the government or public officials. The offence is punishable by a 15-year prison term or a fine of up to three million Gambian Dalasi (Human Rights Watch 2015: 63). Despite a change of government in 2017, Participant 2, a journalist who also served as the information minister, argued that there should be both 'criminal and civil' punishment against the online media. According to them, 'in this era of social media there is a lot of false information and that has nothing to do with professional journalism. We have seen some radio stations and newspapers go to social media pick up stories publish or broadcast them and make those stories even the subject of phone calls'. This argument highlights the concern authorities have on online media, which they believe lacks professional orientation.

Conclusion

In this chapter, I have shown how a range of laws have been used to regulate the practices of independent journalists in The Gambia. Through a doctrinal legal analysis of these laws, I highlighted how the political repression of journalists escalated to the highest level when the government of former President Jammeh started arresting, prosecuting and convicting journalists for criticizing the president online. At the same time, the Information and Communications (Amendment) Act 2013 was introduced, forbidding criticism of government officials on the internet, and introducing 15-year prison terms for spreading false news online. Whereas the Constitution 1997 of The Gambia and international treaties look to protect press freedom, the country's Criminal Code repudiates this concept, which is a step backwards to the standards applied during colonial rule. I argue that this is compounded with legal uncertainties, as the constitutional protection for media freedom has proven ineffective.

While the legal analysis showed a pattern of sedition and false publication charges against journalists for online-related offences, I that established those adopted from the colonial era accorded special protection for both the president and government of The Gambia. I paid attention to the way journalists perceive the legal framework of the media in The Gambia, leading to increasing fear, self-censorship and fleeing to exile. Because of this, combative alternative online journalism websites have emerged outside The Gambia in response to evading the violence perpetrated by the government against the private media inside the country. Evidence shows that The Gambian diasporic online media have immensely contributed to the gathering and distributing uncensored critical information the media inside the country would not publish for fear of reprisals. This is facilitated through websites and online radio stations created by mainly exiled journalists living in the diaspora. Such attempts to circumvent restrictive legal frameworks, particularly in the Global South, can be understood as 'evasive journalism'.

As Darko (2020) observes, it is not uncommon for journalists in the Global South to employ 'evasive techniques' to expose corruption. However, for Darko, evasiveness relates to the ways journalists skirt the boundaries of professional ethics to report news that is in the public interest. In contrast, my use of evasiveness draws on Elert and Henrekson's notion of evasive entrepreneurship. Here, evasiveness relates to how entrepreneurs circumvent restrictive legal frameworks 'by using innovations to exploit contradictions in that framework' (Elert and Henrekson 2016: 1). Although Elert and Henrekson are referring to business, I see parallels here with the activities of Gambian diasporic journalists, such as those involved in the *Freedom Newspaper* and the *Fatu Network*, who have set up news enterprises to overcome the limitations of the law. Elert and Henrekson also acknowledge that such actions can invoke 'a response from lawmakers and regulators' (Elert and Henrekson 2016: 2), leading to stricter regulation, for instance, the introduction of the Information and Communications (Amendment) Act 2013 as an attempt to control the dissemination of news online. Greater attention to the actions of evasive journalists across the Global South can help us to further understand how they navigate complex legal frameworks to report items of suppressed news and limit the possible repercussions for doing so.

REFERENCES

African Commission on Human and Peoples' Rights (2019), 'Declaration of principles on freedom of expression and access to information in Africa', Banjul, https://achpr.au.int/en. Accessed 21 November 2021.

Allan, Stuart (2006), *Online News: Journalism and the Internet*, Buckingham: Open University.

Allan, Stuart (2012), *Online News: Journalism and the Internet*, Berkshire: Open University Press.

Amnesty International (2008), *Gambia Fear Rules*, London: Amnesty International Publications.

Amnesty International (2013), *Annual Report: Gambia 2013*, Amnesty International USA, https://www.amnestyusa.org/reports/annual-report-gambia-2013/#:~:text=Republic%20of%20the%20Gambia&text=The%20inmates%20had%20not%20exhausted,Prison%20conditions%20were%20appalling. Accessed 25 June 2023.

Anansaringkarn, Pattamon and Neo, Ric (2021), 'How can state regulations over the online sphere continue to respect the freedom of expression?: A case study of contemporary "fake news" regulations in Thailand', *Information & Communications Technology Law*, 30:3, pp. 283–303.

Article 19, Access Now and Committee to Protect Journalists (2019), joint submission to the Universal Periodic Review of The Gambia, https://www.article19.org/wp-content/uploads/2019/11/ARTICLE-19_GAMBIA_UPR34.pdf. Accessed 16 July 2020.

Article 19 (2012), 'The Gambia: Analysis of selected laws on media – Overview', April, https://www.refworld.org/reference/research/art19/2012/en/85772. Accessed 1 July 2019.

Atton, Chris (2004), *An Alternative Internet: Radical Media, Politics and Creativity*, Edinburgh: Edinburgh University Press.

Badr, Hanan (2019), 'Egypt's media system: Historic legacies and blocked potentials for independent media', *Publizistik*, 65:1, pp. 63–79.

Beduschi, Ana (2022), *Regulatory Approaches to Online Harms and Human Rights: Three Case Studies*, Geneva Academy of International Humanitarian Law and Human Rights, Working Paper No. 11, January.

Blaug, Robert and Schwarzmantel, Hendrik (2000), *Democracy*, Edinburgh: Edinburgh University Press.

Carter, Edward (2017), 'Mass Communication Law and Policy Research and the values of free expression', *Journalism & Mass Communication Quarterly*, 94:3, pp. 641–62.

Darko, Samuel Appiah (2020), 'Investigative journalism in Ghana: Balancing public interest and individual privacy', *Cogent Social Sciences*, 6:1, p. 1772444, https://doi.org/10.1080/23311886.2020.1772444.

Elert, Niklas and Henrekson, Magnus (2016), 'Evasive entrepreneurship', *Small Business Economics*, 47:1, pp. 95–113.

European Union Election Observation Mission (2017), *Final Report: National Assembly Elections*, Banjul, https://www.ecoi.net/en/file/local/1411210/1226_1507621986_final-report-eu-eom-the-gambia-2017-0.pdf. Accessed 15 January 2022.

Faye, Dawda and Camara, Sana (2008), 'Journalist Fatou Jaw Manneh gets D250,000 fine', *The Point Newspaper*, 19 August, https://thepoint.gm/africa/gambia/article/journalist-fatou-jaw-manneh-gets-d250-000-fine. Accessed 21 June 2023

Flew, Terry and Wilding, Derek (2020), 'The turn to regulation in digital communication: The ACCC's digital platforms inquiry and Australian media policy', *Media, Culture & Society*, 43:1, pp. 48–65.

Foust, James (2017), *Online Journalism: Principles and Practices of News for the Web*, 3rd ed., Abingdon: Routledge.

Freedom House (2021), 'The Gambia: *Freedom on the Net 2021 Country Report*', https://freedomhouse.org/country/gambia/freedom-net/2021. Accessed 22 June 2023.

Freedom House (2022), 'The Gambia: *Freedom in The World 2022 Country Report*', https://freedomhouse.org/country/gambia/freedom-world/2022. Accessed 23 June 2023.

Gambia Independence Act (1964), Chapter 93, p. 1.

Glasius, Marlies and Michaelsen, Marcus (2018), 'Illiberal and authoritarian practices in the digital sphere', *International Journal of Communication*, 12, pp. 3795–13.

Herskovitz, Benjamin (2018), 'Speaking truth to power: Criminal defamation before the African Court on Human and People's Rights', *The George Washington International Law Review*, 50:4, pp. 899–921.

Human Rights Watch (2015), *State of Fear: Arbitrary Arrests, Torture, and Killings*, https://www.hrw.org/sites/default/files/report_pdf/gambia0915_4up_0.pdf. Accessed 23 June 2023.

Hutchinson, Terry (2013), 'Doctrinal research: Researching the jury', in D. Watkins and M. Burton (eds), *Research Methods in Law*, 1st ed., Abingdon: Routledge, pp. 15–41.

Hyden, Goran, Leslie, Michael and Ogundimu, F. Folu (eds), (2002), *Media and Democracy in Africa*, Piscataway: Transaction Publishers, The Nordic Africa Institute.

Independence Act, The Gambia (1964), (c. 93), London: HMSO.

International Federation of Journalists (2006), 'Grave repression of the media in The Gambia: Four journalists imprisoned, two escape, online newspaper hacked', 31 May, https://www.ifj.org/es/sala-de-prensa/noticias/detalle/article/grave-repression-of-the-media-in-the-gambia-four-journalists-imprisoned-two-escape-online-newspap. Accessed 23 June 2023.

Jackson, Robert and Rosberg, Carl (1982), *Personal Rule in Black Africa: Prince, Autocrat, Prophet, Tyrant*, Berkeley: University of California Press.

Mabweazara, Hayes M., Mudhai, Okoth F. and Whittaker, Jason (eds) (2013), *Online Journalism in Africa: Trends, Practices and Emerging Cultures*, London: Taylor & Francis Group.

Mathiason, John (2009), *Internet Governance: The New Frontier of Global Institutions*, Abingdon: Routledge.

Mbaine, Adolfe (2003), *Media Laws and Regulations in Uganda: The Freedom of Expression, Freedom of the Press and the Challenge of New Communication Technologies*, Kampala: Fountain Publishers.

McCracken, Michael (2012), 'The new landscape in Europe: Defamation and the right to freedom of expression', *Human Rights Law Review*, 12:4, pp. 675–702.

Media Sustainability Index (2012), 'The Gambia at glance', https://www.irex.org/sites/default/files/pdf/media-sustainability-index-africa-2012-the-gambia.pdf. Accessed 15 December 2020.

Ndlovu, Mandla (2019), 'Abduction of teachers by state agents condemned', *News 24*, Bulawayo, 29 April, https://bulawayo24.com/index-id-news-sc-national-byo-161494.html. Accessed 25 June 2023.

Newspaper Amendment Act (2004), § 7.C, p.4.

Ngoshi, Hazel (2021), 'Repression, literary dissent and the paradox of censorship in Zimbabwe', *Journal of Southern African Studies*, 47:5, pp. 799–815, https://doi.org/10.1080/03057070.2021.1959780.

Noble, Ian (2018), 'Freedom of expression and media pluralism in The Gambia', *Media-4Democracy*, https://www.eeas.europa.eu/sites/default/files/eud_report_freedom_of_expression_media_pluralism_the_gambia_media4democracy.pdf. Accessed 28 March 2021.

Obia, Vincent (2023), 'Regulatory annexation: Extending broadcast media regulation to social media and internet content', *Communication Law and Policy*, 28:2, https://doi.org/10.1080/10811680.2023.2206382.

Parks, Lisa and Thompson, Rachel (2020), 'The slow shutdown: Information and internet regulation in Tanzania from 2010 to 2018 and impacts on online content creators', *International Journal of Communication*, 14, pp. 4288–4308.

Quaqua, Peter (2017), 'Journalism not a crime: Please repeal criminal defamation laws', *Front Page Africa Online*, https://frontpageafricaonline.com/opinion/journalism-not-a-crime-please-repeal-criminal-defamation-laws/#google_vignette. Accessed 4 August 2021.

Raeijmaekers, Daniëlle and Maeseele, Pieter (2015), 'Media, pluralism and democracy: What's in a name?' *Media, Culture & Society*, 37:7, pp. 1042–59.

Ramchand, Anjali (1990), 'Freedom of the press: Regulation under the Newspaper and Printing Presses Act', 11 SING. L. REV. 130.

Reporters Without Borders (2014), 'The Gambia: The state of press freedom', https://www.refworld.org/reference/countryrep/rsf/2014/en/106433. Accessed 23 June 2023.

Reporters Without Borders (2019), *Egypt Country Report*, https://rsf.org/en/egypt. Accessed 24 June 2023.

Samateh, Bakary (2013), 'Fatou Camara charged with "spreading false news"', *The Point Newspaper*, 11 October, https://thepoint.gm/africa/gambia/article/fatou-camara-charged-with-spreading-false-news. Accessed 21 June 2023.

Sarah, Joseph (2012), 'Social media, political change, and human rights', *Boston College International and Comparative Law Review*, 35, p. 145.

Schäfer, Jan M. (2009), *Protest in Ägypten: Wie Al Jazeera und andere Medien die Kifaya-Bewegung möglich machte*, Berlin: Frank & Timme.

Senghore, Aboubacar (2012), 'Press freedom and democratic governance in The Gambia: A rights-based approach', *African Human Rights Law Journal*, 2, pp. 508–38.

Siapera, Eugenia and Veglis, Andreas (2012), *The Handbook of Global Online Journalism*, Hoboken: Wiley, ProQuest Ebook Central.

Skjerdal, Terje (2013), 'Online journalism under pressure: An Ethiopian account', in H. M. Mabweazara, O. F. Mudhai and J. Whittaker (eds), *Online Journalism in Africa: Trends, Practices and Emerging Cultures*, Abingdon: Routledge, pp. 89–103.

Smith, Williams J. (1884), *An Elementary View of the Proceedings in an Action at Law*, London: Stevens & Sons.

State v. *Ebrima Sawaneh et al.* (2009), HC/293/09/CR/062/AO.

The Constitution of the Republic of The Gambia (1970), Chapter 2, p. 24.

The Constitution of the Republic of The Gambia (1997), Chapter 4.

The Gambia Independence Order (1965), Chapter 2, p. 20.

United Nations General Assembly (1948), *Universal Declaration of Human Rights*, United Nations, https://www.un.org/en/about-us/universal-declaration-of-human-rights. Accessed 2 December 2021.

Universal Declaration of Human Rights [UDHR] (1948), Resolution 217 A (III), Paris: United Nations General Assembly.

US Department of State (1990), *The Gambia: 15 Ann, Human Rights Report*, 20, pp. 101–06.

Conclusion: Afrokology and the Imperative to Decolonize Tech Regulation in Africa

Winston Mano

Introduction

Information and tech regulations are not new. They already exist at varying levels in different forms, but what is changing, as has been demonstrated by this edited volume, is the speed and scope of their effects, with the big question relating to the adequacy of existing regulation. Clearly, digital practices are evolving at a run-away pace, faster than regulations. This rapidly shifting digital environment, which now includes artificial intelligence, necessitates changing the guidelines undergirding the 'rules of the game for this emerging digital ecosystem', as is noted in Chapter 2. More relevant data protection laws and regulations are, for example, needed to achieve fairness and more ethical conduct. There is a need to both 'learn' and 'unlearn' 'lessons from existing research knowledge on new media regulation to inform future regulatory policies' (Obia, Chapter 4). Regulations must protect users from exploitation by the powerful, since 'power is the ability to direct or prevent the current or future actions of other groups and individuals' (Naim 2014: 16). Multi-stakeholderism can help counter the whims of the powerful by collectively developing guidelines and implementation of tech regulation, be it self-regulation, statutory regulation or co-regulation. The main point, emphasized by the book, is the provision of a regulation aligned with international human rights standards as set out in the UN's Articles 19 and 20. However, the global guidance must not result in African tech regulation copying Global North frameworks, such as the way the 'EU's GDPR has effectively become a benchmark for Africa' (Obia, Chapter 4). The chapters in this book collectively identify opportunities, limits and gaps in the regulation of communication technologies in Africa, with a view to bringing more efficacy and an African vantage point. In its pushback on the marginalization of Africa, this book foregrounds and mainstreams research from

'African perspectives' onto the global governance of emerging media technologies, as stated in Obia and Bah's Introduction. This chapter will conclude by discussing the book's key findings in terms of Afrokology (Mano and Milton 2021).

Beyond Narrow Interests

Tech regulation must be critical and responsive to the African context. This means, for example, debunking the narrow technicist stance of embracing communication technologies as a panacea for problems in Africa (see Mabweazara, Chapter 1). Africa's regulatory stance for communication technologies ought to be open to other aspects, especially public interest issues. Human rights issues such as protecting freedom of expression and media freedom must be integral to tech regulation. Africa's regulatory approach needs to push back on the abuse of technology, especially by those wanting to dominate the continent to boost their economic and political power. Internet shutdowns also need to be challenged. The idea of complicating the narrative to include holding to account the powerful, whether politicians, governments or private companies, is important and consistent with historic alternative policy propositions. In *Many Voices, One World*, for example, it is noted that:

> Privately-owned organisations in the communication field wield power in setting patterns, forming attitudes and motivating behaviour which is comparable to that of government, and sometimes – because of the financial resources committed – even greater.
> (McBride 1980: 118)

The problem is with how both private and non-private ownerships take advantage of shortcomings in technology regulation. Across Africa, this is a major issue that justifies the warnings from UNESCO in 1977, 1980 and 1982. The book is a rallying call against the abuse of information technologies to serve narrow interests or as tools of power that widen inequalities between individuals, countries and regions. One troubling concern, which the current book makes clear from the start, is how, for example, taken-for-granted internet safeguards in the Global North do not exist in African countries. In the wake of existing digital authoritarianism and censorship practices, Africa is less able to deal with digital colonialism.

Digital Colonialism

Without adequate regulation, Africa is susceptible to internal and external forms of digital colonialism. Local power blocs and unpopular governments capture digital media by introducing undemocratic barriers to entry for others. The chapters in the book have shown worrying limits on the use of the internet in Africa at critical moments through shutdowns and social media taxes. Chapters in the book have shown how the grey areas in tech regulation result in internet and social media capture that undermines human rights. In Uganda, Kenya and Ghana, for example, existing regulations have not adequately protected the rights of digital users. As discussed by Muthoni Esther King'ori and Maureen Syallow in Chapter 5, there is a need to balance freedom with responsibility in the making of tech regulations such as Kenya's Computer Misuse and Cybercrimes Act, 2018. In Chapter 6, Ndawana Youngson, Joanne Knowles and Elastus Mambwe discuss the problems that arose from the lack of consultation in the introduction of cybersecurity laws in Zambia. In Chapter 7, Bedu-Addo similarly discusses Ghana's struggle to reform its media and communication regulation system in the wake of resistance by vested political and economic interests. In Chapter 8, Yemisi Akinbobola, Vincent Obia and Trust Matsilele argue that regulatory inadequacies have largely resulted in captured public broadcasting both in South Africa and Nigeria. Also, leaving out key groups from the legislative process narrows the available range of perspectives to be considered if the legislation is to benefit all. Without regulatory protection, journalists precariously try to innovate or negotiate the risks on their own terms as discussed by Sulayman Bah in Chapter 9. The sidelining of key voices will result in regulatory capture, a form of internal digital colonialism, that undermines freedom of expression and media freedom.

Meanwhile, another dangerous type of digital colonialism also results from the transfer of tech and regulations from the Global North to the Global South (Mano 2023). Such external forms of digital colonialism are more troubling in the way they undermine African tech futures, as Coleman notes:

> One may believe that strengthening data protection laws will be a barrier to digital colonialism. However, regardless of their relative strength or weakness, data protection laws have limits. An analysis of Kenya's 2018 data protection bill, the General Data Protection Regulation (GDPR), and documented actions of large-scale tech companies exemplifies how those limits create several loopholes for continued digital colonialism including, historical violations of data privacy laws; limitations of sanctions; unchecked mass concentration of data, lack of competition enforcement, uninformed consent, and limits to defined nation-state privacy laws.
>
> (Coleman 2019: 417)

The loopholes in the Kenyan tech regulation are also echoed in other African countries on the continent. Added to this regulatory shortcoming is a rising neoliberal push for reforms in today's Africa, entrenching market liberalism and deregulation. Faced with this precarious context, this book pushes for increased agency in tech regulation among Africans and citizens from the Global South. Challenging technical regulations from the Global North, alongside promoting viable and independent technological regulatory initiatives in the Global South, could advance ongoing debates on the decolonization of regulatory epistemes and practices. A decolonized approach could also lead to more diverse and beneficial technological innovations that leverage human rights. Africa urgently needs to meaningfully engage with broad questions of power and control exerted by private capital in the form of Big Techs (Mano 2021). Based on the foregoing, this concluding chapter will consider the implications of scope and of decolonizing our approach to regulating tech regulation in Africa using the Afrokological perspective.

Afrokology of African Regulatory Frameworks

Theorizing from Africa and the Global South is an important quest for data justice in the emerging global digital ecosystem. This book, *Regulating New Media in Africa: Politics, Law and Governance*, has contributed to an Afrokological turn (Mano and Milton 2021), with evidence and theoretical reimagination that effectively challenges both the local forms of domination and the hegemonic geopolitical dominance of Global North tech regulations. In terms of Afrokology for media and communication studies, the collection adds fresh thinking that refutes the claims that the Global North is the normal order, complete with all regulatory solutions for Africa and other contexts. Crucially, the chapter invokes Afrokology in ways that advance and uphold marginalized epistemes and practices that can help inform and reawaken being African in the world of technological innovations. In essence, Afrokology is presented as a participatory, transdisciplinary and responsive framework grounded in the core values of conviviality and incompleteness. It emphasizes the respectful inclusion of so-called 'other' tech knowledge and lived experiences in regulation, often exploited by Big Tech for profit (Mano 2023). Hence, Afrokology recognizes the African regulatory ideas as valid and pushes for a 'technological pluriverse where different worlds can coexist, not submitted in one reality, but in incommensurability within the sphere of digital communication technologies'. Rooted in decolonization, Afrokology focuses on rediscovering and reclaiming previously silenced African tech knowledge, expertise and lived experience in regulation. It identifies the oppressive and marginalizing forces that are constraining Africa's digital future – both internal and external.

Conclusion

Altogether, *Regulating New Media in Africa: Politics, Law and Governance* highlights the need for a new relational accountability, which not only addresses the misrecognition and underrepresentation of African contributions in the digital ecosystem but also calls on vested interests to unlearn their privileges, to listen and to recognize that Africa has diverse actors in its digital ecosystem. Beyond centring the tech knowledge and research expertise of Africans, rooted in lived experience, this book also humanizes digital ecologies – codes, rules and algorithms – in ways that expose and resist the marginalization and governance of Africans as digital subjects.

REFERENCES

Coleman, Danielle (2019), 'Digital colonialism: The 21st century scramble for Africa through the extraction and control of user data and the limitations of data protection laws', *Michigan Journal of Race and Law*, 24, p. 417, https://repository.law.umich.edu/mjrl/vol24/iss2/6. Accessed 25 June 2025.

MacBride, Seán (1980), *Many Voices, One World: Towards a New More Just and More Efficient World Information and Communication Order – Report by the International Commission for the Study of Communication Problems*, International Commission for the Study of Communication Problems, Paris: UNESCO, https://waccglobal.org/wp-content/uploads/2020/07/MacBride-Report-English.pdf. Accessed 25 June 2025.

Mano, Winston (2023), 'Big tech's scramble for Africa: An Afrokological critique', in W. Mano and L. Mkaouar (eds), *Media Ownership in Africa in the Digital Age*, Abingdon: Routledge/Taylor & Francis, pp. 15–30

Mano, Winston and Milton, Viola C. (eds) (2021), *Routledge Handbook of African Media and Communication Studies*, Abingdon and New York: Routledge.

Contributors

Dr Yemisi Akinbobola is an associate professor and research degrees coordinator at Birmingham City University and a global authority on gender and media in Africa. She is the co-founder of African Women in Media, where her research and enterprise have shaped policy. Her work led to the Kigali Declaration on the Elimination of Gender Violence in and through Media, and she served on the committee that drafted the Lusaka Declaration on Press Freedom in Africa.

Dr Sulayman Bah is an academic and journalist specializing in media law and journalism. He has extensive university teaching experience, holds multiple degrees in journalism and law and possesses practical, international journalism experience across various media platforms. He serves on the UK's Independent Monitor for the Press Code Committee of experts.

Dr Kobina Ano Bedu-Addo lectures journalism, media and communication courses at the Ghana Institute of Journalism (GIJ), now part of the University of Media, Arts and Communication in Ghana. He is a co-founder of the Communication and Social Policy Research group at the same University. Dr Bedu-Addo has extensive experience working for Advertising, Public Relations and Broadcast Media firms in Ghana. He studied at the GIJ in Ghana, and Lambeth College, the Open University and the University of Westminster, all in the United Kingdom. His research interests focus on how technologies, economics and politics shape media and communication policy in African jurisdictions, the regulation of media and communication spaces in the post convergence environment in Africa, how new communication technologies recast journalistic production and consumption in the digital platform era and the futures of public journalism and public service broadcasting/media in African digital media platform ecologies.

Oliver Carter is professor of creative economies at Birmingham City University. His research explores hidden economies of cultural production, with a particular focus on the intersections of technology, law, and commerce.

DR ESTHER MUTHONI KING'ORI has wide experience in journalism, media and communication studies. She holds a Bachelor of Arts in communication from Daystar University, Nairobi, a Master of Arts in communication studies from the University of Nairobi and a Ph.D. in communication (media studies) from Daystar University, Nairobi. Her Ph.D. thesis investigated the ethical frameworks of news bloggers who are not mainstream journalists. Dr King'ori is a lecturer at Strathmore University, Kenya where she teaches communication and media studies. Prior to joining academia, she worked as a journalist and news editor with several media organizations in Nairobi, Kenya. Her research interests are in media ethics, media regulation, film studies and media framing.

JOANNE KNOWLES is a senior lecturer in media, culture and communication at Liverpool John Moores University. Her research interests include media organizations and their politics, values and related operating decisions, as seen in her work on ITV and broadcaster identity and her collaborative work on journalism and media ownership, as well as work on gender and popular media and organizational use of digital media.

DR HAYES MAWINDI MABWEAZARA is a senior lecturer in media, culture and society at the University of Glasgow, UK, and senior research associate at the University of Johannesburg, South Africa. He is an associate editor of *Journalism Studies* and *African Journalism Studies* and serves on the editorial boards of several high-impact journals, including *Digital Journalism*, *Communication Theory* and *Journalism Practice*. He has published widely on digital journalism in Africa and is the author, co-author or editor of five books, including *Media Capture in Africa and Latin America: Power and Resistance* (Palgrave, 2025).

ELASTUS MAMBWE is a lecturer and researcher in the Department of Media and Communication Studies, University of Zambia, Lusaka, Zambia. He completed his Ph.D. in film studies at the Centre for Film and Media Studies, University of Cape Town, South Africa. His thesis examined the development of postcolonial Zambia filmmaking through the juxtaposition of political economy and the small national cinema approach. Elastus' research interests lie in media industries, screen studies and mass communication. He is a member of the South African Communications Association.

WINSTON MANO is a full professor and member of the University of Westminster's top-rated Communication and Media Research Institute. He is a course director for the MA in media and development and founder/editor-in-chief of the *Journal of African Media Studies*. He is the director of the Africa Media Centre and was co-director of the Chevening Africa Media Freedom Fellowship programme (2020–23). Mano has published widely and his research interests span Afrokology, decoloniality, African radio, music, media audiences, digital communications policy and development, China-African media relations and African media and democracy. Mano is a senior research fellow at the University of Johannesburg, South Africa.

DR TRUST MATSILELE is a senior lecturer of journalism at Birmingham City University, UK. Matsilele researches the changing journalism ecologies with a particular focus on Southern Africa. Of late, he has been investigating how generative artificial intelligence reconfigures journalism practices. He also studies social movements and the role that digital media plays in shaping participatory cultures.

VINCENT OBIA is a Leverhulme early career fellow researching African approaches to AI regulation and digital media governance at the University of Sheffield. He completed his Ph.D. on new media regulation at Birmingham City University and was previously involved in research and teaching at the University of Lagos, Nigeria. His research interests include new media regulation, platform governance and the inequalities between the Global North/South in the use, design and regulation of new media technologies.

DR ANNE MAUREEN SYALLOW is an accomplished academic researcher and lecturer in the School of Humanities and Social Sciences, specializing in media, security and conflict. With extensive publications in areas such as international relations, media and migration, media and security and refugees, Dr Syallow is a recognized expert in her field. She serves on several key boards at Strathmore University, including the School Exams Board, Board of Postgraduate Studies and the Research Committee Board. A dedicated mentor, she has supervised numerous graduate and undergraduate students and is a certified research ethical reviewer for Strathmore University's Institutional Research and Ethical Review Board.

NDAWANA YOUNGSON is a lecturer in the Department of Media and Communication Studies, University of Zambia. He graduated from Liverpool John Moores University with a Ph.D. in media, culture and communication. His research interests are in journalism cultures, media policy and regulation, media history, cybersecurity and internet freedom, and media and politics.

Index

n refers to a note; *t* to a table

www.ingramcontent.com/pod-product-compliance
Ingram Content Group UK Ltd.
Pitfield, Milton Keynes, MK11 3LW, UK
UKHW051841120626
472074UK00002BA/5

9 781835 95244